CS-70

DATE DUE

St. Martin's Paperbacks by
Eugene Izzi

THE TAKE
THE EIGHTH VICTIM
BAD GUYS
THE BOOSTER

THE BOOSTER

EUGENE IZZI

SMP

ST. MARTIN'S PAPERBACKS

This novel is a work of fiction. All of the events, characters, names,
and places depicted in this novel are entirely fictitious or are used
fictitiously. No representation that any statement made in this novel is
true or that any incident depicted in this novel actually occurred is
intended or should be inferred by the reader.

BAD GUYS

Copyright © 1989 by Eugene Izzi.

Library of Congress Catalog Card Number: 88-29736

ISBN: 0-312-92330-9

Printed in the United States of America

St. Martin's Press hardcover edition published 1989
St. Martin's Paperbacks edition/October 1990

10 9 8 7 6 5 4 3 2 1

To the Broham Brothers
my sons
Gino and Nick

1 When winter rolled around, Vincent got fat. Not every day and not every winter, but on the average he could make more money on the typical January morning than he could in the whole month of, say, July. Especially if the wind was blowing and it was snowing.

As it was this morning.

Six in the morning. Shivering some, but he had it under control, standing on the corner of 147th Street and Gately, waiting for the dummy to come along who would make him fatter.

Last year's Buick rolled into the 7-Eleven parking lot. A woman left it running but Vincent felt lucky today, nothing less than this year's model would do. He let it pass.

The thing was, he could get pneumonia if he got too choosy.

Vincent Martin was wearing a pair of faded blue jeans over long underwear, the pants legs over heavy construction boots, the kind that laced all the way up to mid-calf. A heavy white sweater over a sweatshirt, a brown-leather bomber jacket over that. He was wearing a ski mask but had it rolled up atop his head. It was for emergencies only. And for warmth. He was cold.

It was January 27th, and there was a foot of snow on the ground. A bitter northeast wind drove in off the lake, sending the early morning 7-Eleven customers into the store leaning forward, their hands in their coat pockets. He watched a guy come out with the morning paper under his right arm and a cup of coffee in his right hand. The guy went to open the door of some old beater with his left and the hawk wind grabbed the paper, swirled it into the air and took it away like Dorothy's house leaving Kansas and going to Oz. The guy made one short move for it before getting it through his thick skull that it was a lost cause, spilling the coffee all over his work pants. Vincent saw the steam coming off the pants and lip-synched, "Shit," with the guy.

And then he saw it. Today's piece of work. He began walking toward the public phones bolted to the outside brick walls before the fat guy even pulled into the parking space.

The fat guy was wearing a three-piece suit and a camel's hair topcoat. A white shirt and a green tie. Smoking a cigar, and leaving the Eldorado running as he ran into the store for his morning coffee and his paper, so the car would stay warm. From his appearance and the way he walked, Vincent knew he was a guy who figured nobody would mess with anything that belonged to him. Like he was a badass, like maybe fat meant strength. The fat guy had about twenty hairs on his head, combed all the way over to his ear, so people would maybe think he had a full rich Clairol head of it. Vincent turned his back as the fat guy walked past him.

The 7-Eleven door hadn't swung shut on him when Vincent made his move. He hung up the phone and strolled casually over to the Cadillac, got in and put it in reverse, slowly backed out of the space and then put the car into drive. He pulled carefully out into the Sibley Boulevard traffic, which was whizzing by him like mad. The car smelled of cigar smoke, and the fat guy had the climate control up around 110 degrees, so Vincent powered the window down to solve both problems at one time.

He got four grand for the Caddy. He was feeling fatter every day.

He put the money in his lockbox and headed for home. He had taken a cab from the fence's warehouse to the bank, and from here would go to Van Buren Street, intending to walk the two miles home. The cabby tried to engage Vincent in conversation part of the way, enjoying the prospect of the big fare he was making, driving the big guy in the leather jacket from Calumet City to the Loop, a thirty-mile trip. Vincent answered him in short yeses and nos, and finally the cabby gave up. But he did ask Vincent for twenty dollars good-faith money when Vincent told him to wait outside the bank, and this did a lot to relieve his hurt feelings. Vincent handed him the money without a second's thought.

What the cabdriver saw when Vincent got out of the cab was a tall man, maybe six foot, with wide powerful shoulders under the leather jacket. From the way the coat was buttoned on the bottom the driver could see the man had narrow hips, no belly or ass. Maybe mid-thirties. Blond hair and piercing blue eyes. The cabby was impressed by the way the fare moved; like he was moving underwater only faster than it looked; then he got it; the guy walked like Chuck Norris from the movies, knowing every step he was taking before he took it, like a karate guy. Eyes looking straight ahead but seeing everything around him.

The cabdriver liked movies, imagined the big fella going in to rob the bank, saw himself driving away from the cops, evading them all with his dexterous driving before pulling into an alley and after a fifteen-minute karate battle beating the guy and taking all the money for himself, but the fare blew it for him; he came strolling out a minute later, those wide shoulders filling the doorway almost, holding the door open for some fat hag. The woman said something to him and the blond guy looked startled, then said something back.

The guy was smiling when he got back into the cab, but didn't say what had gone on at the bank, and as he'd already insulted the driver once, the cabby did not ask. He had his pride. But when the blond guy got out of the cab on Van Buren Street and gave him the full fare and told him to keep the twenty dollar good-faith dough, it went a long way to soothing his damaged ego. He told the blond guy in broken English, "Ave ay goot day."

Sometimes, Allah be praised, things went well for a cabdriver in the big city.

Guido Baggio thought that Raymond Parilo looked like a frog. Anytime now, he expected Parilo to open his mouth and have nothing but a deep booming "rrr-iii-biitt" come out. He'd have rather heard that than what Parilo was actually saying.

"They got to go," Parilo told Baggio and his superior, mob crew underboss Jerome Montaine. "There's a rat in the fucking mob. All these guys, since Campo went down and Tombstone rolled over, all of them, they're fighting for position, planning to get rid of me. They think I'm the one to blame, cause I'm Tombstone's brother-in-law. Well, I got a surprise for them."

They called Baggio "Guy Bags," as if hearing that name on a tape recording would throw off the FBI. He shifted in his seat, not liking what he was hearing. He turned his head to look out the window at the breathtaking view from Parilo's apartment, ninety stories up in the Sears Tower building. On the way to this meeting, Montaine had told him that Parilo was over the edge, and had to go. Now he was seeing it for himself, up close and real, and he had to agree: The guy was bad news.

"You paying attention, or what?" Parilo was standing right over him, his hands on his fat little hips, shit, the guy looking like Edward G. Robinson in *Little Caesar*. All he needed was a cigar.

"Yeah, Raymond," Guy Bags said, "I'm hearing you. But ain't it a little drastic, whacking all these guys out? I mean, some of them, they're pretty heavy guys, they got friends, too, you know."

"Hey, I want your advice, I'll ask your boss to ask for it, okay? You're up here on a pass. And something else you ought to keep in mind, Bags, if you ain't with *me*, hundred percent, then you're with *them*."

"I'm with you, Raymond." Bags said it softly and with conviction. This maniac was talking about killing four of the mob's top underbosses, so taking down a captain of his own crew wasn't something he'd lose any sleep over.

Bags looked over at his boss, Parilo's top underboss; Jerry Montaine looked back at him with reptilian eyes that told you nothing. As if he were watching a movie, and matters of life and death weren't being discussed. He knew what Montaine was trying to tell him, though. Shut the fuck up, was what the man was telling him.

Parilo was right about one thing, though. He *was* here on a pass, Parilo letting him up as a favor to Montaine. Parilo probably thought that he was doing Bags a big favor, and more than likely getting off on showing the place to a guy he figured to live in a rathole on the South Side. But what Bags was seeing wasn't encouraging.

The view, the apartment, yeah, he had to hand it to the guy, it was unique. But Jesus Christ, talk about paranoid. There were two guards on a couch outside the front door, and plenty more armed morons roaming the hallways and the stairwells, loyal to this goof and ready

to kill anything that smelled of threat. Parilo had the
fear so bad he never left the apartment anymore unless
he absolutely had to, and never after dark. As if the mob
wouldn't whack him during the day. Montaine had told
Bags, weeks ago, what Parilo was holding that was so
important, and they'd begun plotting then. But before
he would embark on a plan that could get his entire
family murdered, Bags had to see for himself. Montaine,
just as paranoid, had said okay. So here they were.

"So the thing is," Parilo said, speaking to Montaine
but staring right through Guy Bags, "you're *all* either
with me or against me. I'm gonna whack out every single motherfucker working against me. The others, I got
a way, keep them in line."

Bags knew it was time to jump in again, but he was
genuinely a little afraid. The guy had already told him
to shut his mouth once.

He said, "Raymond?" and Parilo stared at him,
maybe in awe. Bags rushed on. "Okay, I agree, whatever you say goes. You want them guys dead, we'll take
care of it. But what about the others? They got pull, a
lot of clout in New York. What *do* we got, keep them in
line? I'd hate to think, they'll let you do what you got to
do to their friends, then they'll lay back in the weeds,
waiting to get the drop on you. If that happens, where'll
we be?"

"Worried about your own ass, Guido?"

"All our asses, Raymond. You lose, sure as hell, I'm
dead. Jerry might be forgiven, the loyal underboss, but
a crew captain, they'll kill me for the fun of it."

"Don't you worry about it. I got just the thing."

"You better show him, Raymond." It was Montaine
speaking, softly but with power. Bags knew that Raymond respected Montaine, nearly loved him, and never
made a move without talking it over with Jerry.

Parilo looked at Montaine, hard. "He's your man,
right, Jer?"

Montaine pursed his lips and nodded his head, once. "Like blood."

"Like you are to me?"

"Nobody's that close, Raymond, but he's working on it."

Parilo nodded back, liking the answer. He stared at Bags for a moment, sizing him up. Montaine looked away, as if Parilo's decision either way didn't matter, and Bags thought it was a good move. Parilo was going to need all the help he could get if he was going to pull his plan off, and if Montaine thought that Bags was indispensable, worthy of trust, then Parilo had better get the same idea.

Parilo left the room and Bags sighed under his breath. He looked at Montaine, rolling his eyes at Parilo's insanity, but Jerry just let his gaze move on by, staring off at the wall, appearing bored.

Parilo came back in, carrying a couple of small tapes. He shook them in Baggio's face, as if he was holding gold panned out of a supposedly dead mine.

"Evidence," he said. "Tapes Tombstone made with six of the guys, used to be Campo's top advisers. He told me to hang on to them until he wanted to make his bid for early parole. The Campo tapes, they nearly wrecked our thing. They got Tombstone ten years on an Army camp in the Witness Protection Program, and they got Campo about thirty life sentences, state and federal, and two death penalties. These," Parilo said, shaking the tapes again, "are his insurance."

"And you're gonna use them for leverage, Raymond? Whack out the bosses, ain't on tape, then use the tapes to keep the loyalty of the other six?"

Parilo nodded.

"What about Tombstone?"

"Hey," Raymond said, "fuck that stool pigeon." He disappeared for a couple of minutes, and Baggio let his mind run free.

The man was totally out of control, over the edge. You didn't go around whacking out four of the toughest made mobsters in the country and then hold the others in line with just some tapes. Christ, these guys, they'd *shit* on tapes. They were used to being recorded.

But recorded by the Gee, on the telephone or in the back booths of restaurants. Not recorded by a guy they trusted with their lives. A guy like their boss, Tombstone Paterro. Christ, they had let their hair down with Paterro, told him everything they did.

With a shudder, Bags decided that if Parilo wasn't stopped, the crazy son of a bitch could really pull it off. If that happened, the mob would be in ruins.

It was almost there right now, but killing four of the few men who still knew how to operate the right way would be the icing on the cake. This guy didn't know it, but he was doing the Gee's work for them.

Which meant that Montaine was right. Parilo had to go.

Parilo came back into the room, rubbing his hands together. He looked hard at Bags. "You with me, Guido?"

"All the way, boss."

"You *better* be," Raymond said, then said, "Now, let's get down to the planning session, huh? We got a lot of work to do, we're gonna pull this off."

Ted King stood against the far wall outside in the hall, looking at the concrete ceiling and surreptitiously staring at the two whackos on the couch. By all rights, he should be sitting there and one of them should be standing, but once you lose face in the mob, it's hard to get back. He'd made his bed, he had to admit, and nowadays it seemed that the damn thing was made of nails.

Ten years ago, when he was twenty-three, he was an up-and-comer, a contender. His cousin Bags had got him his button, and he'd done six solo hits. He was a man to be reckoned with.

He'd beaten the first rap, got off on felony probation back in the days when you could pay the right people and business was conducted in the courtroom hallways. It had been a criminal assault charge; he'd busted up a guy Bags had wanted to teach a lesson to. The mob had stood behind him because he'd been doing their business. So he had been, technically, a convicted felon when he'd got nailed for the drunken-driving charges. Even then, it was a boys-will-be-boys type thing, and Bags had got him off the hook.

What had done him in real good was when he'd got drunk and had walked down Rush Street trying to cap the moon with a .357 in each hand.

Convicted felon in possession of a weapon—two years federal with no chance of early parole. The boys hadn't been able to do anything for him there.

Upon his release he'd been given some money; not enough to cover his lost wages, but he knew better than to complain. He did most of his drinking undercover, sometimes with Bags but usually alone. Had even promoted himself a couple more hits. But then Bags had gone hard on him when he got himself hit with another DUI charge, had sent him down around the docks to collect the chump-change the wallopers bet on basketball and football. He'd done it though, again without complaint. He'd been patient.

And it was starting to pay off; he had been getting his status back, when the accident happened.

But now, three months after his last release, it looked as if he was finally going all the way to the top.

He didn't know much, just that Bags had called him at the apartment he'd rented for Ted upon his release and had told him there was a big meet on. He picked Bags up and was told there was something in the wind

that could make them all rich and put them on top.
They couldn't use their own people, Bags had said, because this was sensitive, something that would never be
sanctioned. Bags had told him this as they'd driven over
to pick up Jerry Montaine, and as soon as Ted had met
the underboss, he'd gone deaf and dumb; he would
have gone blind, too, except he was driving.

He knew the way to play it. Don't speak unless spoken to. Say yes, sir, when asked an opinion. Stand tall
and look tough (which was hard at only five-seven without the lifts in his shoes and a face that was choir-
boyish); and never, ever make a wrong move.

When Bags had told him to drive them to Sears
Tower, Ted knew that for some reason he was back in
the middle of things, at least under consideration for a
top spot in something really big.

He had never complained or whined over the phone
to his cousin. Had always accepted his fate with class.
Never tried to blame the cops who'd busted him, or the
judge who'd sentenced him. But most of all, he'd been
patient. Had played his cards close to the vest, had
taken the lowly assignments given him without complaint. He'd shown he was a stand-up guy. If he could
just stay away from the booze, it looked as if he was
finally going to be rewarded for his efforts.

Thinking this, he reached into his topcoat pocket for
the roll of wintergreen Certs. He popped two in his
mouth so no one would be able to smell the two shots
of gin he'd poured down after Bags had called him.
There was no use in panicking, quitting booze altogether. As long as he could handle it, he figured, he'd
be all right.

He stared at the ceiling, getting impatient now,
thirsty, too, thinking about maybe slipping downstairs
to one of the bars and sneaking a couple, and when the
door to the apartment opened he felt relieved.

Until he saw the look on Bags's face.

Even Montaine, old Stoneface himself, looked white around the gills, but Bags, he looked like he'd just got caught beating off in the bathroom. Terror was on his face, awe, and confusion, too. Mostly disbelief. Ted pushed himself away from the wall and walked to the elevator, then had to wait until one of Parilo's private army put a key in the little hole to bring the thing up to their floor.

They were silent in the elevator. Ted had to bite his tongue, dying to ask them things, but knowing his place. In the car, they started talking to each other in normal voices, and Ted took in what he could.

"Crazy," he heard that word a lot. Something about "the plan," as if they'd been working on something together for some time. Then they started talking about another guy altogether, Bags telling Montaine that the guy was old, but the best there was. Wiseass but solid. A stand-up guy. Guy could do the job alone, no problem.

Then they started talking about *him*, as if he wasn't in the car. Montaine asking Bags if he was reliable, if his "problem" was behind him. Bags assured him that Montaine could trust Ted as he trusted Bags himself, and Ted King felt proud. Then he felt a tap on his shoulder and tried not to start.

"Yes, sir?"

Jerry Montaine, the underboss himself, said, "Hey, can I count on you?"

"With your life, Mr. Montaine."

"No, it's *your* life on the line, King." Then he sat back again and said to Bags, "His *and* yours, Guido. You got to understand that."

When they were seated in the Embers restaurant, the two men started treating him more like an equal. They told him things and he nodded and kept his mouth shut, taking it all in. Feeling good, one of the boys.

They explained to him that they were going to be

trusting him, that they couldn't use their own people
for this, because what they were about to do had never
been done before. They would, from time to time, have
people backing him up, helping him out, but it was
their show, the three of them, and when it was all over
the rewards would be great.

Ted refused a drink, ordered ginger ale. The look he
saw in Bags's eyes told him it was a wise move. He sat
back and basked in the glory they were allowing him,
listening, making comments when asked. He felt on top
of the world, part of the gang, one of the boys. He was
in heaven.

Until the old bastard none of them were prepared for
came in and everything started going to hell.

Vincent left the cab, shaking his head, thinking that it
took all kinds to make a world. Like the old broad
down at the bank, trying to hold the door open for her
and she gives him the line, she didn't need any man
holding doors for her. So he'd asked her if that meant a
blow job was out of the question, and that had stopped
her cold. And then the Iranian cabby, Jesus. He'd be
happy to rub elbows with a few solid crooks, make him
feel like the whole world wasn't going crazy for a
change.

He walked down Van Buren to the corner of Clark,
deciding to wait awhile before heading for the warmth
of his South Loop home. Around the corner and two
buildings down to Bolo's bar.

Nine in the morning and there they were, the retirees,
lined up at the bar drinking Bolo's beer, milking their
glasses for all they were worth, savoring every last drop
of the free ones Bolo poured for them every morning, a
gift for living to retirement age. In their line of work,
few men made it that far.

Tony and Tommy and Vito and Pez and the Animal,
Two-Finger and Gino Papa and Angelo, Leo, the usual

crew, the motley crew, the retired thieves and grifters and con men and boosters, taking it easy now that eyes had failed and hands were shaking, now that they'd lost their touch. Drinking free beer and shooting the breeze about the good old days. Sometimes, these old guys gave Vincent the shivers, and he could imagine himself there in twenty years, when the legs were gone and no one would work with him anymore, no one would trust him to keep up his end of the score. But not this morning. Today, like always after a score, he felt good looking at them. They were the closest thing he had to family.

"Bolo," Vincent said, "let me buy the bar a round." And he dropped a twenty on the bar as Bolo smiled and went over to the grateful retirees, the oldest of whom was fifty-nine years old.

Three weeks without a drink and look at the changes. The bar stools had been there since the Immaculate Conception, old three-legged stools with real red-leather padding, rubber tipped on the bottom so the floor wouldn't get scratched. Hardwood floors that were washed, polished and waxed weekly; swept up daily by Bolo before dawn. After which he would throw the sawdust down. Peanut shells covering the floor surrounding the retirees' stools already. Peanuts were free. The old Wurlitzer juke in the corner, wooden, a throwback to some earlier time, maybe the twenties; Vincent wasn't sure and never asked. Seventeen tables surrounding a dance floor; four booths against the far wall. A joint. A real honest-to-Christ joint in the heart of the Loop, surrounded by the enemy.

When anyone with blow-dried hair walked in, all conversation would stop and Bolo would make a big deal out of turning off the VCR under the TV mounted on the wall, then the TV itself, then he would walk real slow down to the stool where the yuppie was sitting and say, "What do you want?" giving the guy the glare.

Bolo would burn the joint for insurance before turning it into a Rush Street gin mill. There were his customers, and then there was the rest of the world. If the interloper was ignorant enough to stay for more than one drink, one of the regulars would start in on him, say something like, "Hey, dickhead, there ain't no waitresses in here gonna be wearing no referee's shirts," or, maybe, if the guy still didn't get the hint, "Hey, asshole, what the fuck you doing here, mistake it for a fag joint or something?" Usually by this point the guy would finish his drink and take off, if he had any sense. If he didn't, then it was time for someone to go to work, go make friends with the guy, buy him a round, steal his watch right off his wrist while shaking hands.

Bolo had put in track lighting sometime in the last three weeks, that's what it was. The change. Made the entire joint look different. Usually the only light came from the Budweiser and Old Style signs hanging all over the walls, or from the TV. At night the shaded fluorescents over the two pool tables in the back room would throw some light into the room, or if push came to shove, Bolo would flip on the overheads, if someone wanted to match dollars. Vincent decided that the track lighting up there took some of the character away from the place. Although he had to admit it would flatter the women, the angle the lights were set at; they would look great in the mirror behind the bar.

Vincent noticed that the light set in the ceiling nearest the east end of the bar was positioned differently, toward the bar instead of away from it the way the rest of the lights were. He felt a lump come up into his throat when he saw why. With the lights on, the damned thing would be pointing at his picture, which was hanging there right in the middle of the dozen or so pictures Bolo had behind the bar, all of them fighters, from Rocky Graziano to Muhammad Ali.

A picture of an eighteen-year-old Vincent Martin in

boxing shorts with eight-ounce gloves on his hands, staring menacingly into the camera. Or trying to. To Vincent now, on January 27th, twice as old as he'd been when the picture had been taken, he looked like a scared skinny little kid trying to look bad. He was saved from further reflection by Bolo, who was placing his change on the bar in front of him.

Bolo said, "The hell you been, Champ?" He gave Vincent an accusing glare, as if Vincent were a child caught playing hooky. Which from Bolo's point of view wasn't too far off the mark.

If the retirees were Vincent's family, Bolo was his father. His teacher, his best friend. Bolo was a couple of inches taller than Vincent, skinny now, running around behind a bar sixteen hours a day. Enrico Rubolo, the greatest safecracker the world had ever known, retired now and running a bar and enjoying his middle age.

Vincent said, "You gonna get me a beer, or what?" and Bolo smiled.

"Sure, kid. Schlitz?" He waited for Vincent to nod, then strolled slowly over to the cooler, throwing it over his shoulder, the little dig. "Didn't know if you were on the wagon, or dead, or busted, or what." He snapped the lid off the bottle on the opener attached to the bottom of the bar, then brought the bottle to Vincent, who was smiling.

"I was, for a while."

"They cut off your phone?"

"Nonpayment of bills. The lights, too. And the gas." Vincent was taken away from the game by one of the retirees, who remembered his manners and yelled out, "Yo, Vincent, *salud!*" Other ex-thieves chimed in, calling out *salud* and *skol* and *cheers,* so Vincent raised his bottle to them and nodded, poured some beer down his throat—

And nearly died, it tasted so good. Man, three weeks without a taste, then suddenly downing one, feeling that familiar warmth in his gut, spreading out. Good and cold, too, the way Bolo always kept it. He closed his eyes as he drank, put away half the bottle before lowering it to the bar. And spotted Bolo staring at him with a strange, strange look in his eyes.

"What's the matter?"

Bolo made a big point out of looking over his shoulder at the picture of Vincent eighteen years ago on the back wall, surrounded by some of the greatest fighters of all time, there in his Everlast shorts with his hard lean muscles bulging, looking angry and tough. He looked back and said, "Oh, nothing," giving it maybe 25 percent, letting Vincent know exactly what was wrong.

Instead of responding, Vincent put the bottle to his lips and drained it, slammed the empty down on the bar and then looked at Bolo challengingly and said, "How about another?" which effectively ended that line of conversation before it really began. . . .

Two beers later Bolo said, "Yeah, that's good, sock it away for a rainy day, kid, but Jesus, are you ever pulling exposure, working every day like that."

Vincent said, "Bolo, we've been over this ground a million times. And my answer's still the same. If you do it right, you don't get caught."

Bolo slapped a hand on the bar. None of the retirees even looked over at them. "Goddamnit, Vincent, that's stupid, talking like that. What if some stroke, he comes out of the store, sees you driving away, he happens to have a three-fifty-seven under his coat, or what if a squad just happens to pull in as you're backing out? The way I taught you, there's no room for error at all, and here you are, *boosting*." He made the word sound filthy, beneath them both; to Bolo, boosting was a repugnant and repulsive act. Bolo held up his hand.

"Listen to this a second, will you?" he said, his anger set aside momentarily, his wise eyes gleaming. He walked to the middle of the bar and picked up the remote control for the VCR-TV, turned the sound up. The retirees were waiting with smiles on their lips, knowing what was coming. On the screen a dapperly dressed cop circa 1963 was talking rapidly and toughly to a suspect wearing a pompadour haircut and a sharkskin suit. The cop said into the suspect's face and from the speaker into the attentive bar, "Where'd you down the merch?" and the bar went up for grabs, the ex-crooks hooting and howling, saying to each other, "Where'd you DOWN THE MERCH?" cackling, getting a bang out of it.

Bolo came back to Vincent's end of the bar, turned the sound back down on the TV and laughed for awhile. He said, "Down the merch," the same way he'd said "booster" earlier. "Vincent," he said, "I was a safeman in this city almost forty years, and I never in my life heard cop, fence or crook say 'down the merch.' Jesus Christ, where do they get these guys?"

"The hell are they watching?"

"Another show, from the same guys who brought you that Miami thing, this time set in Chicago in sixty-five. Guy says 'down the merch' to me, I say to myself, cop.

"Vincent, you should see the crowd, Friday nights, they make me tape "Miami Vice" and show it later, so I can fast-forward the commercials out. Whenever one of those guys comes strutting out, the regulars, they start whistling and catcalling; you'd think they were in the joint, spotted some seventeen-year-old fish coming on the tier."

Vincent said, "Yeah?" He pictured the Friday night crowd blowing kisses at a couple of guys wearing thousand-dollar pastel suits over undershirts with 9mm pistols or .357 Magnums in shoulder holsters. He couldn't think of a single cop he knew who still wore a shoulder holster.

On a roll, Bolo said, "Last Thursday, the usual afternoon dregs of humanity come in, punks trying to join the crowd, cops dressed like hippies; too early to give them the look or say anything; what the hell, they liven the joint up. Two punks, shooting pool, maybe twenty-three. Quiet little mouses when they come in, minding their own business, looking around, checking the place out. Couple of beers, they start talking shit to each other, calling each other motherfucker, I'm expecting them to ask me if I know anyplace where they can 'down some merch.'

"So they're shooting pool and Gino Papa comes in, flush; he ain't what you'd call active anymore, but now and again he pops a score for some pretty good bread; he's buying a round, waving the dough around, having a good time."

Bolo went away for a second and Vincent looked over at Gino Papa, a tall Italian man dressed impeccably, his iron-gray hair combed straight back old-country style, watching the screen, shaking his head from time to time at the inanities he was seeing there. He looked skinny, but Vincent knew from experience he was as strong as a bull and twice as mean if you got him going. Bolo came back, waving down the customer who had called out to give Vincent one; it was an unwritten rule in Bolo's bar, the old-timers, meaning anyone over fifty, could not pay in the mornings. He put his right foot up on the sink behind the bar, hitched his pant leg up and continued.

"So these mice, all of a sudden they got three beers in them and they're Joe Louis. They come back in here, get another round, order it kind of snotty, right? Not anything you want to slap them over, just a surly, on-the-muscle tone. They spot Gino Papa and they say to him, 'Ey, you buyin' a fuckin' round, or what?' and Gino looks at me, gives me the wide-eye, like what the hell are they doing here, but he's smiling, and he goes, 'Sure,' and he turns to me and he says, 'Bolo, give the children a can of soda or something, okay?' like they're a couple of his grandkids. Not ever one to step on a joke, I says to the kids, 'What'll it be, lads, Kayo or maybe some strawberry?' and they get pissed; all the customers are laughing right at them now, throwing shots at them. Vito says to them do they want some bubble gum, and someone else asks if their die-dees are wet.

"By now the kids are red as that old Firebird you used to drive, and they look around; there's Gino Papa, the guy who started it all, laughing at them, a wad of money in his hands, and this first punk, he says to his partner, 'You ready?' like they're going to teach these old-timers some manners, and Gino, he can't stop laughing, he gets this old dago accent in his voice; he was born on Eighty-seventh Street, for Christ's sake, and he says, 'Ready? To do what, go inna back and makea de love?' and then he throws a kiss at them." Bolo repositioned himself, removed his right foot from the sink, hiked his left pant leg and put his left foot up. He leaned his elbow on the bar and he was laughing now, remembering, his slender body shaking up and down as he spoke.

"These kids, Vincent, you want to feel sorry for them, but they are such assholes, you just can't. Big weight-lifting jerks, got the muscle between their ears.

"The talker, he says to his partner, 'Fuck this.' Everyone is laughing at them both, pointing fingers, making remarks, and his buddy, he's watching the kid walk over to Gino, he looks about half-scared, he goes, 'Ey, Mikey, maybe we better—' but that's as far as he gets, the guys, they hear the name, Mikey, they go nuts. Leo, he watches the TV all day long, he shouts out, 'Mikey, hey, the kid's name's Mikey!' and he says to the kid, real loud, he says, like in that old commercial, 'Hey, Mikey, he'll eat *any*thing!' and the kid goes nuts, he starts shouting like Bruce Lee, making karate noises, and he jumps at Gino.

"Gino, he doesn't even drop his drink; it's afternoon now and he's got a Dewar's on the rocks; he steps back and to his left, sticks out his right foot and Mikey falls into the sawdust while Gino puts his drink on the bar, takes his suitcoat off, puts it on the stool. Gino says, 'Yo, Mikey, I got something for you,' kind of singing it out like, as if he's calling him home to dinner, smiling. That's when the kid makes a big mistake.

"He rolls over and he gets to his feet, pulls a switch out of his back pocket.

"Now, everyone knows the rules. You don't plan scores in the joint, you don't do any business, and no violence if you can help it. That's why God made alleys, settle the beefs. But this kid doesn't know any better.

"I'm walking around the bar by this time, about to kick this kid's ass for him, and Leo's on him, the kid takes a swipe at him with the blade and Leo grabs his arm, twists it up behind him and you hear this big old snap, it's broken, the kid turns white and faints.

"I turn to the other kid while the guys take Mikey out back into the alley and I asks him his name; for Christ's sake, it's Jamie. He's sweating bullets and about to pee his drawers. I says to him, 'Jamie, you better get on home now,' and he says to me what about his buddy Mikey and I asks him if he wants to go out, in the alley, check on him, and he gets my drift, shakes his head, calls me sir now every other word out of his mouth, 'No sir, I think I'll just go on home sir if you don't mind,' and he sidles to the door, out he goes, running his ass off."

Bolo went over, shut off the set as the closing credits rolled across the screen and started rewinding the tape. The Animal asked him to put in the funny movie with the black kid playing the cop from Detroit going to Beverly Hills to fight crime, but he was shouted down by the rest who wanted to watch another episode of "Crime Story." Bolo put the new tape in and handed the remote to Animal, telling him to turn the sound up whenever.

He looked at Vincent's empty glass and said, "Another?"

"No, I just come in here for the ambience."

"Wiseass. I like wiseasses. Like Mikey was a wiseass." He went and got another Schlitz out of the cooler and smiled when Vincent told him to set up the bar. He even poured a couple of ounces of draft Michelob into a glass for himself. "So, where the hell you been?"

Vincent shook his head. Then: "Wait a second. What the hell happened to Mikey?"

Bolo looked surprised. "Why don't you go over, ask Gino and Leo what happened to him; the Animal, he went out there too. You could ask him, maybe he'll let you eat the remote for a while."

"You're kidding me, Bolo."

Bolo said, "Hey, kid, you know the score, you want to play, you gotta pay."

Vincent didn't say anything. Maybe the kid got what he deserved; he would have escaped with just a good ass-kicking if he hadn't pulled the switch. Jesus, though, to die for losing your temper when you were drunk. After a while he asked Leo if he wanted to shoot some pool.

Eight ball, last pocket for twenty a game and a drink. Short, fat, bald-headed and unassuming, Leo had played them all: Willie, Fats, Fast Eddie, and couldn't lose to anyone of amateur talents such as Vincent, but it was worth the money and the price of the booze—which Leo had switched to as they began playing, Cutty, neat—to hear the great stories Leo could tell.

Stories about Leo and the old-timers scoring, going in, cold; back thirty years ago when you had to peel the safe layer by layer, in the old days when you didn't have things like portable drills and diamond-studded bits that could cut through Swedish steel like a hot knife through butter. Working with a chisel and a hammer and crowbars, for Christ's sake. The Stone Age.

Getting busted and having your head split open by the cops who wanted half the take at least before cutting you loose. The good old days, way back before Operation Graylord when a crook could get away with murder—literally—if he had the bucks in his pocket to square the beef. When everyone with a badge was for sale and the judges worked for them most of the time.

Back in the days when if your crime partner ratted you out, everyone went looking and he wouldn't be safe in a bomb shelter a thousand feet under the ground. Not like today, when the punks would get popped, first time out of the box; some safe-and-loft cop from the old days would scare him, kick his ass a little bit and tell him what the colored guys would be doing to him for the next thirty years up in Stateville, and he'd sell his mother to get out from under. Back then it never happened.

When Ogilvie had been governor and Winston Moore ran the county jail, Leo had been busted on a bum murder rap; he'd angered a mob boss by refusing him a piece of his last score and the gangster had set him up. They'd hung Leo up by his wrists, shackled him to a water pipe in the basement of the jail complex at Twenty-sixth and California and beat him with a rug beater for three hours straight. He didn't tell them a thing. Today Leo still had the scars on his back and chest, but the gangster was long dead so Leo figured he was ahead of the game.

Vincent could tell some cop stories himself, and he did while they shot pool there in Bolo's bar, the baddest crime joint in the city of Chicago, where anything goes and most nights did.

Like the night he'd been popped on some Mickey Mouse beef he knew nothing about but still had to go on in and take the heat for; a dumbass homicide dick handcuffing his hands behind his back and then to his ankles, forcing him into a kneeling position and sticking his head into a filth-encrusted toilet. Christ, to this day he could still get sick remembering the stench. The cop letting him up long enough to ask if he was ready to sign a confession, then sticking his head back down, Vincent fighting to keep from drowning. His lawyer had gotten the case thrown out by showing the judge, at the pretrial hearing, pictures of Vincent all beat to shit. The judge had listened to the cops tell him that the suspect had "fallen down," and then had asked Vincent what had happened. Vincent had not answered. It was against his code to rat out anyone, even a cop. Which the judge seemed to respect, because he let him go, after telling him that he had a right to file suit against the officers for violating his civil rights.

When he told this story, Leo nodded his head wisely and continued clearing the table, a six-ball run that left his last pocket the right side, which he neatly banked twice and sank. Leo said, "I always heard, even when you was a kid, that you had a lot of heart."

At noon Bolo's afternoon replacement came in, as he did on Monday, Wednesday and Friday , and Bolo called Vincent-who-had-always-had-a-lot-of-heart over to the bar. Vincent went, still steady on his feet; he'd only had maybe seven beers all day, but it was on an empty stomach.

Vincent said, "The hell you want, I was starting to wear him down."

Bolo laughed, and said, "Kid, you couldn't wear Leo down with a goddamn baseball bat across his bald head; hell, he was shooting eight ball when you were still crapping your drawers." He told Eddie, his replacement, to give them both a Schlitz and then added, "As a matter of fact, he could take the baseball bat you were gonna nail him with, use it as a cue and still whip you with his left eye taped."

"Yeah, but I could take him in three rounds."

"Don't be so sure about that, either, kid."

They were in the booth farthest from the bar, in the back corner. Away from the toilets, away from the small dance floor; a business booth if ever there was one, except for the fact that Bolo did not allow business to be discussed in the bar. Ever. So it shocked and surprised Vincent when Bolo asked him if he still thought he had it in him, to go unarmed and willingly into a house with a safe with the express intention of cracking it.

Vincent looked pained. "Bolo, how long you known me? What was I, eleven, twelve, when the old man died? Jesus, you *taught* me! Am I ready, Bolo, goddamnit, do I still have it in me? After what happened to Tino? I ain't never going in again, ever, no sir."

Bolo said, "You didn't kill Tino. He fucked up. Besides, if anyone was at fault, it was your lookout. He ran on you worse than a dog."

"Well, he paid the price."

"That he did, but it didn't bring Tino back, now did it?"

Vincent said nothing, just looked at Bolo.

"And you wound up doing, what, seven?"

"You know as well as I do how long I was away."

Bolo nodded. "Seven." He looked at Vincent for a short while, squinting, as if he were looking through him. "And the seven, it wasn't lucky for you, was it. Cut the balls and the heart right out of you."

"You want to test my balls, Bolo?"

"Don't get tough with me, kid. I don't need that shit from you; I've known you too long. Now answer the question."

"Hey, Bolo, I still got my balls, understand me? I score Caddies these days, make twenty, thirty grand a week. TVs, VCRs, still in the boxes, right out of the stores. I fight when I have to and I mind my own business. I never rolled over in the joint, got in the best shape I been in in fifteen years. I'm back now, and if I got the right thing, yeah, I'd go in. With the right guys."

"But you ain't looking."

"I'm doing okay."

"You're doing good?"

"Yeah, I'm doing all right." Indignant now, angry that he was defending himself to someone who should know better. He almost added, At least I'm not tending bar twenty hours a fucking day, but he knew where the lines were drawn and he never got so drunk that he'd step over them. Just as there were things Bolo could say to him but never quite did, because it would be stepping over the line.

But he was coming dangerously close with this business of having lost his balls in the joint.

"So how come you're drinking like a goddamn rummy and living alone all of a sudden?"

Vincent looked up, angry. "Who am I supposed to move in with, my wife?"

"Your ex-wife, you mean."

"Let it go, Bolo."

"None of my business, kid?"

"You know, you're the only guy in the whole world calls me kid?"

"I got a right, don't I?"

Vincent didn't know if Bolo had the right, the way he was talking to him. "Goddamnit," he said, "I'm getting sick of this third-degree bullshit. You want to tell me what the hell this is all about?"

2 Bolo took his time, checking Vincent out. "You been out what, two years now?"

"Two years right before Christmas. They gave me four to seven, I did the straight bit."

"You know, I got a guy, comes in takes over for me three days a week, spells me till eight, then I come back on till two. The other four days I open and close myself."

"A lot of hours, Bolo."

"Night, I got a waitress comes on, makes three, four hundred a night in tips from the high rollers."

"I know Evlyn, Bolo."

"How well you know her?"

Vincent just looked at him.

"What I'm saying, Vincent, I'm saying this girl, she's what, twenty-seven, twenty-eight, been working here three years, never even looked at another guy twice; you come home, Jesus, all of a sudden she gets wet panties. Every time you come in, she's falling over herself trying to get next to you, but you ain't buying. I ask myself, Bolo, why is that? I figure one of two things." Bolo held up his right fist and popped his thumb up.

"Number one, you're carrying a torch for Camille."

Bolo shot up his index finger and Vincent said, "Don't even say number two, all right, Bolo?"

"Which was gonna be?"

"That I went fag in the joint."

Now it was Bolo's turn to just look at Vincent.

"Bolo, I don't think I want to talk anymore." Vincent rose to leave but suddenly a vise had his right hand and he looked down to see Bolo hanging on to his wrist, the veins in Bolo's hand popping and twitching as he squeezed. Vincent could have broken away but for Bolo to grab him like that—it had to be important. He sat down.

Bolo said, "I got to know a few things, kid, and the only way I know to get an honest answer out of you is to ask."

"So, ask."

"You go fag in the joint?"

"Not one time."

"What's with Evlyn, then?"

"She used to be married to a drunk."

"I see, now."

"I took her out a few times, Bolo, it didn't work out."

"But she's got a torch for you, kid."

"Anything else, Bolo?" Vincent wanted to get off the subject of Evlyn. He wouldn't admit it unless Bolo asked him straight out, but the thought of her did hurt.

"Can you get off the booze, kid?"

"For Christ's sake, Bolo, I ain't had a drink in three weeks."

"That wasn't the question, Vincent."

Vincent was angry now. The guy sitting there with maybe a thousand scores under his belt and half a dozen kills getting all holier-than-thou and nearly accusing Vincent of being an alcoholic.

Vincent said, "Yeah, if I have to, but why should I?"

"We'll get to that."

"When?"

Bolo smiled. "Soon." Then he said, "I have ears all over, Vincent, you know that? Still, in the department, in the joints, I know what's going on. I don't hear anything sissy about you, but all of a sudden you're throwing away an education maybe six guys in the world still alive ever had, and I want to know why."

"Tino—"

"Tino, my ass." Bolo was staring hard now, giving him the glare like Vincent was a yuppie just walked in off the street, and Vincent didn't like it. Not after twenty-five years of being Bolo's apprentice and helper. Crime partner.

Bolo said, "You use Tino's death for your excuse, but it's got nothing to do with scores. I lost three partners before I was your age, kid, and it never even slowed me down. I'm going to ask you one more time, why ain't you scoring the way I taught you?"

And Vincent could tell by the way Bolo said it that he could either tell Bolo the truth or risk losing his friendship.

Bolo had taken him in when Vincent's father had died and had taught him everything there was to know about scoring. Vincent could pick a lock while most of his contemporaries were beginning high school. He could fight like a contender, was Golden Gloves regional champion three years running and had had a shot at the Munich Olympics before he'd blown it messing around with the general's daughter. He owed Bolo everything and nothing; their friendship was never one based on guilt. But he knew Bolo, had seen him banish men he'd known all his life for lying to him once about something important, and he knew that if he lied now he'd be treated the same.

But Jesus Christ, how could he tell him the truth?

Vincent read a lot, a habit acquired in prison, so he pictured himself as a guy in a bar in a book, and when he spoke it was as if he was reading the lines out of a novel. He spoke slowly and clearly, his tone dead, lifeless and droning, monotonous.

Vincent said, "Because I am afraid." There. It was out. The big dark secret.

Thinking back nine years, remembering . . .

Tino Anuerrino, his crime partner, or one of them. He preferred to work with Bolo, but Bolo was only working part-time those days, one, two scores a month, while Vincent couldn't rest unless he was working once a week. Tino was tall, black-haired, muscular, a professional like himself. Patient and fearless, he'd done time, more than he should have, but he hadn't ratted out his partners, so he'd gotten extra time tacked on for being stubborn. Tino of the coal-black eyes and the huge hands. Who never said much and never joked, but there could be five hundred cops surrounding a score and he'd stay and do his job, find a way to get you both out.

They'd set the joint up as Vincent had been taught, patiently, checking the neighborhood, the patrol times. They knew the alarm system and could beat it blindfolded. They knew when the family would be gone and what time they would be coming back. The mark: a real estate broker who took his wife out to dinner every single Saturday night, and who bought her a bauble about once a week.

Then Philip the lookout, backing out of the job, and Vincent making a rare mistake and not doing as he'd been taught and blowing the score off; Vincent instead getting a punk who hung around, trying to suck up to them. Vincent thinking, What harm could it do? He'd only be a lookout, sitting in a car with a police scanner radio and a walkie-talkie. There was half a million in the safe, according to the source in the insurance company. Half a million dollars couldn't be put off; it was serious money.

So Vincent forgot one of Bolo's most important rules: Never work with rookies or men unknown to you. He forgot it just one time. And paid the price.

The kid panicked while they were inside and a squad car passed. He had raced away, tires screeching, drawing the heat who were probably just driving by but who would never admit it later. They came out of it, the cops did, as bona fide heroes. They caught the punk a block away and the kid ran out of the car swearing up and down that he had nothing to do with it, nothing at all, while the cops heard Tino's voice whispering urgently, coming from the walkie-talkie on the seat. . . .

And they'd barged in, guns drawn, as Vincent was loading the bag. Tino had grabbed Vincent around the waist and was running him—still carrying the bag with half the take—toward the rear escape route they'd set up when the cops opened fire.

Miraculously, Vincent was only wounded twice, both wounds bleeding a lot but superficial. Tino, on the other hand, was deader than the proverbial doornail. The punk had turned, rolled over on him, and had mysteriously "disappeared" the week Vincent got convicted. Four to seven, he'd served the whole bit.

And he now knew why Tino had taken the chance and tried to run from two cops with pistols drawn. Anything, even death, was preferable to doing long hard time in Stateville Penitentiary.

And he sat across from Bolo, grateful to Bolo for saying earlier that the lookout had fucked up, because they both knew that it hadn't been the lookout.

It had been Vincent.

He sat across from that middle-aged surrogate father and told him something he had never told anyone. He said it again, unwilling to look his mentor in the eye.

"I am afraid," Vincent said.

And Bolo said, "Shit, Vincent, you asshole, is that all?

I thought it was something really bad . . ." His voice trailed off, thoughtfully. Vincent looked up at him, grateful, but Bolo was off somewhere, faraway.

Vincent had seen him like this before, more than once. But not for years. His thinking look. Turning things over in his criminal mind, the finest criminal mind Vincent had ever run up against. Bolo would sift and sift and turn and simmer and then bring it all to a boil and then he would have the answer.

Bolo sat that way for a long time. Vincent was mesmerized. Bolo seemed gone to a place Vincent could only imagine, the lines there on the forehead, the mouth shut tight. He could almost hear wheels spinning.

At last Bolo focused on him, shook his head, almost seeming surprised that Vincent was still there across from him in the back booth away from prying eyes and meddling ears.

"I'm getting old," Bolo said.

"Yeah, me, too, but it beats the alternative."

"Don't interrupt. You known me since I was what, your age? The age you are now? Thirty-five, thirty-six? I made millions, kid, and blew it all. All I got in the whole world is this bar and a couple hundred grand for a stake, won't last me five years I head to the islands, Florida. Not the way I blow it. I work like a dog, Vincent, but I spend, too. Sportsman's Park, Arlington, Balmoral, all the pony tracks. Vegas in the winter twice a year, Bahamas in the fall. Canada for two weeks in the summer, the only time all year I don't hustle anyone or anything, just sit and fish like a square john. Like a working stiff. I got no wife, no kids. Just you, the guys here at the bar and my memories.

"I want to get out from under, Vincent. I got maybe fifteen, twenty years left to me if I take it easy, lay off the booze and the cigarettes. I'm sixty years old, for God's sake."

"That's middle age."

"Middle age," Bolo said, eyes twinkling, "is fifteen years older than whatever you happen to be." Then he lapsed back into earnestness. "I talked to Evlyn, Vincent." He held his hand up to ward off complaint. "She told me about you, waking up sweating and shaking in the middle of the night, and it reminded me of when you first come home from the war back in '72. Nightmares and the night screams all over again. The joint made you as bad as that war did.

"I know about the booze, too. How much you're drinking, and how you act when you get a good snootful. What you do after you leave here. Kicking ass on some guy walking in the park, taking a chance on another bust just because you're drunk."

"That was one fucking time, Bolo!" And Bolo looked at him long enough that he amended it to two or maybe three.

Bolo said, "I talked to Hank Greely down at the gym, trains killers would fight Attila the Hun for two bills; you're in there beating them into rabbits, they run when they see you coming.

"So I figure we've had it, kid. You're burnt out from the goddamn joint and I'm burnt out from too much living. You can't keep a good woman because you can't get away from the past, and me, I've had too much past." Bolo got up and took both of their empty bottles to the bar and while he got refills, Vincent got up to use the can.

Standing at the urinal thinking, This is it. It had been coming for a long time. He knew, in the back of his mind, that someday it would indeed come, this moment, but he always put it off or when he did think about it, thought of it in some far-off distant future.

Bolo was a guy used to the fast life; fast cars, fast women, fast horses, fast and wild rolls of the dice. He wasn't the type to sit back the rest of his life and play around in a gin mill, even if it was the place where the very best crooks, fences and players hung out and spent small fortunes.

He washed his hands and went back to the booth, taking a couple of deep breaths before he sat down.

Bolo said to him, "I wasn't being nosy before, Vincent. I had my reasons. What I just said, I knew these things for a long time, about Evlyn, about the gym, about mugging stiffs for the hell of it. About your boosting. What I had to find out was if the rabbit was in your blood, if you'd lost your heart. And I figured it ain't and you ain't." Bolo leaned across the booth and stared Vincent dead in the eye, his breath smelling of stale beer and peanuts.

"Kid," Bolo said, "I taught you a long, long time ago, never be afraid of being afraid. I never went on a score in my life when I wasn't afraid. What you do, what a man does, he works through the fear and kicks its ass. You say to me, I am afraid; well, I say to you, there's a lot more things in life to be afraid of than going back into the joint, which, I might add, I ain't never been and don't ever plan on being. So you're scared, so what? You gonna let it run you? That's what I got to know, Vincent. And real soon." Bolo winked at Vincent and said, "On account of I got a way to get us both from under, you're willing to give it one last shot."

3 A way to get out from under, Jesus Christ. That was all Bolo would tell him right there; he had to talk to some people, he said, then he'd get back to him. In the meantime, he told Vincent that as long as he was already hitting it, to go ahead and get plowed, but starting tomorrow, he was off the booze. And then Bolo had taken off, leaving Vincent alone in the booth with a puzzled look on his face.

A way to get out from under. Vincent had 317 grand in 4 different safe-deposit boxes, 100 grand in 3 of them, 17 grand in the fourth. Unlike a lot of thieves he knew, he'd never come up with a solid figure, an amount he'd quit at. Most of the guys he knew, like Fabe Falletti, one of the best high-rise thieves who'd ever lived, put the number at a million. One million tax-free dollars to live on the rest of your life.

Vincent could come up, right off the top of his head, with numbers larger than that, earned and blown already, back when he was scoring like a champ. Unafraid still. But then again, he wasn't exactly living quietly back then, either. He had a car once that he'd paid $142,000 for. Bolo had taken one look at it and had told him, shaking his head and grinning, that he'd send him a cake with a file in it on his goddamn birthday.

Jimmy the Polack had wrecked the car driving drunk one night and the insurance company had refused to pay off, as he had no business driving it, and Vincent had told the Polack that he should have reported it stolen and let Jimmy do a few years for boosting it. Jimmy had sworn that he'd pay it off, but he'd been killed in a running gun battle with some colored numbers runners who'd thought, wrongly, that Jimmy was trying to rob them. Christ, on PCP or something, the idiots. The Polack had never wasted his time with anything that wouldn't bring him at least thirty grand.

Horses, that had been another one of his downfalls. Betting a grand a race, more if he'd been drinking. Easy come, easy go . . .

And women, Lord, Lord, the women. Tall women, short women, skinny women with small pebble-hard breasts and voluptuous women with large, yielding ones. Until Camille, God, how he'd blown money on the broads.

Camille had caught his eye right away, sitting in the bar at the Hyatt Regency, listening to Booker T do his thing. Long red hair falling in waves down her back, maybe five feet seven or eight, no fat at all—the girl worked out harder than he had when he was fighting, for Christ's sake—just firm hard flesh. And the things she could do with it.

Camille had helped him settle down, he had to admit that. The outfit was after him to come into the stable, making stupid threats, and Bolo had told him to chill out for a while, get them off his back, leave him alone as they surely would if he didn't buckle under.

The outfit being the Chicago arm of the Mafia. The bane of all professional crooks, demanding that you come to work for them, making it look sweet. They'd set up every score, get you in with movies taken, floor plans ready, every alarm system set up and ready to be taken down. Sometimes even the combination to the safe would be supplied if it was an inside job and the mark wanted to make a score himself off his insurance company. The outfit would supply everything, money, cars, all details down to the number of mice living on the premises. Then they would fence the jewels themselves, wash the cash, take all the chances afterward.

The fly in the ointment being they didn't pay you anything, maybe ten cents on the dollar for jewelry and coins, fifty cents per dollar for washing cash. They kept the rest, the outfit did. And of course, if you were busted, you were on your own; they said they'd take care of you, but Vincent knew of at least three guys in the joint doing heavy time who never got a dime from the outfit for their families. And they'd work you every night until you went down or burned out.

Vincent knew fences of his own, and they weren't like the fences you saw on television shows or read about in novels by guys who never came any closer to a score than they did to the Pulitzer Prize. Fences were not fat little Jewish guys squeezing every cent out of a burglar. Maybe the junkies, granted, they might be stuck with some inane pawnbroker who ripped them off blindly, but no professional thief worth his salt would sit still for such nonsense. Fences were businessmen who made at least 100 percent profit on everything they took in, so by God when they found good, stand-up professional thieves, they would kill to keep them happy.

Vincent knew a fence who never handled anything but weapons. One who handled only diamonds. One who handled only electronic equipment such as TVs and VCRs and stereos. He did a lot of business with that fence at the moment. And he knew one he was working with almost every day this winter who handled only luxury cars. And these guys paid top dollar. If they didn't, Vincent would never work with them again; he'd simply find someone else.

But he knew about the outfit fences. Man, they'd run

you into the ground and they'd work you till you dropped and they'd make a fat killing off the sweat of their stables and they paid nothing at all. So working with the outfit didn't seem like such a sweet deal to him.

Another problem being, though, that the outfit killed guys who didn't see their point of view.

So Vincent, with nearly but not quite a million dollars, had married Camille and had bought a lovely tri-level in Forest Park and had bought a Cadillac for himself and a Mercedes for his heartbreakingly beautiful twenty-five-year-old redheaded wife, and the heat had indeed gone down, just as Bolo had said it would.

But stealing was in his blood. It was like eating. It was something he just had to do.

And then the deal had gone bad with Tino; Tino had been killed and the lookout, the little rat fink of a prick, had taken a swim late one night in Lake Michigan wearing chains around his legs, but wide awake and knowing it was coming, his executioners being two guys who would have died for Vincent.

And Camille, well. Vincent had broken another of Bolo's hard-and-fast rules. Which was: Never tell a woman anything about your business. And it had cost him just as dearly as the first mistake had. Camille had known all along where the money was, almost a half-million, even after the cars and the house and the lawyer fees, and naturally she'd divorced him while he'd been serving his time. When a man's in the joint, a woman doesn't need his permission to divorce. And naturally she'd taken the money and gone off, she wrote in the letter, to Try and Forget.

Half a million dollars would make for a good beginning for anybody.

Funny, sitting in the back booth, trying to come back to the here and now, Vincent still had no desire to look her up, try and get his money back. Or her. He didn't even have the urge to see if she'd really gone away to

Forget or if she'd just run. It didn't matter, and he was afraid of what he might find out if he did look her up.

And now old Bolo had a way out for them both.

Vincent knew the date, remembered it well. Bolo would never remember, as he wasn't sentimental, but January 27th was the day that Vincent had been born, thirty-six years ago today. He wasn't, as Bolo had mentioned, getting any younger.

If one big score came along, one superscore so big he'd never have to work again, never have to even think about the relatively risk-free boosting again, let alone scoring safes, could he give it all up? Maybe buy the bar from Bolo, have someone run it during the day and work a regular five-night week? Christ, Bolo had to make a fortune in the joint, the guys in here spent money like it was going out of style.

And the things he set up, he got a piece of that action, too. Putting a couple of good people together, or introducing someone to the right fence, that was worth 10 percent of whatever was going on. That also had to account for a couple of grand a week, averaged out.

Vincent knew all of the same people Bolo did. Maybe even more, as Bolo, in spite of his thousands of scores and the millions made and blown, had never spent a night in even a county jail, let alone the penitentiary. The joint was a breeding ground for meeting people—if you were good, could take the heat, and kept your mouth shut.

Nowadays, though, there were very few people who could, and Vincent had always had a jacket for being tough, no-nonsense, gutsy and ballsy. He took no shit from anyone on the inside. With his connections, he could make a billion dollars if he owned this joint, did the right thing with it. Ran it right.

The question was still nagging at him, though.

If he could make one last score, *could* he retire? Could he walk away from the overwhelming high of taking something that didn't belong to him? The thrill of knowing that if he was caught in the act, he'd be going away again for a very long time?

Could he?

Half the thrill of scoring—whether it was boosting or honest-to-Christ scoring, busting a safe in a house or a business—was knowing that you were getting over; were something more than your average working stiff on the street, going to a nine-to-five job and punching a clock. Another part was taking no shit from anybody, having no bosses. Never having to put up with any nonsense from anyone. Making more money in one night than his old man or his uncles had in a year.

Getting over. If he were put against the wall and somebody put a pistol in his mouth and said, "Tell the truth," he'd have to admit that getting over was the best part. The pure unadulterated joy of doing it, breaking the law and not giving a damn, telling the cops and the judges and the screws in the pen and everyone else that you were better than they were. Tougher. Smarter. Badder.

That was the best part.

On the other side of the coin, there was the joint.

The penitentiary, where he had resided for seven long and brutal years. Guys hollering to him when he first went in, that first terrible night, screaming what they were going to do to him when they went over to his house later that night. Going in and seeing some big ugly colored guy lying on the bottom bunk in a two-man cell with his pants around his ankles, pulling his Johnson, saying to him, "Come on down here and meet your new daddy, honey." Vincent had attacked, kicking the shit out of the guy, beating him half to death before the screws had raced up into the gigantic round tier and had clubbed him off with their sticks. They'd beaten him senseless and he'd spent three long hard weeks in solitary confinement, the Hole, but when he'd gotten out, he'd been put in a different cell with a white guy for a roommate and he'd never been bothered by the big black guy again. Although he wasn't the last colored guy to try him out, see what he was made of.

All these years later, his hands were still misshapen from that first bloody year, trying to keep his honor and virtue with a couple of thousand guys who wanted to marry him. After a year or so, they'd let up, when they'd finally figured out they'd have to kill him before getting him to say I do. He wasn't worth it when there were maybe a dozen young white guys coming in every day who would drop trou in a hot New York second in exchange for protection from the gang rapists, who took turns until your mind went or the shock killed you.

Vincent even hated the term. *Penitentiary*. Christ, he'd never met anyone inside who was truly penitent. Maybe some of the young guys who'd got caught stealing cars or some of the older guys who'd just done something stupid while drunk, or the white-collar-crime guys coming in with their big round eyes looking around with that "What in the hell am *I* doing here?" look. But none of the pros. They weren't penitent. The only thing they were sorry about was the fact that they'd been caught. And like Vincent, they spent their time figuring out how they'd messed up, what they'd done wrong, and they were all certain as could be that the same mistake would never happen to them again. Not to them. To some other stiff, maybe, who didn't cover his ass and made stupid mistakes.

Could the fear of going back to the pen overcome his desire to score, to get over?

He didn't know.

But Vincent was anxious to find out.

Leo said to him, "Hey, Vincent, I thought you was gone." Pulling up his zipper, walking over from the can.

"Come on, I'll let you win some of your cake back; I'm getting bombed, man, can't hardly see."

Vincent smiled. He said, "How much you beat me for, Leo?"

"I don't know, a couple of bills, maybe. I'll tell you what, I'll play you double or nothing, one game, last pocket, and I'll play you left-handed."

Vincent said, "Some other time, Leo."

Bolo had told him to get off the booze and to get into fighting trim. And there was no time like the present.

4 Sean Kent was promoted to detective sergeant at 8:54 A.M. on January 27th. And it was as simple as that. He walked into the squad room, surly and mean, as he usually was in the morning, no one saying anything to him and not saying anything to them right back. Maybe, he guessed, the place had something to do with it.

Anyone would have their morning wrecked, tromping up three flights of stairs to the 1st Precinct Detective Squad. A mile away was the great and modern building at Eleventh and State where the elite cop squads worked, all soft colors and humidifiers and good working furnaces, and here he had to tromp up the steps, smelling urine and vomit, looking at institutional green walls that hadn't been painted since the place had been built, before he had had even a cup of good coffee. And the city of Chicago had been incorporated over 150 years ago.

Looking at the usual mass of humanity in the downstairs station never did much to cheer him up, either. Junkies handcuffed to metal benches, hookers cowering in the cage while their pimps, dressed like ostriches— they still wore big hats with feathers in them—hollered at the desk sergeant to hurry it up; time was money, Jackson.

An entire district comprised of 22 square city blocks, over 10,000 citizens of the city of Chicago, some of the richest, too, and there were only 24 detectives to cover the entire area.

And the bad guys were winning, making larger inroads every day.

He lumbered when he walked, stomping over to his desk, angry. He'd noticed half a handful of hair in his brush this morning after he'd shampooed it. The hair was going rapidly now, running away from him in direct proportion, it seemed, to the extra number of inches bulging at his waistline. Six feet tall, on the nose, weighing in last Sunday at 231¼. Stomping to his desk while he took off his fifteen-year-old topcoat and having to look up at his partner, who was standing at his desk, a cup of steaming coffee in his hand.

Sean took it gratefully, smiling his thanks, almost having to bend his neck back to look into Bigum's face. He sat, sipped, watched Bigum sit down in his own chair at his own desk directly across from Sean's, so close the tops nearly touched. Pencils and pens were caught in the tiny space between desks. He looked at the envelope on his bare desktop, bare except for the phone and the pad of paper, his ashtray and his old coffee cup now filled with pencils. Then he looked back over at Bigum.

LaVar (Bigum) Barnes was quite simply the largest man Sean had ever seen. He was six and a half feet tall, which wasn't extraordinary, not the way kids were growing these days, but he was huge. Hands as big as toy poodles and almost as hairy, curly little black hairs popping out from the wrist on down to the fingertips. Sometimes Sean wondered if the guy shaved his nails. Bigum had a sixty-inch chest and a thirty-eight-inch waistline, the dirty dog. Size fourteen feet. All of his facial features seemed to have been added as an afterthought, as if God had invented this gigantic hunk of carved ebony and had then stuck eyes and a nose and a mouth and ears into the top of it, like a youthful deity playing with a Mr. Potatohead. Even Bigum's teeth were big, horsey teeth, bucked a little and whiter than a photographer's flash. He was showing them now, the gigantic choppers, showing a lot of pink gum, too.

Bigum said, "Looks like someone done left you a love letter on your desk there, Sean."

Sean looked at the plain envelope on the desk. Blank. Maybe a Bigum-style joke. He'd open it and a finger would fall out or something. But it looked flat, safe enough. He finished his coffee and checked his watch. 8:54. Once 9 A.M. rolled around, he wouldn't have time to play around anymore with Bigum or anyone else; they had a war on crime to wage, and they were sustaining more casualties every day. He picked it up and slit the seal and pulled out the single folded piece of paper inside, read it. And smiled. He looked up at Bigum, who was studiously ignoring him, looking around the room, as if he hadn't seen it a zillion times before, checking out the stiffs in the cage looking at him as if they were gazing at a reincarnation of Bushman, come back to life out of the Museum of Natural History, where the world-famous ape was stuffed and adorning a glass cage for eternity. The stiffs looked away hurriedly when they noticed Bigum staring at them. Looking like an ape someone had dressed up in a cheap suit and had dropped into a chair that was way too small.

Sean said, "From now on, son, you call me sergeant." Then he nonchalantly refolded the letter and put it back into the envelope, stuffed it in his inside jacket pocket. On the left, right next to his heart.

Bigum said, "I *ain't* your son, I ain't never gonna *be* your son, and you don't even know my *mammy*, so don't give me none of that racial shit; I don't play that racial shit." But he was grinning, and he added, "Sergeant, sir, ya'll."

And, with the exception of Bigum saying that Sean now made over two hundred dollars a month more than he did and would therefore have to buy two lunches for each one Bigum paid for, that's all there was to the promotion.

A half hour later they were in their unmarked green Plymouth with the little bitty skinny antenna stuck smack dab in the middle of the trunk. The unit with absolutely no extras. No whitewall tires, no radio, no hubcaps, no air conditioning, but thanking God that the thing at least had a heater. It was an undercover car the type of which was known and recognized throughout the city to every player, pimp, thief, grifter, gangbanger and child over the age of six years as the car belonging to the enemy, the Man.

"Now that you're a sergeant," Bigum was saying as he drove, "maybe you can buy us a real flashy car, maybe a Caddy or a Lincoln, eh?" Grinning his wide toothy grin, joshing, enjoying himself. "Maybe something got a special seat made so I can sit in it without my head hitting the top of the roof?" He sneaked a look at Sean, who was studying a rap sheet that was perched on his lap, holding it in place with his left hand while his right held the constant cup of White Hen Pantry coffee.

Sean answered without looking up. "Bigum, your head hits the top of seven-forty-seven jumbo jets, for crying out loud."

"For crying out loud, for crying out loud," Bigum mimicked. "You the only partner I ever had in sixteen years who don't ever swear. You scared you're gonna shock me, or what?"

Sean looked at him. "I don't swear?" he said.

"Never heard you once, Sean."

"Honestly?"

"For real."

"Okay," Sean said, "listen up. I'll swear one time, just for you, okay?"

"Thank you, Sean."

"You listening?"

Bigum turned the corner of Hill onto Wells, heading for Old Town, where Jesus Silva lived. He said, "I'm all ears."

"And chest and mouth and head and muscle and—"

"And Johnson, don't forget that, Sean. I got a big wild Johnson bar here twixt these massive thighs." He shot another glance at Sean, then looked back to the road. "I'm waiting."

Sean said, "Shucks."

Bigum said, "I knew you couldn't do it." And had to end the game because they were pulling over in front of the tavern above which was the apartment where they were supposed to serve their warrant.

Greed never amazed Sean anymore. Not after twenty-three years and four months as a Chicago cop. He'd seen young guys kill their mothers over welfare checks and welfare mothers kill their sons because the boys had beaten mom out of the check playing cards. He'd seen babies roasted alive in ovens and listened to parents whacked on angel dust explain that they'd done it to burn the devil out of the kids. He'd seen cops he'd gone through the Academy with get busted and go to the joint for taking money that did not belong to them. And judges and lawyers and politicians were in fancy federal joints on Army camps while the cops, they had to settle for Stateville, where they had to serve their time in P.C., Protective Custody, called Punk City by the cons because that was where the stoolies lived.

By these standards, Jesus Silva was a saint.

But a greedy saint.

As they mounted the steps, Bigum said that he wanted to take the lead, as he and Jesus were old buddies. Sean would enter first, introduce them, then Bigum would take over. Sean told him that was jake with him as long as Bigum didn't get into any police brutality, in the event of which he would have to rip Bigum up some, show him who was boss. Bigum smiled.

Sean knocked on the outside door to the apartment, the two of them standing on a rickety wooden stairway a flight above city concrete with a twenty-mile-per-hour wind howling at their topcoats.

A soft sleepy Hispanic voice said, "Who is it?" Masculine. Jesus Silva, possibly.

Sean said, "We have the place surrounded, Jesus; open up, it's the police." Then stepped back as far as he could on the right side of the door, looking down at the ground beneath him, his bulk up against the rotten wooden railing. Bigum didn't even move. He'd rather get shot than fall twenty feet to the ground, and there wasn't a wooden railing made that would hold his weight if he leaned too hard on it.

The precautions were unnecessary, however, because they heard a sharp intake of breath behind the door and then the chain was slapped off and the door was thrown wide and Jesus Silva was standing there in his jockey shorts, skinny and small, looking about thirteen years old except for the demon goatee there on his chin.

"C'mon in, officers." Like he had nothing to hide, a good neighbor trying to get a couple of civil servants in out of the howling wind on a late-January morning. Jesus walked into the small apartment and took a ratty bathrobe from a hook on the closet door. An unmade bed with filthy sheets was pulled down from the wall. A couple of dishes were in the porcelain sink, looking as if they'd been left by the previous tenant. No works visible, or other sign of drug paraphernalia.

"Jesus Silva?" Sean said, making it formal, pronouncing it with the Spanish inflection, hay-soose.

"Hey, Jesus!" Bigum said, pronouncing it as in, Christ. "How you getting by, my man? Jesus, Sean, it's Jesus!" Acting as if he and the Mexican junkie were long-lost war buddies.

"Jesus, goddamn, boy, tell me, what you doing scamming insurance companies, huh? Ain't that a little over your head?"

Jesus shriveled, swallowed up in the robe. He smiled shakily at Bigum. "How's it going there, Officer Barnes?"

Bigum walked rapidly over and Jesus shrank back, Bigum stopping just short of making physical contact. Using his tremendous size to intimidate the much smaller man without actually doing anything that could be considered illegal or threatening in a court of law. Sean leaned against a wall and watched, trying not to smile.

He said, "You two know each other then?"

"Knowing each other, *knowing* each other? Why, me and Jesus here, we been knowing each other what, ten, fifteen years, ain't that right, Jesus?"

Jesus said, "It is Je-sus, sir, not Jesus." Then grinned sheepishly. "Although many women, sir, they think I am some kind of god."

Bigum said, "I believe that, Jesus, they figure you're a goddamn faggot, huh?" And throwing his head back, he gave a harsh barking laugh that seemed to shake the windows. Sean thought, poor Jesus.

Bigum said, "Hey, Jesus, we got a warrant for your arrest here, son!" Smiling man-to-man, as if they both knew that it was a jive-time charge but Bigum had to go through the motions, do his job.

"What is the charge, sir?"

"Insurance company done sworn out a complaint, Jesus, said you run a game down on them, used a half dozen aliases to collect money on insured cars over and over again, got greedy, eh? Stopped buying old beaters and insuring them one at a time, started insuring the same car with four different companies, calling it in stolen when all the time you probably didn't even pick it up from the junkyard, did you? Just sent in the title, sold it back to yourself over and over again, making a killing. Didn't know that the insurance agents, even your own people, who you used, got these little old computers these days, numbers pop up more than one time, boom, a little red flag starts waving, they know someone's being a naughty little boy."

Jesus's shoulders sagged and he looked even younger, if that was possible, than he had when they'd entered. Bigum was cornering him now, never touching him, but the implied threat of his size was scaring him worse than if Bigum had.

Bigum said, "You in a heap of trouble, boy. Looks to me, now I don't know all the legal things they can throw at you, but at least five in Joliet, you be bumping dickheads in there with guys make me look like a midget"—poor Jesus was shaking now at the thought—"and like I say, I can't know for sure, but if you used the mails to make your claims, you might be looking at some federal time on top of it, and you know how *they* are. Man, you rob a bank, you do five, but you play with the mails at *all*, they throw twenty at you." Bigum's grin widened and he finished up with, "Time you do both bits, you be a shriveled-up little meskin, they be calling you Rosita instead of Jesus."

Jesus said, "Look, Officer Barnes, you always been good with me, you know? I mean, your word is good with me." Bigum smiled and nodded his head as if Jesus's opinion of him mattered. Jesus said, "What I want to know is, I'll believe you if you say we can, what I want to know is, can we discuss this?"

Bigum said, "Now, Jesus, you know I don't take no bribes." Smiling, but his voice threatening, his tremendous forehead lined with a new concern.

Jesus hurried to reassure him. "No *bribe*, Officer Barnes, no, sir. What I meant, what I was trying to say was, if I give you something, maybe you could leave, huh? Let me get a head start?"

"You mean drift away with one of the pieces of ID you got, make yourself a new name?" Bigum rubbed his chin thoughtfully. "What about your parole officer?"

Jesus smiled, looking frustrated, but what are you going to do? "I guess, he will have to live without me, eh?"

Bigum said, "My man, anything is negotiable. But you don't mind, while me and you chat a bit, if my associate here takes a look around, now, do you?"

Jesus jumped right on it. "No, no, sir, not at all." Then gave Bigum his patented sheepish grin. Sean wondered how many billions the kid could make if he could bottle it.

Jesus said, "As long as, you know, he don't take my ID away?"

"Oh, he won't mess with your ID at all," Bigum assured him, then said, "Now, what did you want to tell me, of your own free will, Jesus?"

"Can I sit down?"

"Why sure." Bigum plopped down on the bed and it groaned but held, and Jesus perched on the edge of a chair. He reached over and plucked a cigarette out of a pack sitting on a tiny table in the studio apartment, a table littered with cigarette butts, ashes and matches, without an ashtray in sight.

Jesus said, "This morning, the fellow I buy the titles from, he is late. I am there buying three new ones; I have the cash money. As I am waiting for the fellow to come along and see me, I watch as a worker there pushes a button and the steel door, it rises, and in drives this other fellow with a brand new Cadillac car. He comes in, my title fellow, he comes out of his office and ignores me and hands the other fellow a fat yellow envelope, the other fellow takes it and says, see you in the morning and my fellow says to him, so long, and then he called the other fellow by his first name." He looked at Sean walking around the room, picking up all kinds of evidence against him. He looked at Bigum, sitting on his bed breaking the springs, the poor bed moaning and groaning and sagging to the floor. He said, "I tell you the name of the fellow I buy titles from to cars that do not exist, and the name he called the fellow who most obviously steals new Cadillacs for him, and you will let me go, right?"

Bigum looked at Sean hard at work searching Jesus's drawers. He put his finger to his lips in a shushing gesture, nodded at Sean's back, then nodded his head twice at Jesus and grinned. Jesus grinned back, widely, then winked.

Jesus said, "My fellow's name is Robert Barecki; he owns the junk car shop on Seventeenth Street in Calumet City. The name he called the other fellow by was Vincent."

Bigum said, "Don't ring no bells, but tell me, my man, what does this Vincent look like?"

"Tall, although not as tall as you or your friend there, but he is not fat." Jesus's eyes widened and he said, "I did not mean to say that"—then stopped, maybe thinking that he would only make it worse by trying cover it up. "Maybe one hundred and ninety pounds, around there. A powerful blond-haired man who walks funny, very slow appearing but he is really moving fast; do you know what I am saying?"

"Did you happen to hear a last name, Jesus?"

"I do not think so, but the fellow, Robert, he called

him Vincent, but then the fellow who works there and
who opened the big steel door for the big blond fellow,
he seemed to be calling him Marty when he said goodbye."

"You can get dressed now, Jesus."

As the young man dressed, Sean came and showed
Bigum all the things he had found. Several different
driver's licenses all from the State of Illinois Secretary of
State Office. Official. The kid had greased another kinky
political appointee. Several thousand dollars cash. Half a
dozen titles to the same car, only the numbers being
different, the description exact. Then a half-dozen titles
to seemingly different vehicles, with the numbers being
exactly alike. Hundreds of insurance policies, the agent's
surname almost always being a Spanish one. Easier to
pay off a soul brother than a whitey.

Jesus eyed them warily as they went through his
things wordlessly, glancing at him every few seconds as
if to make sure that he wasn't going to make a run for
it. He smiled at them, trying to appear reassuring, but
by now Sean guessed that his facial muscles must be
ready to collapse from the phony smile planted there all
this time, and the smile didn't work for anything at all
except to make Jesus look even more frail and waiflike
than he was.

Dressed, he came and stood next to them, hands in
his pockets, smelling of fear-sweat and morning breath.
He said, "I can go now?"

Sean said, "No, you can't go now. Jesus Silva, I am
placing you under arrest and charging you with theft by
deception and—"

"Please, Officer Barnes, sir!" Jesus shouted, desperate
now, wondering what was going on.

Bigum took his handcuffs off the back of his belt and
spun Jesus around effortlessly, clamped the cuffs to his
wrists behind the young man's back, by the numbers,
but not tight.

Jesus said, "But you promise me . . ." Tears welled in his soulful brown eyes; his little bebop goatee bobbed up and down.

Sean said, "He lied to you, Jesus." Softly.

Back in the squad room on the third floor of the 1st Precinct station house, with Jesus in the cage sobbing, waiting for a bluesuit to come and process him before the short trip to Twenty-sixth and California, the dreaded county jail, Bigum filled Sean in on Jesus's previous encounters with the law while Sean sat at the computer terminal. He was pouring information in, trying to come up with a Vincent or a Marty somebody who was around 6 feet tall and 190 pounds, with blond hair.

"He was running another scam, four, five years back, taking money from his soul brothers and telling them he'd get their family into the country from Mexico. Not taking too much, the way the guys do over in California or Texas, just a couple hundred here and there, but the thing was, he wasn't doing anything about it, not bringing anyone in, just telling the poor folks he was scamming, that he needed more time or money or whatever." Bigum's voice was edged with disgust.

"Imagine, Sean, ripping off your own soul brothers, Jesus." And Silva looked up hopefully from the cage, saw that Bigum had not been speaking to him, then put his head back into his hands and continued sobbing.

Sean said, "Bigum, if you're through with your one-man civil rights march, there, I got something here on a guy named Vincent Martin."

He hit a printout sheet and got the vitals, the priors, Vincent's previous arrests and his one conviction. He took the picture over to the cage and showed it to Jesus.

"Is this the guy you saw coming into the place driving the Cadillac?"

Jesus looked up, dry-eyed, but his body was shaking. He looked at the picture and said, "I have never seen that man before in my entire life."

Sean called over to Bigum, "It's the guy all right."

5 Only the prospect of working with a dirty cop upset Sean more than some son of a gun getting off the hook because he was protected. Sean lived in the real world. He knew that today's police department was influenced more by politics than ever before, that the right bad guys paying off to the right people at the right time could walk away from crimes, thumbing their noses at the cops and their badges. Laughing at them.

But that still didn't make it right.

He'd come out of his lieutenant's office red-faced and angry. The man had dared to tell him that this Barecki character was federal, they had him under their all-powerful gaze, so that made him off limits. Besides, the guy didn't live or work in Chicago. The lieutenant told him that he'd executed his warrant; the Mexican guy had filed dozens of false police reports and now he'd been arrested; they had enough work to do without taking on the FBI, stepping on toes that would rear back and give you the entire foot right dead in the behind. Sean had asked if he could follow up on the Martin character; he lived within the city limits and had a record and the lieutenant told him that if he couldn't find anything better to do, maybe he was in the wrong line of work. No crime had been reported, no warrant issued. On any given night, they had maybe two dozen burglaries, attempted or achieved, and didn't he have to look into some of those?

At his desk, looking through the day's work, he filled Bigum in and said, "Thanks for coming in with me, your backup really helped my case."

Bigum said, "I told you, dummy. Go on in there talking to a politician like the man's still a cop and try to run a game on him. This Martin guy, he's playing the game, he'll get caught, sooner or later. In the meantime, we got enough to keep us busy right on through till suppertime."

"Now you sound like the lieutenant."

"Yeah? Then how come it is that you make sergeant and I'm still just a measly old little detective plainclothes, making two hundred a month less, if I'm so much like the boss man?"

"Maybe they're prejudiced, upstairs."

Bigum said, "I heard that, man. If only I was a lady, I'd catch rank fast as you."

"Twenty-two years to make sergeant is catching fast rank?"

"Our problem is, Sean, we too goddamn honest."

And Sean said, "I heard that."

Bigum immediately became defensive. He said, "Are you making fun of me?" Squinting at Sean.

"Bigum, who on God's earth is dumb enough to make fun of you?"

"You dumb enough, Sean, you want an answer."

"The question, Bigum, was rhetorical."

This satisfied Bigum, and he grunted, looked at the pile of garbage on his desk. He said, "You know, now that you a sergeant, how about you complain to the Man, tell him we're through doing stuff the uniforms do for everyone else?"

Sean looked up, trying to find out if his partner was

kidding. He decided from the look stamped on Bigum's face that he was serious. Sean sighed.

"We've got," Sean said, "a little old lady on Lake Shore Drive to go and talk to about the burglar who kicked in her door and robbed her blind in the middle of the night while she slept."

Now Bigum sighed. "They never forget, do they?"

Sean said, "They've got better memories than the elephants."

Bigum said, "Are you making fun of me, with that elephant jive?"

But this time he was smiling.

What *they* never seemed to forget was the fact that Sean Kent and LaVar Barnes were two totally honest, incorruptible cops. Neither man had ever taken a dime that he didn't earn, which wasn't that unusual even in Chicago. What set them apart from the rest of the honest cops was the fact that neither man had ever allowed a partner to take money that the partner hadn't earned, and this caused them both more than their share of grief.

Sean had been counting the days, three years ago, just waiting for retirement, disillusioned and frustrated, drinking too much—alone—his friends from the force having dropped him long before due to his unshakable convictions. They had promoted him to detective after having him run the Officer Friendly Program for three years, one of the few postings he had ever held where he didn't have a problem. He wasn't a publicity hound and never went to the press or the headhunters, the policemen at the Office of Professional Standards, never ratted or squealed.

But what he'd do, was, he'd kick the stuffing out of any partner who sullied him and the badge he'd taken and the oath he'd sworn to by accepting money that he hadn't worked for. Within five years of his graduation from the Academy, Sean was considered a social out-cast.

Bigum, although much larger and stronger than Sean, went the other route. He testified in a trial against his own partner, a crime more serious than child molestation within the ranks of the fiercely fraternal and protective department. And had signed his own professional death warrant.

The resultant publicity had forced the administrators to promote him, but nobody would work with him. Death threats were phoned and mailed to him, sometimes a dozen a day, even a year after the trial. His wife, so used to the easy and close relationships that they'd had with other police couples, left him when everyone else did, when the death threats and the loneliness and his being gone sixteen hours a day finally became too heavy.

He'd been investigating, on his own time, a major Mafia figure who was apparently breaking the strict code of the outfit by selling dope, on the off chance that he might catch the guy with his drawers around his ankles, when he'd been shot in the leg.

After he'd announced himself as a police officer and the mobster's guards had panicked and run, he'd pulled himself to the car and called in for help.

His mistake being that he'd given his car number to the dispatcher.

He passed out, and was therefore unaware that the only police officer on a force of 13,000 who had responded had been a white dude named Sean Kent.

In the hospital, they went through the mail together, the "Get well" cards with obscenities scrawled in the message sections. Sean would come in and look at the leg hanging in the cast and would ask how Bigum was doing and Bigum would always say that he couldn't kick. A big joke to someone who'd been shot and abandoned—maybe even set up—by his fellow officers.

Upon his release they'd asked for and had been granted permission to work together.

By the strict rules of the book, a detective's job was not to begin until the crime had already been committed. So the 1st Precinct lieutenant was well within his rights to assign them to following up the occurrence of major crimes. Where he stepped overboard was in sending them out to interview burglarized widows and mugged conventioneers. With the amount of crime committed within the precinct, it had become standard procedure for uniformed officers to take down crime reports on the fly, report to the scene and do the work, tell the victim to call the insurance man, take the muggee to the hospital. That freed the detectives to follow leads and chase down killers, rapists and thieves while the trails were hot.

Not so in the cases of Sean and Bigum.

The lieutenant had allowed them to work together—with their unblemished records he could hardly stop them—but that didn't mean that the lieutenant had to treat them as detectives, as men.

He loaded them with busy work, giving them the job of following up after crimes in which there was no possible chance of an arrest or conviction.

What he didn't plan on was their tenacity.

Sean and Bigum would put in their eight hours, doing the busy work, never a minute more or a minute less. And then they would go to work.

Chasing down hot leads, creating investigations on their own time, going after whichever criminal they felt needed to be off the streets the most. And usually, they would get their man.

They'd throw their hands up in the lieutenant's office when he'd ask them, "Why wasn't I informed of this investigation?" and they'd say that it was a spur-of-the-moment thing. They'd used a judgment call and gone after it alone. The miraculous breaks just always seemed to happen after regular working hours.

The irony of it was beginning to become apparent to the rest of the detectives. Two guys with nothing to do all day going off when they weren't supposed to and having a combined arrest record that was higher than any other team in the precinct.

What the hell, the record had gotten Sean promoted, hadn't it?

So Bigum had known that it was a lost cause to go into the lieutenant's office and try for permission to go after the Cal City chop shop dealer. But he also knew that the first time they stepped out of bounds, the very first time they did one single solitary thing that could even be considered in a court of law to be objectional, it would be over for them. They'd be in deep, deep trouble.

So Sean had planted the seed, and when they went after this car thief, this Martin character, and after they busted him, Sean would raise his hands palms up in the lieutenant's office and get the innocent look on his face and he'd say, "But Lieutenant, I told you about this guy the other day, remember? When you told me I couldn't go after the Cal City dealer?"

Thinking about it, driving to the little old widow's home that had been burglarized the previous evening, Bigum smiled. He drove, whistling between his teeth, as Sean studied Martin's sheet there in the passenger seat next to him, his Styrofoam coffee cup in his hand, reading glasses perched on his nose.

Sean was smoking and going hmm . . . and ahh. . . .

"This one's a pistol," Sean said. "Heavens, he's got two Silver Stars from Vietnam, along with twenty-one felony arrests, one conviction." Speaking as much to himself as to Bigum, wanting to hear himself think, try and put something together by hearing about it instead of just thinking about it. Sean believed that the intellect was limitless, but sometimes you had to use your sense of hearing to put it into high gear.

"Say where he was at?" Bigum said, interested.

"No, it doesn't; I have his citations here in front of me from the Department of Defense, copies of his awards, but no, it doesn't say where these acts occurred."

"You wasn't a good cop, I'd ask for another partner, you know that? Anything I hate, it's a wiseass partner."

"Pleiku ring a bell?"

"It's across the Central Highlands, a hot spot when I was there." Sean didn't respond to this, so Bigum waited, expecting something good. He wasn't disappointed.

"Oh, yes," Sean said, "the second incident occurred in a place called, I can't seem to make it out, the darn ink's smudged, something, oh, I've got it, someplace called the A-Shaw Valley."

Bigum looked over at him, startled, and smiled. He said, "No, *shit*?"

Sean said, "No kidding."

"First Marines?" Bigum shouted, amazed.

"No, Army."

"Hundred and first?" Bigum said, under control but surprised.

"That's right, Bigum," Sean said, gently.

"Routine patrol went in there, expecting engagement the next day, Intelligence fucked up, reported large NVA activity a ways to the north. A company of Airborne Rangers walked in, Sean. Seven GIs walked out."

Sean said, "I always wanted to hear the real story . . ."

"Then why didn't you ask?"

"Because you're so humble, I didn't want to embarrass you."

"Yeah, well, let me tell you. We come in, the First Marine Division, and we fought there in that asshole of the world of a valley for three days and three nights until finally we killed every goddamn gook that was breathing and then we killed them again a couple more times to make sure they was dead. Christ, they had the high ground and fought like animals on us. Never backing up."

"Thank you, Bigum," Sean said softly.

"What for?" Bigum was genuinely surprised.

But Sean just shook his head.

Bigum said, "So maybe we should go ahead on and look into this war-hero fellow a little bit tonight, what do you think?"

"You think you'll be free tonight?"

Bigum said, "I'll have to check out my social calendar, Sean, but I be*lieves* I got me a few spare hours for this evening, if the cause is righteous."

Thinking that what he liked best about Sean—excepting the fact that he was a partner, something Bigum hadn't had for awhile until Kent came along—was that he never got predictable or boring. And he never pushed him too far like a lot of his partners had over the years, venting their frustration and resentments on him and trying to convince him they were doing it because they were so tight or some other bullshit like that; testing him out to see how he handled stress. Shit, put an M16 in his hands and outnumber him twenty to one with little Asian fellas, he'd show them how he handled stress.

Like now, saying, "Thank you, Bigum." Jesus Christ in Heaven, the guy was thanking him for doing his *job*, for going off to war instead of running off to Canada. For doing what his country wanted him to do.

Partners like that were rare, even if they didn't know how to cuss like a man.

"We talk to this old lady, and then you buy lunch, huh, to celebrate the promotion?"

"Hey, *you're* supposed to buy lunch, Bigum, to congratulate me."

"Shit, you serious?"

"Of course I'm serious. My goodness, can't a man be serious with you once in a while?"

"Nah, you buy lunch or I ain't eating." Giving it a pause, timing it just right.

Then adding, "Besides, I can afford to skip a meal, as I went ahead on, soon as I seen the envelope there on your desk, and made reservations for us at Ditka's City Lights." He smiled, fighting it but unable to keep it from his lips. He nodded his head twice, without conscious thought, hardly nods at all; his massive head just dipped a couple of times as if he was listening to a catchy beat no one else could hear. Then he said, "So you want me to buy lunch and dinner too, huh?" Giving the grin the go-ahead, beaming widely, the cat out of the bag. He risked a look at Sean, and the little old white cat was just looking at him, maybe thinking about saying something nice but not knowing how to do it without throwing in some kind of jive-time wiseass remark. Thinking of a way maybe.

Bigum grinned and grinned, thinking that his partner wasn't the only one pretty good at being unpredictable.

6 The Animal was bombed, Vincent could tell as soon as he walked past him. Trying to get out, wanting nothing more than to get some fresh air and a good rest. Thinking about what Bolo had told him would put him to sleep right away.

But he couldn't get past the Animal, who reached past him and grabbed his arm. Even through the leather jacket and the sweatshirt, Vincent could feel some pain as the huge man squeezed his bicep.

The Animal said, "Vincent, I got to talk to you." Imploringly; Vincent about to pull away and make a stand when he noticed the pain in the man's eyes, a pain he'd never seen before and never expected to see at all.

The Animal was Vincent's height, but barrel-chested. He was called Animal because of his face. His eyes were too close together, for one thing, with simian brows, bushy, thick, growing in one line there above his eyes. Animal's forehead was massive and protruding, like an ape's. His lower lip jutted out at least an inch beyond the upper; a matter of his jaw once having been broken and then set improperly. In prison, sometimes, you got less than the best of medical care.

Vincent gently pulled his arm away, looking into the Animal's hurt black eyes, and said, "So talk."

The Animal said, "Not here."

Vincent was hesitant to go anywhere with the Animal; he'd never liked him much because the Animal was a killer. Literally, it's what the man did; he killed people for money.

Vincent said, "I don't know, Animal . . ."

But the Animal said, "Please," and the fact that he spoke a word Vincent had never heard him use before convinced Vincent that the man really wanted to talk. That and the haunted lost look in his eyes . . .

They went outside, around the corner and into the alley, huddling there, Vincent ready in case this was some kind of a trick, although that was paranoid thinking; Jesus, the Animal knew how close Vincent was to Bolo, whom the Animal adored.

Vincent had his hands in his jacket pockets, ungloved, his ski mask rolled up on his head like a watch cap. "What's wrong, Animal?"

The Animal looked around to make sure no one was in the area, his heavily hooded eyes darting nervously. At last sure they were alone, the Animal said, "Vincent, remember in the bar back awhile, they wanted to watch some show and I wanted a comedy, remember?" As if it was a matter of life and death that Vincent remember.

Vincent said, "Yeah, Animal, Jesus, what—"

"Vincent, I got to get my mind off it, I got to, or I'm gonna fucking die!"

The Animal wasn't given to exaggeration or dramatics, so Vincent was surprised. The big stone killer standing there in the alley hopping from foot to foot like a little kid having to use the can, staring at Vincent as if Vincent was his only salvation.

Vincent said, worried, "What?"

"You give me your word, you got to give your word, Vincent, this goes no further?"

Vincent said, "You think I'm a fucking rat, or what, Animal?" He used a tone both men had heard countless times in the joint, the challenging, fuck-you voice that generally preceded some mindless act of violence.

As the gusting wind drove snow into their faces, Vincent took his hands out of his pockets, assumed a protective stance, ready to move if he had to, listening to some garbage from a drunken hit man in an alley, Christ.

"Vincent, you don't understand, I can't talk to anybody else."

"Hey, Animal, you ain't going to be talking to *me* much longer, you don't stop insulting me and get to the point."

Desperately, breathlessly, as if afraid that if he didn't blurt it all out at once he would never again speak about it, the Animal said, "They're coming to get me in my sleep, Vincent, Jesus, Jesus, oh, Christ, Vincent, you got to help me!"

Vincent, remembering what Bolo had told him in the booth earlier, allowed himself to feel frightened, telling himself it was okay to feel it; the brave man worked through it, kicked its ass. . . .

Then said, "*Who* is, Animal?"

And the Animal said, "Every one of them, Vincent, every guy I ever killed, they're coming after me in my dreams, coming to get me." And then he wailed and whimpered, jumping up and down, terrified.

Vincent walked slowly down Van Buren to North Clinton, heading for home, thinking about the Animal and from time to time shivering from things that were much more chilling than the bone-numbing cold.

Garbage cans rattling from the wind, that's how strong the wind was blowing, the hawk. Taking the breath from their mouths and blowing it away. Vincent wondered if the Animal's wail had carried, maybe down to Madison Street, chilling winos filled with antifreeze, making them hallucinate werewolves before them, coming after them. That's how he'd sounded, like a werewolf in a movie howling in the woods as he stood in an alley off Van Buren Street in the heart of the Loop on a January afternoon.

Christ Almighty. The guys the Animal had killed were coming after him in his dreams. He'd told Vincent that they were reaching for him, their arms waving slowly, maddeningly, their dead rotted faces mouthing his name, calling to him. As they made their slow progress toward him, he'd try to run, escape them, but he could never move; he was rooted to the spot.

Vincent had told him that it was just a dream and the Animal had told him that it happened every single night without fail; as soon as he put his head on the pillow no matter how drunk he was, it would come.

And they were getting closer every time. . . .

The previous night he could smell them, rotted flesh having that smell all its own and he'd smelled them, felt their long fingernails scratching his body and he'd screamed silently in his dream and they'd started laughing.

Vincent shook himself and started as a car drove past him, the driver honking the horn at him, and he lifted his arm halfheartedly and waved.

Animal telling him that he owed him, that because he loved Vincent and because he respected Vincent and because he would die for a stand-up guy like Vincent, he had been one of the two guys that had murdered the skinny little punk who had ratted Vincent out almost ten years ago. And now the kid was coming at the Animal along with forty-five other men and three women; the kid's hair filled with seaweed and his dead mouth filled with sand.

Forty-nine kills, half of them in towns he couldn't remember, performed against people he could never remember, and that was how he knew the dream was real. Twice he'd just wired a car, been paid and shown the

ride, and the guys who'd caught it were never seen, but
now they had faces, names, now he knew every one of
them and remembered them and they were coming after
him.

The Animal kept saying the word *dream*, and Vincent
said if it was a dream, then why was he worried, and
then he'd changed it to nightmare. As if that wasn't another word for dream, only a bad dream.

Vincent asked him why he didn't ask someone for
help and the Animal had shouted, "What do you think
I'm doing now?" Vincent had said professional help and
the Animal had just looked at him.

Vincent getting it then; how do you walk into a
shrink's office and tell him what the Animal had just
told Vincent without going away to the fruit farm or
the penitentiary one?

The Animal said, "It's not a dream." In anguish, and
Vincent could not tell him it was . . .

. . . because maybe it wasn't. . . .

And the Animal had left him, apologizing, going off
with a stagger and a start into the afternoon, to his car,
Jesus, offering Vincent a ride.

And Vincent had headed home.

Five twenty-five North Clinton, above an abandoned
warehouse, the entire top floor his.

His sanctuary, his refuge.

Two alarm systems each independent of the other,
both so well hidden it had taken Bolo an hour to find
and disarm them. Time enough. At least no gang-
bangers or small-time B & E punks would be in there
boosting what he'd worked for.

Vincent entered the gigantic single room, reset the
alarms and locked all three deadbolts behind him. Two-
inch bits of steel bolted to the iron fire door, going into
the steel frame around the door. Safe and secure. There
was a skylight, but it was on both alarms systems, the

tiny wires attached on the inside, the glass panes shatterproof. No other windows in the room.

Evlyn had said to him, "God, it looks like the library," the first time she'd seen it, and she'd come close. All four walls, from floor to eight feet up, were filled with hardcover books, resting in bookshelves Vincent had built himself. Wide shelves, stopping halfway to the sixteen-foot ceiling, the rest of the wall all the way up stone. An impregnable fortress without television or radio. Just books, a fireplace, a huge leather couch that folded out to a queen-sized bed. Home. The couch in the middle of the room, facing the fireplace, with a lamp next to it.

Vincent pulled the switch that would unfold the Levolor blinds over the window; he did not want to see the bright sun or watch it set as it would do anytime now. He went to the single walk-in closet, opened the door inside against the far wall and turned the bathroom light on so he could see what he was doing, hung up his jacket and removed his jeans and sweatshirt, put the hat on a shelf above the hanging clothing. Tons and tons of hanging clothing. Vincent liked clothes. And books. Books most of all.

He dressed in fleece-lined gray sweats, pulling his socks off, wanting the feel of the highly polished hardwood floor beneath him. Even though it would be very cold. The fire would warm them soon enough. Three thousand square feet of open space in the South Loop belonging to him, surrounded by his books, with wooden floors under his feet, leather cracking beneath him and a warm fire to gaze into as he digested what he'd read.

Heaven compared to a four-by-eight cell he'd shared with another man, one of them always having to go to the bathroom or farting or coughing, cramped in there all night with nowhere to go even if the cells had been left unlocked.

He'd debated with himself about the closet when he'd bought the building. He hadn't wanted anything to break the bookshelves, wanted to give the impression of millions of books side by side in oak cabinets, but he'd also not wanted his clothes there where he could see them all the time. So he'd built the closet and put the bathroom inside it; even the single phone was mounted on the bathroom wall. There would be no distractions when he was reading.

Vincent walked out of the closet and closed the door behind him, then looked at it. The door blending in with the cabinets but damnit, it still wasn't a bookshelf. Maybe he should go ahead and put one there with wheels on it or something, or better yet on hinges, so it could pull away from the wall. But then it wouldn't be flush against the floor like the others, would still look out of place.

To hell with it.

Vincent went to the fireplace and admired the stacked wood piled on both sides, adjusted the piles as he stacked some in the fireplace, making them look balanced and even. Order was very important to him when he was home; balance. As he had none in his ordinary daily activities. He got the fire blazing just right, the flames illuminating the room; with the blinds closed, the place was very dark.

He went over to the D section of the nonfiction shelves, looked for dreams. There were seventeen books there about dreams and dreaming. He found one that was written by someone with a PhD. and took it down, walked with it to the couch. He sprawled out, reached for the button with his foot and stepped down, and the little area of his tremendously spacious home where he was sitting was illuminated brightly.

Knowing now that, no matter how sweet a deal Bolo had going for them, his thinking about it couldn't lull him to sleep, not after his ordeal with the Animal, he began to read.

7 There was a power struggle going on in Chicago. One that could not really be called political but nonetheless had strong political overtones. It was a struggle for power within the outfit.

For thirty years Tomasino Camponaro, aka Tommy Campo, had ruled Chicago with an iron fist. Thinking himself immortal and untouchable, he had surrounded himself with underbosses who carried out the tasks he assigned to his strong right arm, Angelo (Tombstone) Paterro. The underbosses controlled the gambling, prostitution, loansharking, pornography and burglary rings in the city. They controlled the docks and the construction workers' unions. They had access to or were paid tribute by the black and Puerto Rican gangsters who were suddenly organizing and taking control of their own neighborhoods, perhaps tired of watching white men make all the hay and collect all the money from their parents and neighbors.

They kept their control easily because they murdered anyone who stepped too far out of line; thieves who had refused to pay tribute would take a late-night swim in Lake Michigan, with iron chained to their feet. Pimps and numbers runners who skimmed a little too much cream off the top were there, too, the lake being a

notoriously equal-opportunity resting place. No preju-
dices at all. The fishes did not care who slept with them;
everyone tasted the same.

And then the unthinkable happened.

Campo began to lose his grip a few years back when
he'd allowed one of his underbosses, Roland DiNardo,
to import drugs. He hadn't had knowledge of the for-
bidden crime until it was too late and DiNardo was already the subject of intense scrutiny by the Chicago
Narcotics Squad controlled by Jimmy Capone, one of
the few incorruptible cops to ever carry a badge in the
fair city. But to mob watchers and fellow gangsters
alike, it had been a sign that Tommy was maybe not on
top of things. Instead of cutting his losses and admit-
ting to administrative errors, Tommy had compounded
his mistake by having the underboss murdered in the
county jail as he awaited trial.

The other underbosses tried to understand; after all,
DiNardo had been selling drugs, but their boss's lack of
loyalty bothered them.

It even bothered his number-one man, Tombstone
Paterro. Who began secretly taping their private conversations. Paterro kept dozens of incriminating tapes in a
safe hidden in the den of his home. When a zealous
undercover cop had tried to take down the entire mob
structure, Paterro had decided to use a just-released psy-
chotic ex-convict to take care of the cop and a soon-to-
be-indicted underboss who had trusted the undercover
agent, and the house of cards began to feel the wind.

The decision to kill the underboss had been entirely
Paterro's; Campo had been manipulated into it by the
wily Sicilian. The decision to use outside talent had also
been his. Serious inroads had been made in Campo's
organization due to the murder of DiNardo, and to
have another underboss murdered within a year of DiN-
ardo's death might have brought them enough heat
from the national commission to force Campo and Pa-

terro into retirement. So he could not use his own people. His mistake had been in not telling the young killer to leave the underboss's wife alone.

She was the daughter of one of the nation's most powerful crime bosses, and the young man, in his enthusiasm, had killed her.

And had then called Paterro, using a telephone that had an authorized wiretap attached to its lines.

His back against the wall, looking at page after page of indictments but truly worried only about the state charge of murder, which would put him away in a dungeon in Joliet for the rest of his life with no chance of parole, Paterro decided to do the unthinkable.

He ratted out his boss.

Never in the history of the Mafia had such a powerful figure turned on his master, and within months Campo was serving one life sentence, then within the year another, and on January 17th, this time in a federal court, he'd been sentenced to a thirty-year term, the max, under the RICO statute. His state trials were under appeal and there were more to come. For all practical purposes, Tommy Campo was through in Chicago.

Paterro himself had been sentenced to a ten-year federal term and was working with the authorities, helping them to tear down the mob in the city. He was doing his time in comfort, guarded by federal agents on an Army post in Florida, working on his tan and living with his wife in a cottage that had once housed a lieutenant-colonel. Not quite what he'd grown accustomed to, but better than a four-by-eight cell in Stateville any day.

And the underbosses had converged on the corpse of the Campo empire like piranhas on an unsuspecting Brazilian swimmer.

Mob war raged. Bodies were turned up daily. The cops sat back and smiled, enjoying it. Not working too hard to clear it all up, not looking for arrests or evi-

dence. Bringing in the ones who were crying that they
were next, looking for immunity. Telling them that it
was a buyer's market these days, a boom town for police
officers. Reduced sentences, maybe, immunity, never.
Those days were long gone. The cops had fun tearing
apart what was left and watching the men of respect run
for cover.

The national commission had, since the days of Al
Capone, looked upon Chicago as the retarded brother
of the mob. The civilized mobsters who were more
businessmen than crooks shook their heads and waited
for the fallout to stop before moving in and taking over,
putting things back in order and straightening out the
mess. When the time was right, they'd come in and
shatter whatever resistance was still left, replace the
fallen walking dead men with their own people. Put
high-tech wizards on top to replace the dinosaurs who
still believed that swagger and bluster were the equal of
true power.

But it would be some time before they could come in
and do what had to be done. These dinosaurs did not
face extinction happily.

Lined up behind their leaders, the old underbosses to
Tommy Campo, the soldiers and street punks saw this
battle as the best thing that ever happened to them;
fought valiantly and bravely to improve their chosen fig-
urehead's position, make him the most ruthless and
powerful man in the city, so they themselves could reap
the rewards their loyalty would surely bring them.

While the body count continued to rise and the mor-
ticians got fatter than Vincent Martin could get in a car
lot full of Eldorados with the keys in the ignition.

Bolo knew all about the power struggles and the
gasping outfit fighting for its life. He knew even more
about what was going on than a lot of the mobsters did.
He knew, for instance, about the blacks and the Hispanic mobs growing more and more powerful each day,

consolidating their power bases, joining forces against the dying old guard. Ready to take over when the smoke cleared. He knew, too, about the bloody battles that would be joined when the national commission sent their troops in thinking there would be no more blood spilled. He knew the minority gangsters would one day rule their mobs the same way Tommy Campo had once ruled his, and he figured this for a good thing. Because Bolo thought the dagos had gotten too big for their britches.

He'd always paid his tribute, like all the best burglars had. Ten percent, right off the top, for the right to work whatever area he'd chosen. But he'd never gone to a mob fence in his life and he'd never worked for them straight out. And had taught Vincent never to do so.

Bolo had it in his mind that the crooks were going to smother each other quite soon, that they were in the violent throes of a death dance. And so he wanted to get some of the millions out of their pockets before they blew it all on defenses, or the state or federal government took it all away from them.

So he decided, for the first time in his life, to go to work for the outfit. One score, one night's work. His own way, with his own people, doing it in his own time. And not for any piece of whatever he found there in the safe or squirreled away in the house. If the mob wanted him, if the outfit thought they needed the best, then they'd have to pay for it.

Two million, cash. Half up front and half paid out on delivery. Bolo would have to have his money before he would even consider turning the take over to them. They talked all the talk and scarfed up the books and movies about loyalty and honor, the outfit guys did. But he knew they did not walk the walk. In Bolo's opinion, the outfit guys would sell their mothers to black pimps if there was enough in it for them to live really well for awhile.

And so he was smiling as he cabbed to the Embers restaurant on Wabash, the very same restaurant where Angelo Paterro had first come in contact with an undercover cop named Jimbo Marino. He was smiling because these guys were so stupid, they'd never change. Using the same joint that had been the scene of the beginning of their own violent end.

It was snowing now, heavily. Two years ago Chicago had been the recipient of the mildest winter in recorded history; January days in the sixties, for God's sake. Last year had been normal, cold and snowy. This year was a goddamn killer.

Bolo paid the driver and threw him a ten-dollar tip for the nine-minute ride, waved away the guy's thanks and entered the restaurant.

Two jamokes in suits—big guys, but Bolo sized them up and guessed that Vincent could take them both out in maybe three seconds—nodded at him as he checked them out, one of them giving his head a sideways shake, as if Bolo did not know that the people he had come to see were inside. Assholes.

Ted sipped his ginger ale and listened. There was much to learn. When his opinion was asked, he gave it, but he never jumped in. Never tried to impress Montaine or Bags with his insight, startle them with his wit. He was patient, playing it by instinct, by ear. So he was shocked when Montaine asked him what he thought of the deal.

"I think you need a couple more guys, go in with this thief. At least one. Keep him honest. I also think it should be done at night. No matter how many cops you got in your pocket, someone sees a guy hanging off the top of Sears Tower in broad daylight, maybe he'll walk right in, tell security instead of calling the cops. Those goons of Parilo's find out, your plan'll be dead before it gets off the ground. They'll shoot the guy off the wall."

He sat back and sipped his ginger ale, trying not to appear nervous. Montaine was looking at him with a new respect.

Montaine said, "Ted, your cousin told me you were sharp," and Ted nodded. "But Parilo won't leave the apartment after dark. He's paranoid. Hell, he just showed me the tapes not two month ago, and that was only after I balked about his plan to whack out guys I've known all my life."

Ted felt that Montaine was waiting for him to say something, but he didn't want to appear eager or foolish, so he kept his mouth shut.

Montaine said, "I told you before, we'll have guys backing you up. Like when you deliver big dough or think you need help. But you, Ted, let me ask you something, how you feel about heights?"

"I can do it, Mr. Montaine, you want me to."

"There's a little more to it than that," Bags added.

Ted raised his eyebrows.

Jerry Montaine said, "Soon as you open the safe, soon as you're certain the tapes are all there, Ted, and you feel secure about getting out of the place without the guy's help, I want you to blow his fucking head off. Preferably inside of the apartment."

"No wonder you don't want too many guys involved in the robbery."

"That, and, the less who know, the better chance we got of pulling it off. You know thieves, Christ, they get two drinks in them, they're off to the races, bragging to each other about past scores, upcoming scores, doing the honor-among-thieves bit. Then they get all surprised when the cops show up when they're in someplace they just told forty other guys about."

"Then the guys who dropped the dime watch the booster get arrested, and go in and grab the score for themselves." It was the first time Ted had spoken without having been asked a direct question, but he felt safe.

And Montaine didn't call him on it. His cousin Guido didn't even give him a dirty look.

Montaine looked at Bags and said, "When this is over, Guido, you find a good spot for this man, you hear me?" And Ted King, for the first time, began to loosen right up.

Bolo was wearing eighty-buck slacks and a tailored shirt, over long underwear. He had on two pairs of heavy wool socks. He was wearing brown New Balance running shoes. His waist-length woolen jacket was new and had cost him two bills, no jewelry; and as he sat down at the back booth, he felt grossly underdressed, and if these goofs weren't going to hand over 2 million to him—serious money—he might have gone ahead and laughed at them.

They looked like movie gangsters, early afternoon and they were wearing pinstriped three-piece suits and sipping scotch out of rock glasses, holding their pinkies out as they drank so the soft lighting would show the world the diamond sparklers set in heavy gold on their little fingers. Two of them side by side, looking like a couple of dummies straight out of Marshall Field's west window, both ugly enough to need a couple grand worth of clothes, plus diamonds everywhere to take the attention away from their mugs. Next to him was a little guy, much younger than the two outfit gents, dressed in cheap imitation of them. Some kind of bodyguard, or maybe one of those karate kids who seemed to forget that a kick in the balls would fell any man; the skin on his nuts was no thicker than anyone else's. Bolo ignored him and nodded at the two outfit guys.

"Guido," he said, "Jerry." The gangsters almost winced at the familiarity Bolo assumed.

Guido Baggio, smiled stiffly, trying to maintain his regal composure and bearing, then said, "Bolo." The name rolling off his tongue the way Bolo himself had

said the word *boosting* to Vincent that afternoon. Jerry
Montaine did not even nod. He just sat there smoking
his English Oval nonfilter cigarette, staring toughly, trying to intimidate a guy who didn't know the word.

Bags said, "I hope you understand, Bolo, that with
the situation the way it is these days, the times as they
are, we can't allow even our oldest and most trusted
associates to speak with us without first getting checked
out." He nodded at the young kid next to Bolo and
said, "This is Ted King. He's gonna give you a quick
frisk and—"

"He touches me one time, I'm out of here," Bolo
said. He grunted. "Kid's wearing an off-the-rack suit
from Sears, a goddamn pair of shoes cost maybe six
bucks, a phony diamond pinky ring. Jesus, he touches
me, I'll break his fingers." He addressed himself to Jerry
Montaine. "Since when you guys hire people got no
class?" That got a tight smile from Montaine. Telling
them what the kid was wearing, down to his shoes,
without even glancing at him for more than a second
seemed to have impressed him.

Beside him, Ted King said, "Hey, I don't need this
shit," and Guy Bags without looking at him told him to
be quiet. Ted grunted, and Bolo could feel the kid's eyes
staring knives at him. He showed his disdain by not
even bothering to acknowledge Ted's existence.

Montaine said, "My friend Guido, he tells me you're
the best."

Bolo smiled. He couldn't resist rubbing it in a little
and so he said, "Hey, Jerry, how do I know this kid
here ain't wearing a wire?" Smiling so Montaine and
Bags would know he was kidding, just giving the kid a
little ball breaker. Bags smiled and Montaine grunted.
From beside him he could hear the kid suddenly breathing heavily. Under him the fake leather was whispering
as he moved slightly, his left side now mostly protected

by his arm. If the kid, Ted, got tough, he'd elbow the hell out of him.

Montaine said, "Are you?"

Bolo said, "Jerry, there was a colored guy, Safeman Willy, he was the best in the entire country. He got killed by the Central Investigation Unit right before they disbanded, came into his house and shot him down like a mad dog; the guy never raised his hand in anger once in his life." He paused and fished an English Oval out of Montaine's box, lighted it with the Dunhill that had been sitting atop the box, started to put it in his pocket, then said, "Oops," put it back where he'd found it.

"There was another guy, Fabe Falletti, used to score like a champ three, four times a year. He's retired or dead, no one knows what the hell happened to him. Couple years ago he just up and disappeared." He took a deep drag off the butt, stubbed it out—the cigarette almost totally unsmoked—and let the smoke ease out his nostrils.

"Outside of those two guys," Bolo said, "I'm the very best safeman there is."

Beside him, Ted King said, "Humble, too, eh, Mr. Montaine?" and Bags shot him a filthy look, waved a hand at him shortly.

Montaine said, "Guido tell you what we want?"

"He tells me you need a safeman for a job." Bolo held up his right index finger. "One job. One time only, then I'm back in retirement."

"He tell you what we pay?"

Bolo thought, Jesus Christ, if you guys are so tight, why don't you talk to each other? but he kept his mouth shut, nodded, not wanting Ted to know what was involved. He was obviously no bodyguard, just one of their nephews or something, called to duty during the manpower shortage.

Montaine, as if reading Bolo's mind, said, "That's

good, because now we all know what's going on. And for two million fucking bucks, Mr. Bolo, I don't need no wiseass coming in here talking to me like we're family, calling me by my first name."

Next to him, Ted grunted, and Montaine looked at Bags sharply and said, "One more sound out of your cousin, Guido, and I'll suck his eyeballs out of his head." Guido looked at Ted threateningly, an I-told-you-so look. Ted sat mutely, wondering how things could go wrong so suddenly. Bolo guessed he was too cowed to even apologize.

He said, "Fellas, you want some man going to tremble and shake, you're not going to find him. Not a professional safeman. But I'll tell you what you do, if what you're looking for is a fawning asshole to kiss your ring and go out and blow an alarm off, get himself in a jackpot, why then, you use Teddy here. He's more your type than I am." Bolo smiled and turned his full attention to the young man for the first time.

Seeing a short, compact kid, maybe a welterweight, going bald already, shit, he couldn't be forty yet. Dumb-looking, wouldn't be so bad, though, if he hadn't been trying for a tough-guy sneer. Probably did time in some minimum-security state farm and had convinced one of the local bad guys he was stand-up and ready to help them win control of the city.

To Ted King, Bolo said, "You a safeman, Teddy?"

Ted King said, still sneering, "You call me Teddy again, old man, I'll show you what I am."

Bolo smiled. Bags and Montaine were both older than he was, and he knew they wouldn't miss the reference to age as a sign of weakness.

He looked at the two mobsters and shook his head. Bags was staring knives at Ted, but Montaine was ignoring the kid, looking at Bolo hard, his mouth working, grinding his damn capped teeth, maybe getting ready to swallow his pride.

Bolo said, "I got a business to run." Got up and turned again to the young man in the cheap Sears suit who was grinning at him thinking he'd scored some scare points.

"All you got to do, Teddy, is grow a set of balls big enough to let you make a move. Then I'll show you what you're made of." And he turned his back on the kid, knowing that the gangsters would stop him from doing anything stupid in a public place.

Bags said, "Bolo."

Bolo began to walk away.

Montaine said, "Mr. Rubolo," in a cracked, angry voice.

Bolo kept his face straight and turned to him, an inquiring look set politely on his face. "Mr. Montaine?"

Montaine said, "I'd appreciate it if you'd sit back down, maybe we could get back down to business here without a bunch of nonsense getting in our way." He turned sternly to Ted King and said, "Teddy. Go wait in the bar." Ted looked, white-faced and shocked, at Guy Bags, who shook his head violently, pointing it toward the front of the restaurant.

Bolo thought the kid was going to cry.

His face beet-red now, staring at Bolo with hatred shining out of filling eyes, Teddy got up out of the booth and stalked toward the front of the place. Bolo sat down.

"No more of this Mr. stuff, okay, Jerry? Just call me Bolo," he said, poker-faced, ready now to talk business since all the ego garbage was out of the way and they all knew who and what they were dealing with.

He knew that forever more he would be Teddy to them; they'd call him that now just to piss him off. Just to show their contempt until he proved himself. And wouldn't that be a ton of fun, proving himself to Montaine by whacking out that wiseass son of a bitch. In the joint, out in Vandalia where he'd picked corn for the state and cleaned the garbage off the highways, he'd tried to get the other cons to call him Barracuda. He was slender and powerful, like a barracuda. Some of the guys had asked him what his name was and when he told them Barracuda, they'd just laughed at him. Doing short time in a minimum security joint wasn't a place to look for trouble, so he'd let it go. He knew that the cons who abused the privileges were sent to Stateville over in Joliet and although he knew he was a pretty tough guy, he didn't intend to ever go to that place. They ate barracudas for *lunch* in Stateville.

He was mad about the old guy calling him Teddy, and he was mad about the guy making fun of his shoes. They'd cost him three hundred, because they put two inches on his five-foot-seven-inch frame.

He walked up to the bodyguards who'd met them when they'd entered and said, "Everything okay? Bags wanted me to check." And the guys looked at him like he was something that had crawled up out of one of the kitchen sinks, and he felt his face going red so he swaggered away from them, giving it everything he had, swaying his hips, his toes pointed out, swinging his arms.

Into the bar. He looked at the skinny young bartender wearing the white shirt—pencil-thin arms pointing out of the short sleeves, eyeing Ted because he had come in with Baggio and Montaine, men of respect—saw the fear there in the guy's face. He said, "Hey, you, get your ass over here and get me a fucking White Label, rocks, eh?" And the guy came on the run, saying yes sir right away sir, mixing the drink, pouring it freestyle. He put it in front of Teddy with a flourish.

"There you are, sir," the bartender said. Then stood there, waiting to get his money.

"You got a problem? You want something?" Ted gave the guy the glare, seeing him start to shake.

"No, sir, no problem, sir—" Jeez, ready to start bawl-
ing, about to lose the price of a drink because he was so
scared of Ted King. Teddy took a ten out of his pocket,
threw it on the bar and said, "Keep the change, kid."
The bartender maybe two or three years older than
Teddy was.

"Thank you, sir," the bartender said, smiling gratefully. Man, if they were in the joint, a fish acting like
this guy, Teddy'd have himself some head running before suppertime.

Feeling good, forgetting for the moment about the
old fart inside who'd insulted him, hurt his pride and
challenged him, Teddy said, "Don't worry about it." He
raised the glass to his lips and took a small sip, his little
finger out, his zircon flashing.

"I'm not taking him in with me. You want the job
done, you got to understand that, it ain't gonna happen."

Bags said, "Bolo, try to see it from our point of view,
will you? Here we got a guy, got no respect—now
don't take an attitude, all right?—but let's face it, you
don't like us and we don't like you. We got a business
deal. We're paying two million dollars to you for whatever you get out of that safe. Now, you didn't last as
long as you have, never doing any time, being stupid.
You got it figured what's inside that safe is worth a lot
more to us than what we're paying. With your attitude
toward us, how we supposed to know you ain't gonna
grab the money and the goods, take off, sell it somewhere else?"

"You said it yourself; I ain't stupid. And I got my
honor, my pride. One time, I went out on a score for a
guy, a divorced doctor, he wanted jewelry from his
ex—old lady, millions' worth he'd given her and she'd
kept it after the divorce. He couldn't understand why
she wouldn't give it back. He pays me, I go in, make the

move. Meantime, this doctor, he been playing footsie with some chick he was supposed to be healing; the woman's old man finds out, she cried rape, she was under some drug the doctor gives her, blah blah. The doc gets nailed, goes to the county for ninety days; the trial takes two months; he beats it; he's cleared. Forgets all about me, what with his troubles, and in I stroll as soon as his shingle's hung up again with his duffel bag full of diamonds.

"The point I'm making is, all this time I'm drawing exposure. Taking a chance. By my way of thinking, soon as the job's done, I could have dumped the jewelry; I didn't tell the guy to fall in love with some married dame he's getting paid to look up her snatch. But I didn't because when I make a deal, it's made. There's no way for either party to break the contract, ever. The doc had gone away for five years instead of five months, the deal would have been the same. He'd have walked out of the joint and I'd have been waiting for him." Bolo sat back and sipped the beer he'd ordered. He'd invented the story on the spot and he knew these guys would fall for it. Even if they didn't, he'd blow the entire deal off before taking a piece of garbage like Teddy inside with him; it just wouldn't work.

Montaine had been watching and listening, no longer angry now that they'd gotten down to business. He said, "The kid, he can wait outside; as soon as you come out you turn the stuff over to him, right?"

Bolo stared at Montaine, trying to hide his shock. They'd given in so easily. He decided to meet them halfway. He said, "The kid, Teddy, he can drive, how's that?" Figuring the jerk couldn't get him in any trouble just sitting out there waiting in a car. Not if what these men had told him was true.

Bags said, "He can drive just fine."

Montaine said, "He drove us over here."

Bolo raised his hands palms up, dropped them to the table. He said, "So when do I get the downpayment?"

Montaine said, "You'll have it tonight. Someone will bring it over to the bar. It'll be safe there, all the Italians hanging around there all night."

Bolo had no problem with this. They wouldn't dare rob the money back from him before the score was taken off. He nodded, smiled, and said, "Pleasure," and was gone.

Montaine watched him leave, staring at his back, thinking now of all the things he should have said to the man that would have cut him right down to size. He hated guys who thought they were better than real men of respect. Outsiders with no respect for anything, thieves like this Rubolo character. They were erratic and unpredictable. They could not be controlled. Fear could not be instilled in them. They were outsiders, mutants.

He said, "This guy, you swear his word is good?"

"He says something, it'll happen."

"Guido, can you trust the kid to hold up his end? Or should I maybe look around, try to find someone else I can trust."

"Hey, Ted's my father's sister's kid. He's got the blood. He's family. He'll do what he's told and he'll do it right. Besides which, the way this jagoff was talking to him, it'll be a pleasure for Teddy, whacking him out. Maybe he'll even get a nut."

"If he got any balls to shoot nuts out of."

"Ted?" Bags said, watching Teddy rush out of the bar and stare at the safeman's back, his hands balled into fists. "He got more balls than he got brains."

Montaine said, "That, I believe."

"I go to the first doctor," Bolo said, "and he tells me, cancer. I says to myself, oh, man, sixty years and now this. When I'm ready to give it all up and retire. Then I says to myself, I says, Bolo, how do you know this guy ain't stupid? Somebody had to graduate, the bottom of the class. Maybe he mixed my X rays up with somebody else. I feel okay, strong, like a twenty-year-old kid. So I come to you, and what do you tell me? Cancer. So, okay, I got cancer. But hey, doc, let me ask you a question, how you going to get your bill paid? By the time you take me to court, I'll be dead."

The doctor was smiling, puzzled. He'd had men threaten physical violence, he'd had women and men break down and cry, he'd had people laugh at him and tell him he was foolish. He'd watched as finally they'd all come to accept one simple thing—the game was over. But he'd never had one like this character. Wanted only to know how he could get out of paying the bill. The doctor had the urge to tell him that he'd sue the estate; he knew the man would appreciate the joke, but it would have been in poor taste. So he said, "Mr. Rubolo, what I'd like to do is check you into the hospital this afternoon. The growth can't be worked on, it's too far advanced. As a matter of fact, I'm amazed that you haven't felt any discomfort . . ."

"Well, there was some, you know, lower back acts up, you figure you're just getting old. Hauling beer cases around, whiskey, day and night, these things happen."

"Well, I've seen many good things come out of chemothera—"

"No, uh-uh, just forget about that noise, doc. What good things—hair falling out, teeth rotting, losing weight, withering away to nothing, nah, fuck that noise. I want to eat, drink, make merry here for a while before I throw in my cards."

"Mr. Rubolo, there are really some wonderful things being—"

"Hey, doc, there any miracle cures in this hospital? This radiation business, it gonna cure me?"

"Well, I . . ."

"Right." Bolo was sitting on the chair set across the desk from the doctor. He'd known right off when the doc had asked him into his private office instead of seeing him in one of the sterile white-walled rooms with the stainless-steel sink. The first sawbones had been right. He stood up and asked, "How long you figure, doc?"

The doctor stood along with him, his face concerned. Marcus Welby himself. He said, "Mr. Rubolo, there really is no way to tell, with the chemotherapy and the proper drugs, I would say maybe eighteen months to two years. But why don't you—"

"Why don't I get out of here and start living the rest of my life, is that what you were going to say?" Bolo turned and walked toward the door, swaggering, unafraid. At the door he turned and smiled at the doctor. He said, "Oh, yeah, don't worry, doc, I'll pay the bill on the way out, all right?"

The doctor just stood there staring at him.

He called a cab from the nurses' station. Je-sus. Dying. Well, he'd be all right, one way or the other. If the outfit guys didn't whack him out, which they would have to do after the way he'd spoken to them this afternoon, then he'd come up with something else. He stood in the hospital waiting room, there by the sliding-glass front doors, watching for his cab in the swirling snow out there, shivering already. At least he felt okay.

For now, at least.

And he'd be taking care of his family. All the family he had, anyway.

One of the things that aggravated Bolo the most in the entire world was the fact that somewhere along the line Vincent had gotten it into his head that he had no feelings. Vincent would listen to Bolo tell a story and he'd say, "You're a cold man, Bolo." Smiling. Sure enough, Bolo had never gone in for the hugging and kissing business much, not even with women. But if he was so damn cold, how come there was a picture of the kid hanging in the bar right up there with the champs, Frazier, Ali, La Motta? In the middle with the spotlight on him, like he was the best of the bunch?

The boy's father had died drunk, a blessing in disguise and the kid didn't even know it. The drunk, Vincent's father Lonnie, being maybe one of the meanest guys he'd ever run across, probably would have busted the kid's head for him a million times he hadn't caught some liver thing ate him up in six months. If he were such a cold man, why'd he let the kid move in instead of letting the state take him away? He owed Lonnie, sure; Lonnie had taken a bit for him in the fifties and had never ratted him out, but he didn't owe him lifelong responsibility.

And after the joint, the kid losing his touch, maybe. Vincent had no idea how much Bolo really did know, which was almost everything, if you got right down to it. Like how much Evlyn cared about the dummy who didn't even know it. The pretty young kid in love and Vincent only worried about her comparing him to her ex—old man. A stupe, that's what he was. Letting someone like Evlyn get away. Sleeping with her a couple nights a week when he wasn't bombed. Not wanting her to see him drunk, ever.

Bolo suspected that Evlyn was the real reason behind Vincent's three-week dry spell on the water wagon. Trying to see if he could make it without the booze. Vincent probably figured himself already for a coward who'd lost his balls, so maybe he was a drunk, too. A lush. The way Bolo figured it, Vincent wasn't either. Just a stupe. A jerk about broads.

The cab pulled to the outer curb and Bolo stepped from the hospital, the doors rushing in soundlessly, reminding him of the TV program he and Vincent used to watch, Saturday mornings when Vincent was a little kid, then the reruns years later when he was a teenager, late at night after Vincent had dropped out of school and was training to be a fighter. What was it? He got into the cab and gave the driver the address of his tavern, sat back and got it. "Flash Gordon." Doors were always swooshing open and shut on that program with Buster Crabbe, and that broad, who was she, played Dale Arden? He remembered how the two of them would laugh like hell because every episode Dale would scream her lungs out when the Clay People or the evil asshole Ming the Merciless would grab her. Bolo understood how they felt because he himself would sure like to take a grab at old blond-haired Dale one time. She was a real pisser, that one.

He'd lied to Vincent today, too, for maybe the first time since the kid was small and would ask him where he was going at night. Had told Vincent that he was broke. Jesus, only a total idiot could have blown the kind of money he'd earned in his life. The fact of the matter was, he enjoyed working the bar umpteen hours a week. Opening early during the week and at three Saturday and Sunday. He got plenty of rest on the weekends.

What with the bank accounts and the stash under the bar in the fireproof safe, he had maybe three million to leave the kid. The kid had to have some kind of stake himself, boosting everything in sight every day for the past two years. And with the two million he'd get for this job, the kid could live the rest of his life like a king off the interest, after Bolo was gone. Live the rest of his life and wonder if he'd lost his balls. Go back out there someday and give it a shot, so scared and paranoid that he'd blow it, get himself in a trick bag and baboom, right back into the joint.

So Bolo would rest his mind before he died. Take the kid with him on a cakewalk like this mob heist. Show him he still had what it took. So later, after Bolo was dead, he would have no reason to go out there and mess up the rest of his life. Maybe settle down with Evlyn, too, if Bolo had anything to say about it.

And the kid thought he was cold. Maybe because he didn't go to church now that he was sixty years old, as Bolo had seen happen a million times. Well, not him. He'd lived his life. Sixty years and he'd never gone to any man wearing a funny skirt down to his shoes and asked him for help. He wasn't about to go now. Hell, the doc had said, what, eighteen months, two years if he took the treatments and the drugs. He could get the drugs a hell of a lot cheaper than he would ever get them from a store, on the street. Any kind of drug. Maybe try that stuff he'd heard about a few years ago, the stuff they were passing out in Mexico but you couldn't get in the United States because the AMA didn't want to lose the billions they were raking in on the cancer boom in this country.

What was the name of it? He'd have to ask Vincent. Vincent would know, all the damn books he read. Like some kind of schoolteacher instead of a thief.

With the drugs and if the mob didn't whack him, maybe a year. Hell, he knew lots of guys probably wouldn't live until January 27th of next year. Vincent's birthday. Kid hadn't even mentioned it there in the bar that afternoon, probably using it as another reason to think that Bolo was cold.

Bolo thought, I may be old, but I ain't cold.

Smiling, Bolo paid the driver, dropped him a ten and the guy, ignorant son of a bitch, he just grunted like it wasn't enough. He tromped through the snow to the door of the bar, just planning on stopping in and seeing how things were going before heading upstairs to plan for a while. Plan the last score. The final score. Sounded like the title to a book, or a movie or something.

Bolo walked into the bar and said hey. The television was off now, music blaring. He learned right off that he'd been right in the cab, some people wouldn't last the year; he'd outlive some of them because the first thing Tommy the bartender told him was that the Animal had killed himself.

8 Ditka's City Lights. Sean was in his glory. Bigum in his element, surrounded by men his own size for a change. Professional football players. Those who hadn't gone to Hawaii for the Pro Bowl right after the Super Bowl last Sunday. My God. The coach himself had gone over and shook Bigum's hand; Bigum had introduced Sean to Mike Ditka himself.

The coach left and Sean had to ask, "How do you know him?"

Bigum was acting smug, cute. "We old friends. Hell, they wanted me to play the game for them, years back, I told them I had a thing to do for my uncle first, then I'd get back to them."

"You're kidding me."

Bigum smiled. "Yeah, I'm kidding you. Me and the coach spend some free time over at the Misericordia homes, playing with the kids got some bad breaks. He's a nice guy, buys his share of the rounds, you go out after."

"Jesus, is that—"

"Sure is. Pull your head in, man, get hold of yourself. Look like some kind of tourist, sitting there with your head on a swivel, sticking out of your scrawny little collar there."

"Size eighteen is scrawny?"

"Look around you, Sean."

Sean said, "I see what you mean."

"It seems like a shame to leave, don't it?"

"Bigum," Sean said, "let's you and me get drunk, play with the players awhile, get away from it all for just one lousy night."

"I could get behind that, Sean, on one condition."

"Which is?"

Bigum smiled wide. "You say, motherfucker."

"Bigum, that isn't fair."

"Hey, you the one want to stop fighting crime, not me. I'm ready and raring, hot to trot, about to go out there and find Mr. Vincent Martin and put the fear of God into him something powerful. Least you can do, you want me to give up my fun, is say a little old word like that."

"I will not."

"You in the wrong line of work, Sean."

"You eat here often?" Sean now tried to change the subject.

Bigum shrugged. It looked like an Alp during an earthquake. "Now and again, you know how it is, man needs a place where he don't feel like a fr—out of place."

"This works for you, but where can I go?"

"The way you are about language, why don't you try a monastery?"

"You ready to go, Bigum?"

"You ain't gonna say it, are you, Sean?" Bigum was grinning broadly now, playing one of his favorite games, trying to get Sean to give up the silly thing he had about not swearing.

"Let's go find this Martin character," Sean said.

Bigum grunted.

* * *

Vincent woke up cold, feeling cramped. He shook himself and wished he'd at least brought a pair of socks out with him for later; for now. He dreaded the thought of going over to the bathroom, even though his bladder was bursting, because the floor would be freezing. Thirty-five grand for a furnace downstairs, and the vents were above the bookcases and now they were blowing hot air, but heat rises. The floor would be like ice. Three hundred a month in the winter for gas bills, even without a stove to cook on. And he had to freeze. Should have put vents downstairs, too, pay ten times as much but at least he'd be warm.

He jumped off the couch at once and was shocked full awake because the floor was indeed cold. Vincent danced over to the closet, threw the door open and rummaged through the little dresser under the clothes for a pair of socks, ran into the bathroom and shut the door behind him. Ahhh. Much better. The bathroom was tiny, and he always felt claustrophobic in there, but the vent there kept the place toasty warm and now he sat on the lid covering the commode and put the warm socks on. He stood, lifted the lid and did his business, feeling relieved, a little content, almost as good as he'd ever felt since getting out of the pen.

He stayed in the bathroom for a few minutes, warming up, then ran water for a bath, went into the closet and came back in naked and shivering, clean underwear and T-shirt and socks in his hand. He shaved while the water ran and then soaked in the steaming tub, cursing himself because he'd forgotten to bring in something to read. He shampooed his hair, submerged his head and rinsed the stuff off, popped back up and almost smiled because man, was he feeling good. No food, maybe ten beers earlier, but he felt pretty good, which indeed was a change.

Maybe it was because he had figured out something

that might help the Animal. He'd discovered that hypnosis could indeed change the course of dreams; nothing spooky or mystical about it, really; the hypnotist would simply put you under and implant messages that would rid you of guilt, make you feel good about yourself. Perhaps the Animal would give it a try if Vincent went along with him, stayed the night with him and loaded him up with coffee. If worse came to worst, he'd learned that the University of Chicago over on Fifty-fifth Street had a whole department devoted to dream research. Scientists, they wouldn't care if the Animal had killed his mother and theirs, too, they'd see him as a challenge, an experiment. Doing something for somebody he didn't particularly care for was a new experience for him. Feeling good about it was something else altogether; the feeling had been totally unexpected. If anything, Vincent had planned on feeling a little put out about the whole thing.

But he didn't. As a matter of fact, he felt better than he had since the last time he'd been with Evlyn, what, three weeks back.

If anything, he felt maybe a little bit guilty about the way he constantly avoided the Animal. The man had committed murder for him, for Christ's sake, and he'd avoided him because he'd judged the Animal's lifestyle harshly.

Vincent could think back and try to come up with a time when he'd been fighting, amateur or pro, when the Animal wasn't right there at ringside, sometimes even in his corner if it was a rough crowd and Bolo needed him to help keep the peace. He racked his mind but couldn't come up with a single time. And the times when he'd been a kid, the Animal had never talked down to him or treated him like anything but an equal, slipping him a few bucks against Bolo's strictest wishes, Bolo wanting back then to teach him the value of a buck. He'd taught him that, all right.

Vincent got out of the tub and dried himself, enjoying the feel of the hard muscles bunched all over; he worked out hard every day at the gym or downstairs in the warehouse, no matter how badly he was hung over. Tight gut, hard as a rock. Thirty-inch waist still all these years after retiring. Little muscles bunching and clenching in his chest as his fingers moved.

If only he could get his head in the same shape his body was in. . . .

He went back into the closet and dressed, putting the longies on. It was cold outside. He put on an iron-gray suit over a black six-button silk shirt. He buttoned the collar button but did not put on a tie. Warmed up now, clean and dressed, he went and sat on the couch, waiting for his hair to dry. He did not own a blow-dryer. He put on a gray topcoat when his hair finally dried, walked clear across the giant room and flipped the switch on the alarm, hurried out the heavy steel door and locked both locks behind him.

And stepped into a blizzard. The stairway leading to the sidewalk was old iron, secure, solid, but slippery, and he ran his hand down the rail as he stepped down, cursing, his gray tasseled shoes being ruined, his feet getting soaked already. On the sidewalk he stomped his feet, angry, plowed through the drifts to the man door set in the eighteen-inch-thick stone building's first floor. He unlocked it, entered the warehouse, locked it behind him and flicked on the overhead lights.

Both his cars sat facing the corrugated-steel truck doors. A new maroon Cadillac Coupe DeVille, highly polished and shining in the reflection of the glaring naked bulbs hanging high above. Next to it there was a 1978 Mercury Marquis Brougham. In mint condition. Heavy, solid and dependable, with the 351 Windsor engine and the heavy-duty shocks. The Caddy had front-wheel drive but the Merc weighed much more. He decided to take the Merc.

The downstairs area had no stairway or elevator leading to the second floor, so Vincent had never had it alarmed. Although both of the cars were wired to keep away the petty short-boosters. A professional car thief would eat any alarm on the market for breakfast, so there was no sense in even trying to keep them from the cars when he had one of them on the street. As an extra precaution, he'd never even had the heavy steel roll-up truck door rigged with an electronic opener. When he brought the cars home, he parked in the drive and went around and opened the man door, then had to walk the length of the building to press the button that would roll the door up.

Vincent went to the Merc and shut off the alarm, opened it and got behind the wheel, started it and let it idle.

The downstairs wasn't heated, and served as his garage and gym. In one corner was the massive furnace he'd had installed, and over his head were the pipes for the water and the hollow electric conduits. Against the north wall and extending for ten feet in either direction was a gym mat. Bolted to the concrete block at a height of seven feet was a speed-bag platform, a couple of feet away the Everlast seventy-pound canvas bag that Vincent had wrapped so many times with duct tape that there was no longer any canvas showing anywhere at all. No weights, no benches, no sit-up devices, no rowing machines, nothing hydraulic or needing pulleys or racks. Just the bags and a pair of heavy gloves set upon the platform.

Vincent walked to the truck door and hit the button, watched the door roll up and stopped it halfway. He walked back to the Merc and eased it slowly out into the heavy driving snow, through the snowbank that had been blown against the door, onto the drive leading to the street. He got out of the car and walked back into the building, hit the down button, and stepped through the door before the thing came near his head. He stood next to the car and watched the door roll to the concrete, filling the six-inch crack he'd had cut in the concrete at ground level, so the door would be impossible to pry open with a crowbar. He got into the Merc and drove the two miles to Bolo's bar.

Before Vincent even entered the bar he knew something wasn't right. He stood on the sidewalk outside on a mid-week night at ten-thirty and there was no sound coming from within. The Wurlitzer usually was turned up by now; Frank Sinatra or Tony Bennett or Mario Lanza should be warbling inside, the music reaching a few doors down the street. But there was nothing, not even the driving beat of the latest score from the TV shows the group that gathered at Bolo's liked to watch; "The Equalizer" or "Miami Vice" or "Crime Story." Shows where the musical budget was equal to the star's salary. Something wasn't right.

He wouldn't learn what it was standing in a blizzard on the sidewalk, either. Vincent pushed the door open and entered the place, and his first thought was, It's a funeral.

The place was packed, men speaking in soft low voices, almost whispering to each other. No one was laughing or even smiling. Tommy the bartender was still behind the bar instead of on the other side, sitting there drinking up the free booze he was entitled to along with the ten an hour Bolo paid him. Next to him, serving the customers, was Evlyn.

Evlyn who waited tables and wasn't supposed to be tending bar.

Panic seized at Vincent, clutched at his heart as icy fingers gripped his spine. He rushed to the bar and said in a deadly voice, "Where's Bolo!" Not loudly, but with such intensity that the other men at the bar ceased their low talking and stared at him.

Evlyn was looking at him with wide-open emerald-green eyes, just the touch of a welcoming smile frozen still on her lips. She looked puzzled, then understanding dawned and she softened, hurriedly said, "Bolo's fine, he's in his booth." And Vincent felt himself become weary and weak with relief.

He'd been tight as a drum, tense, ready to tear the joint apart. He'd thought Bolo had died or been hit. He took a very deep breath and let it out slowly, through his mouth. Evlyn was smiling at him now, though sadly.

"Hi, Vincent," she said.

Vincent melted just a little looking at that face. The yellow hair that dye had never touched shone under the new track lighting. Had she sounded hurt? Her feelings bruised because he hadn't called? He'd told her that he was going to need to be alone for a while.

"Evlyn. How have you been?" And she told him that she'd been lonely. He tried a smile, as if to let her know that he knew she was joking, but it didn't work. He said, "Let me see Bolo; I'll be right back, okay?" Evlyn nodded, and she managed to even make that simple gesture convey her hurt.

"You want something to drink?" she asked and now she was staring at him, impaling him with those twin green swords, eyes that touched his heart so gently.

He said, "Not right now," and saw the relief in her eyes. He turned and walked to the far booth to see Bolo and find out what in the hell was going on. Feeling everyone's eyes on him. Staring at his back.

Bolo looked up, sitting in the far booth with—what in the hell was going on here?—a rock glass full of whiskey in front of him. Hunched over it, cupping it with both hands. Staring down into it. Across the booth from him, Gino Papa was sitting next to Leo, their faces telling Vincent someone was dead.

Bolo said, "Sit down, kid; Jesus, it's good to see you."

Vincent slid into the booth next to Bolo, threw an arm around his shoulder and squeezed hard, kidding around, but meaning the hug, too. He'd been scared to death something had happened to Bolo. Vincent said, "What's going on around here?"

Leo said to him, "Didn't you leave with the Animal?" Not accusing him of anything, just making a statement.

"Yeah, he had a problem," Vincent said. "But I think I got a way to straighten it all—" And he knew then why everyone was so glum. He asked, "How'd he do it?"

"Took a header off the Ninety-fifth Street bridge," Gino Papa told him, sounding awed.

"Off a bridge?"

Bolo looked at him, his eyes angry and sad at the same time. "He was born there, you know, couple blocks away. We grew up together, us and a lot more, didn't make it this far. Jesus, I'm the old man in the crowd, you guys know that? Sixty years old and the oldest guy left from the neighborhood."

Leo said, "Come on, Bolo, there's all kinds of guys from the neighborhood older than you."

"Working stiffs." Bolo spat the words out.

"Yeah, but shit, they're still alive."

"Leo, those guys, they ain't never *been* alive." Bolo turned back to Vincent. "He knew the river'd be frozen there, back home. Not wide at all at that spot, maybe forty, fifty feet all the way from bank to bank."

In the bar now there was a muffled burst of laughter as the men started telling stories about the Animal. Things they'd done together. Vincent wasn't the youngest man in the room, there were maybe half a dozen guys younger than he, men the older crooks had allowed into the circle. Stand-up guys who could be counted on. Maybe fifty active or retired thieves, a handful of professional gamblers, guys who made their living at it, not like Vincent and Bolo and the rest of them who went to Atlantic City or Vegas a couple of times a year, or the track, throwing their money away on horses with names that they liked. One fence, that was all Vincent could see. Fences weren't generally drinkers. Family men, most of them. Absolutely no pimps or classless muggers or rapos, they were quickly shown the door without even a word spoken. Who were they going to complain to, the management? The guys laughing now were older men, men who had known the Animal for years, respected him. The younger men were looking around at them, bewildered by the quiet but respectful of it. They knew their place. They were accepted but it would be a long, long time before they were equals, like Vincent, accepted into the crowd as one of them instead of a solid trainee.

Gino Papa said, "Vincent, you know, the Animal always liked you. He said if he ever had a son, he wanted him to be just like you. I remember when you was fighting, Jesus, he'd bet his lungs on you no matter who you were matched up with—" And the three older men stared in surprise as Vincent raced from the booth without even excusing himself, cutting Gino Papa off in mid-sentence.

Vincent tore his coat off and let it drop on the first empty pool table he passed, standing in the dark quiet back room, the only light coming from the bar. Along all four walls chairs were bolted to the floor, three rows of them, the back two rows on six- then twelve-inch platforms so everybody watching a big match could see without any trouble. There'd been big games here; Leo playing any self-styled hustler who came along, taking their money. Making them show two grand before even unracking his cue. Fats had played here, and Mosconi. Vincent sat down in the first chair he came to and put his elbows on his knees. He lowered his head into his hands.

The Animal who had killed forty-nine people had never missed one of his fights and had bet his lungs out. Had told Vincent that afternoon that he was the only guy he could talk to and Vincent had taken an attitude with him because he'd asked that the conversation go no further. The Animal, whom Vincent might have been able to help if he hadn't poured ten beers down his throat that afternoon on an empty stomach. Maybe he would have taken the Animal home with him and they could have gone through the books together, found a way out.

Except Vincent held the Animal's job against him, looked down on him because he killed people instead of—instead of what? Hanging around convenience stores and pizza parlors and video stores, anyplace where people just ran in for a second and left their cars running? The Animal killed people for his living instead of stealing VCRs and stereos and TVs and cars, so that made Vincent better than he was, somehow, right?

Vincent heard the soft shuffle of feet and knew that if it was Bolo, he was making noise on purpose, because Bolo had been the one who had taught him to walk like the Indians, soundlessly and fast, walking with smooth confidence that looked slow and studied. Like a ballerina. He looked up.

Just as Evlyn was reaching out to touch his head. Her middle finger struck his left eye and he pulled back and she apologized but she was smiling and he smiled back and felt a little better.

"Jesus," he said, "Animal, a suicide."

"He always liked you," Evlyn said.

Vincent said, "Goddamn."

He was back at the booth, drinking 7Up, watching Bolo and Leo and Gino Papa getting progressively drunker. Pouring the booze down and telling Animal anecdotes and smiling fondly as they spoke. Whenever one of them finished, another one would start right in after the polite laughter died down. The rest of the bar was livening up, but the TV and the jukebox stayed off. As a sign of respect, perhaps. Evlyn bringing the drinks and giving him a broad smile every time, a secret smile. Because he was drinking 7Up. Having hope for their future, maybe.

He didn't tell any stories—what was he going to say, that he'd forgotten all about the Animal's kindness toward him all his life and had avoided the guy because he killed people?—but he didn't feel left out. Or thirsty, either. He didn't feel the urge to drink.

Nor did he waste his time sitting around talking or listening to other people talk about garbage like God's will or heaven and hell or—Vincent's favorite line from wakes and funerals—he's in a better place. Like where? Last Thursday the Animal and Leo and Gino Papa had taken a young man into the alley and had killed him. Vincent wondered how God would feel about that when the Animal stood before Him copping his last plea for all eternity.

Then he pictured the Animal standing before a great big throne and a gigantic old white guy with a full head of long hair and a flowing silver beard, with a halo. God looking through the ledger and the Animal trying to talk his way out of it and God silencing him with a wave of his hand and then telling the Animal, "Hey, have *you* fucked up." Vincent smiled at the thought.

Then let it drop quickly as the skinny short guy who was going bald and was walking funny stepped over to them, carrying a suitcase.

Vincent didn't like the guy's looks. He looked slimy, slick, like a two-bit actor trying to win an Academy Award by playing a movie gangster when he'd never lain eyes on a stand-up guy in his life. Then he pictured the guy in a tux, with a cute little mustache, teaching little old ladies to tango down at the Arthur Murray dance studio. That's what he looked like. That or a small-time pimp, one. Vincent, without taking his eyes off the guy—who was looking right back at him like some kind of badass—lightly pressed his elbow into Bolo's side and Bolo stopped speaking and turned to the little guy.

"Teddy!" Bolo said, sounding happy to see the guy, and Vincent turned to look at Bolo with wide eyes.

The kid going tough, saying, "I told you once, pal, my name is Ted."

Vincent looked from Teddy to Bolo, his head swiveling around, amazed at the conversation, this kid coming in here and going on the muscle with Bolo while surrounded by guys who would skin him, clean him, debone him and barbecue him for their supper just for looking at Bolo the wrong way.

But Bolo didn't seem to mind; he asked the booth in general to excuse him, got up and walked with the guy into the empty back room, his arm around the guy's shoulders, Teddy trying to pull away but Bolo holding him there. It reminded Vincent of some fish on the tier, trying to get away from a jocker who had decided that he was his brand-new girlfriend.

Then Bolo walked back alone and the guy, Teddy, Bolo had called him, was trailing right behind, walking like his feet hurt. Vincent got up to let Bolo in and Bolo sat, turned and spotted the kid and looked surprised.

Bolo said, "You want something?" and Vincent noticed two things: The kid no longer had the suitcase and Bolo was smiling at him, almost warmly.

The kid said, "Nice joint you got here." He bounced up and down on his toes, twice. He said, grinning, "Real lively." And Vincent wanted to smash him in the mouth and might have if Bolo hadn't put a restraining hand on Vincent's arm.

Bolo said, "Vincent, Gino, Leo, meet Teddy." And

Vincent and the others nodded. Hell, if Bolo wanted to take this business from some wet-behind-the-ears punk, then they had no problem with it.

But the kid stuck his hand out and said, "Good to meet you, Vinnie." Sounding cocky and acting superior.

Vincent stared at Teddy's hand. Finally Teddy pulled it back and—just like in the movies—wiped it self-consciously on his coat. With nothing else to do with it, he stuck it in his coat pocket.

"You come in here, you insult my father, you call me by a name you weren't introduced to me by, and you expect me to shake your *hand*? Tell me something, Teddy, are you an asshole, or were you just born under a dark cloud?"

Teddy stood there uncertainly, maybe just now figuring out that he was in hostile territory. He said, "Look, you ain't showing me a lot of respect, either, calling me Teddy, you know?"

Vincent said, "You ain't worth respect, Teddy." Feeling Bolo's hand on his arm again, ignoring it. He said to Teddy, "Now why don't you just slink the hell out of here before your luck runs out, I throw you through the wall or something."

Teddy said, "I'd like to see you try to throw—" And Vincent didn't even get up out of the booth.

Bolo had a death grip on his left arm, so Vincent reached out with his right and simply grabbed the crotch of Teddy's pants, through the wide-open coat. Teddy, never expecting it, tried to jump back but by that time it was too late; Vincent had him and squeezed just a little. Just enough to get his attention.

Vincent said, "This little thing in my hands, it got any balls hanging down under it?" Squeeze. "I don't feel any. As a matter of fact, I think it's a strap-on, Teddy; I figure there's a pussy there under my hand."

Teddy was turning redder and redder each second, the whole bar now watching the scene, and he reached his right hand under his coat and Vincent squeezed—hard—and Bolo saw Teddy's movement and let Vincent go. He came out of the booth as Teddy dropped to his knees, and he let him go, reached inside and pulled a .38 Smith out of the waistband of Teddy's pants. Vincent stuck the pistol into Teddy's mouth.

"You're used to this, aren't you, Teddy?" Vincent said, quietly, speaking just to him, but knowing that his voice was carrying and the whole bar was listening. "On your knees in front of a man with something long, hard and black in your mouth?" Teddy moved to get up and Vincent eased back the hammer.

"How much pull you got on this, Teddy? A gunslinger like you, a badass, what you got it down to, two pounds? I sneeze, you're gone." Teddy tried to mumble something but Vincent bashed the gun into his upper teeth and he shut up right away. Vincent held the gun steady, hearing Bolo behind him saying his name softly, dragging the name out, his voice rising on the last syllable.

He was about to ease the hammer down and remove the gun, maybe turn him over to Leo and Gino Papa for killing, when the two cops came in the front door.

9 All the way over, in the car, Sean kept saying, "My dear, oh my, I met Walter Payton," in a starstruck voice. Sounding to Bigum like the pope would sound if he'd come face-to-face with God. They'd spotted Payton at the bar on their way out and Sean had just stopped; staring at Walter like he was the Mona Lisa, so Bigum had asked him if he'd like to meet him. Sean had looked at him as if he was crazy and Bigum had told him to come on.

He'd marched right up and said, "How you doing, Walter?" and Payton had looked at Bigum, looked way, way up at Bigum, and smiled, reached out and shook Bigum's hand, and then Walter Payton had asked how Bigum had been. Like they were old buddies. Bigum had introduced Sean to Walter and then they'd thanked him for his time and Payton, always the gentleman, had smiled and autographed a bar napkin for Sean, who would have begged him to but had only had to ask.

They'd walked out into the worst blizzard either of them had seen since the big one back in 1967. Their car was almost covered with the white powder, and Bigum got behind the wheel and started it while Sean wiped the snow off the windows and the hood and the roof and the trunk, all the time with the silliest smile on his face.

Bigum pulled slowly from the curb and Sean had said to him, "You never told me you knew Walter Payton," and Bigum had told him, "You'd never asked." Sean stared at him, angry because Bigum knew all about his passion for football and his near idolization of Mike Ditka and Walter Payton and yet had never told him before that he knew Sean's heroes, personally. He said, "From the Misericordia homes, too?"

Bigum smiled at him, then ended the game. "Sean," he said, "one of the really good things about being my size, a guy like Walter Payton takes a look at you and figures that somewhere in the last twelve or thirteen years you have tackled his ass. He's too nice a guy to ask you who you are, so he asks how you're doing really friendly and hopes you don't ask for an autograph, because he don't want to hurt your feelings by telling you he don't remember you."

And Sean had said, "My dear, oh my," going on and on about he'd met Walter Payton until Bigum told him that they'd better head home; the weather wasn't conducive to driving around town.

Sean said, "Look, the guy works and hangs out at a bar called Bolo's; it isn't two miles from here. Let's stop in, have a drink, check the place out."

"Maybe we better just wait till morning, go stake the car fence's joint out and grab him when he drives up with a new one. Jesus told me he told the fence that he'd see him tomorrow."

"And have to explain to the lieutenant what we were doing out of the city limits."

"Well, I could get in the car with him, make him drive back to Chicago."

Sean looked at him. "How about we drive him into Indiana, then say it's federal, crossing state lines, okay?

Really get him good. Gee whiz, Bigum, sometimes I don't know."

Bigum pulled to a stoplight, skidding in the snow. The windshield wipers were working overtime trying to keep up. Through the windshield it looked as if the snow were attacking them, committing suicide as it tried to get through the glass and maybe eat them. Bigum took his foot off the brake as the car slid halfway through the intersection, muttered something about the snow's mother's sex life, and drove through, thanking God there was no cross-traffic. He said to Sean, "Indiana. It sounds like a good idea to me."

They had a difficult time finding a parking place. The street around the tavern was filled with cars that all looked as if they'd been there for awhile. Mountains of snow covered them, distorting their new streamlined styles. Making them look like huge marshmallow sculptures. The snow was still stark white and when they at last found a place more than a block away and were trudging back through drifts of snow to the tavern, Sean remarked how beautiful the snow was before the dirt and grime got to it and blackened it.

Bigum asked him if that was a racial remark. Reminded Sean that he did not play that racial shit. Sean looked at him, so massive and seeming out of place in the bright whiteness surrounding him.

He didn't respond.

He put his hand on the doorknob and nodded at Bigum, opened it and Bigum stepped through and to the right and Sean came in right after him and stepped to the left while he closed the door behind them.

And they both spotted the man on his knees there in the back of the room and another well-dressed man—a man with blond hair and wide sloping shoulders, maybe six feet tall, who looked a hell of a lot like the picture they'd requested and received through the FAX machine back at home base that morning. A man who was stand-

ing in front of the man on his knees, then turning, hiding something—Sean thought, Heavens, was he having
oral sex with the man?—his back to them now; and the
man on his knees got to his feet and even from across
the room Sean could tell that the younger man was
shivering.

Bigum knew all about attitude and keeping—then
maintaining—control. Control was all. They taught you
that in the Academy these days. As soon as you lost
control, even appeared to, the bad guys had you by the
ass. He also knew that he was tremendously strong and
big and powerful. But he was in a bar with maybe seventy men in it and plenty of them were big and powerful, too, and if they decided to all make a move at one
time, he would lose. In the air—you could almost smell
it—the violence in the room. It was the same smell you
picked up walking through the county jail complex or
strolling the tier at Stateville, where Bigum had started
out as a guard while waiting for his appointment to the
Academy to come through. He had to defuse it—*now*—
because something heavy had been going down here
and these sharks had been smelling blood and suddenly
two cops, the enemy in the flesh, had walked in on
them and the fun was over.

Casually, looking neither right nor left but straight
ahead (he'd lose control if he pretended that he hadn't
noticed what was going on in the back), swinging his
arms, putting a little bebop jive into his step, he sauntered over to the far booth. Sean was right behind him.

When Vincent saw the door open and the great big
gigantic cop walk in first with his partner right behind
him, he spun, handing the gun off to Bolo, who
dropped it down into the space between the wall and
the seat. He stood there watching Teddy get to his feet.
The kid was shaking and looked ready to burst into

tears. Vincent whispered, "The man." Then stood there, watching King Kong and his partner descend.

The black guy surprised him. He reached Teddy and stopped, stood staring down at him with a benign expression while his partner stood right behind him, covering his back, looking not as cool as the black guy, but the black guy, Vincent figured, had probably had more practice being cool in a roomful of hating faces. The white guy was holding his own, though. Maybe as big as Vincent was but fat, no hat on, so Vincent could see the guy was nearly bald. Both men were covered with snow. Water dripped off them to the floor, was immediately soaked into the sawdust. The black guy hip, down and about it; the white cop doing pretty good considering. The black guy looking down at Teddy, obviously waiting for Teddy to speak first, grinning at him as if they shared a secret joke.

Teddy stared up at him, his head all the way back, the black guy inching forward so they were nearly touching. Teddy said, loudly, in wonder, "Jesus Christ."

That was when the black guy surprised Vincent. And the entire bar for that matter. He was laughing now, looking down at Teddy way below him. He said to Teddy, "No, but your *momma* thinks I am." Shaking with laughter while the bar exploded for just a second, guys laughing before they remembered who the big guy was.

Still laughing and jiggling, King Kong said to Teddy, "Tell me, my man, were you really down there running this blond dude some head?" Just like that, making stone fun of Teddy, and the bar relaxed; Vincent could feel it. They'd been ready to take their chances and jump the cops if they had dared mess with Vincent in Bolo's joint with the Animal dead, and the guy had defused the situation just—like—that.

They were still watching, though. In case they were needed.

Teddy seemed smaller than he really was and he backed away, his knees covered with sawdust, his face red as tomato sauce. He backed away from them, heading for the door. He gave Vincent a glare before he left and Vincent heard the door slam behind Teddy as he stood there staring up at the great big cop.

Bolo said, "Sorry, gents, we were just closing up."

The white cop said, "Yeah, I can see that, the place nearly empty and all. Maybe what, only seventy guys left." Going for the laugh but not getting it the way his partner had. Not too bad, though, all things considered.

Bolo said, "Had a death in the family," and stood up.

The black cop looked surprised and said, "Sorry, babe, I don't believe you. Anyone ugly as you, they mommas kill the rest of the babies at birth."

Bolo stepped right up, stood in front of the guy, staring at him, trying to figure him out. Then he took his own shot. He said, "You're one to be talking about heritage, buddy. Couple of years back, your fucking ancestors had missionaries sitting around in big round black pots, with fires under them."

Vincent wondered what the hell was going on here. First the black guy getting down on Teddy, doing a number on him, then Bolo jumping on the black guy, putting him down, and now, Jesus, the white cop, he was laughing like mad, really cracking up. Vincent watched as the black guy took a look over at his partner, shook his head sadly, then said to Bolo, "One thing you got to know, I don't play that racial bullshit, all right?"

Bolo said, "We're still closing." Looked at the white cop who had himself under control now, then back to the black cop. "Even if you guys are Sammy Davis, Jr., and Peter Lawford."

Bolo walked around the bar and started washing glasses, his eyes never leaving the cops. The black giant, man, he was full of surprises, he looked over at Vincent and said, "How you doing there, Vince?" Then winked at him.

Vincent said, "You can call me Mr. Martin."

Bolo shouted over for the two of them to come to the bar and they went, the black guy doing his ditty-bop soul-brother walk, the white guy looking long and cool at Vincent for a second before turning and following his partner. Bolo had his liquor license in his hand.

"You guys see this? This is my license. It's in my own name, I own the joint, free and clear. No mortgage, nothing. I got no record, either, so I'm telling you guys, you don't want OPS on your ass in the morning, coming over here rousting an honest businessman like this, then you better get the hell out. I told you twice already, we're closing."

The black guy said, "Bolo, you wouldn't rat us out, even if we are cops, not even if we raped your sister. Shit, you want to close, close. We just stopped in to get out of the snow, say hello to our old buddy Vince—I mean Mr. Martin over there." He nodded his head toward Vincent before continuing. "How come you close so early, anyhow?"

Bolo said, "On account of suddenly, the joint smells like shit." And the black guy didn't back up a single step or miss a beat, he told Bolo that he noticed that right off, as soon as he walked through the door. . . .

And then they were leaving, walking to the door with everybody in the joint watching them, acting as if they didn't have a care in the world.

At the door King Kong turned and looked at Vincent, cocked his finger like he was shooting a gun at him and said, "See you soon, Mr. Martin." Then they left.

Out in the snow—it seemed to be coming down even harder now if that was at all possible—the first thing that Sean could think of to say to Bigum was, "How'd you know that the old guy was Bolo?"

And Bigum, the wise guy, he had to get cute. He said, "My first hint was the big lighted tube over the door with his name on it and the second hint, the license said Enrico Rubolo on it plain as day."

Sean said, "You mean you read the license?"

Bigum, grinning his Bushman grin, said, "Want me to quote you the number on it?"

At 2:15 Vincent and Evlyn left. She left her car where it was, there at the curb covered with snow, and waited in the warming Mercury as Vincent cleared the snow from the windows. He got back in the car looking like a snowman, his head and shoulders covered with pure white flakes. Evlyn said to him, "That's what you'll look like when you're sixty."

Vincent looked over before putting the car in gear and taking off. He didn't know what she was talking about until she told him. Then he smiled, a little sadly it seemed, and said, "I won't see sixty, Evlyn," and drove off through the raging snowstorm.

They passed many of the men who had just been in the bar, the men wiping their cars off, cursing loudly at the storm, some of them having long drives to suburbs. Vincent ignored them and kept his full attention on turning the corner onto Van Buren. He could see maybe five feet in front of him; he had hardly no traction and the big car was sliding all over the street. Fortunately, there was no other traffic.

Vincent said, "Bolo knows."

Evlyn said, "I know."

"How long has he known?"

She hesitated a moment, then said, "About three weeks, since you stopped coming in. He'd corner me before or after work; sometimes when it wasn't busy, he'd get me on one end of the bar and ask me about you."

"And you told him."

"You don't lie to a man who pays you ten an hour and lets you keep all your tips."

"What'd you tell him, Evlyn?"

Another hesitation, then, "That I'm in love with you, that we've been seeing each other for awhile."

"You know, Bolo, he *expects* people to lie to him, it's all part of the game. It's only the important things he demands honesty about."

"I think our relationship is important."

Vincent knew that he'd made a mistake. They'd been through it time and time again, over and over, Evlyn wanting to know why he wanted to keep their relationship secret and he'd told her that it was for her own sake; if the other men who frequented the bar thought she was spoken for, then maybe they wouldn't leave large tips. The excuse sounded phony even to his own ears. The truth was that Vincent didn't want the pressure, the guys all asking him when he was going to marry her, pushing him into it, giving him a lot of talk about how she was too good to let go.

"I think our relationship is important, too, Evlyn."

Evlyn didn't say anything, didn't even look at him, just sat there staring through the windshield at the driving snow.

10 Teddy—and there was no doubt about it, even in his own mind, he was Teddy since that afternoon when the bastard, Bolo, had laid the name on him in front of his cousin and Mr. Montaine—left the bar in a hurry, his hands shaking, his entire body shaking. He stepped into the freezing night air, stood there at the curb taking huge gulps of it, letting the snow fall into his face as he stared into the heavens. Humiliated, degraded and rejected.

He'd thought, for just a minute there, that he'd found a place where he could fit in. Walking in with the suitcase full of hundred-dollar bills, feeling like a big-timer, he'd smelled the electricity in the air. This was a place for a guy like him. And Bolo, even he had made Teddy feel welcome. Smiling at him, then taking him into the back room—Teddy almost going into shock when the man had put the suitcase on one of the pool tables and just left it there without even counting it. Just leaving it there as if he trusted everyone in the joint. He'd even put his arm around Teddy's shoulders and had shot the breeze with him all the way into the back. Teddy had felt as if he was one of them, accepted. Part of the obviously elite crew that hung around there.

But it had stopped when Bolo had walked back to the

booth. He'd been surprised, Bolo had, to see that
Teddy had followed him, and Teddy had felt foolish,
like he did back in grade school when the other guys
had tried to ditch him and he'd chased after them.
Childish and foolish and unacceptable. But Bolo had
softened, had even introduced him to his son and the
other two old guys in the booth. Teddy had just been
trying to be friendly, hell, what were you supposed to
call a guy who'd been introduced to you as Vincent?
And the big sucker, he'd grabbed Teddy's balls and had
squeezed, then acted like he couldn't feel them. Had
called him a pussy and put him on his knees and made
him suck the barrel of Teddy's own pistol.

Teddy wasn't worried about the gun. He had two
more just like it in the car, and maybe a dozen more at
home. Teddy liked guns almost as much as he liked the
booze. And he *loved* the booze. He wasn't even too worried about Bolo's kid making him look bad. Anyone in
the world, *anyone,* would have taken the gun in the
mouth, sucked it, with some crazy son of a bitch pointing it in his face. Besides, he would be whacking out
Bolo as soon as the score was over with, and his kid
couldn't be too hard to find. Teddy knew even while it
was happening that his humiliation would be avenged.

What drove him wild, though, was the fact that the
nigger and his fat friend had made fun of him. Vince,
when he had the gun in his mouth, had at least been
acknowledging him as a man to be reckoned with, a
man worthy of respect. Or else he wouldn't have used
the gun. But the cop, the nigger, he had offended
Teddy in a way that a fellow crook never could; he had
taken Teddy's manhood away from him and shown him
no respect at all.

He wondered how everything could go from so good
to so bad so damn fast. This afternoon, he was sitting
and shooting the breeze with Jerry Montaine, maybe
the single most important underboss in the city, and

then the old fart, Bolo, had come in and insulted him
and after that it hadn't been the same. He'd gone back
to the table from the bar and Montaine had been cold,
distant. Had gotten up and had split with his bodyguards, without even saying goodbye to him. Bags had
told him that it had been a bad move, having a drink of
whiskey at that hour, and he'd told Bags, what the hell
else was he supposed to do? Had told him that if he
hadn't had a drink to calm down, he might have shot
that son of a bitch on the spot. That had taken care of
Bags, but Teddy knew better.

He hadn't had a drink to calm down; he'd taken it to
get his balls back.

He knew, too, who these cops were. Any mobbed-up
crook in the city who had to make regular payoffs to the
cops knew who Bigum Barnes and Sean Kent were.
They would have to know because Barnes and Kent
were worse than the feds; they never took bribes and
the word was once they were on to you, it was all over;
you could start saving commissary money right now,
because you were going down.

Teddy also knew that they were renegades, outsiders.
Barnes and Kent were hated by their fraternal brothers,
were a couple of outcasts who had made the department
look bad; look crooked. Especially Barnes. How many
times had Bags told him that the guy, Barnes, was a
psycho? How, if he didn't have a badge, he'd have him
whacked out in a hot New York second? How many of
Bags's people had Barnes put away?

And, more importantly, how many times had Bags
bitched to him, telling him that Montaine wouldn't let
him order the hit because the guy was a cop, even
though it was common knowledge on the street that no
other cop in the city would do much hunting for his
killer?

Teddy began to see a way to get his balls all the way
back; with Bags, and with the crooks in the bar. Hit the

puke, and they'd know he was a man to contend with. Besides, the son of a bitch of a black-ass monster, he'd insulted him.

Teddy had been followed by two of Montaine's crew to the tavern. They'd been left with instructions to follow Ted's orders, and he'd enjoyed the power, although he hadn't had to use it. They'd all parked a ways down Clark Street, and the two guards had walked Teddy to the front door, making him feel important, like a big shot. But they'd let him go in alone. If anything happened inside, it would be Teddy's problem. As he walked back to the cars, he thanked God that they hadn't come in. If they had, he would have been forced to kill them both so that word of his humiliation would never get back to his cousin. He had enough problems with Guy Bags—having to kiss his ass in front of his friends, like Teddy was some kind of lackey or gofer— without him learning that Teddy had taken a gun in his mouth and been insulted by a nigger with a badge.

He waved to the two guards in their big Lincoln Continental, his cousin's car, but the two guys, they acted like they owned it. The big ugly guy in the passenger's seat powered down his window and asked him if everything went okay and he'd nodded, had put a look on his face as if to say, what could have gone wrong? The guards pulled into the street without another word and Teddy had watched them drive off, thanking whatever there was now that Bags had insisted on two cars, one for interference. He got into the Cadillac Eldorado that Bags was letting him use and started it, warmed it up, his eyes never leaving the tavern door for a second.

Teddy popped the glove compartment and pulled out the .38, feeling like a new man already just holding it in his hand. He bent over in the seat and pulled the fifth of Dewar's White Label out from under it. And felt complete, whole, a real man once more.

Teddy had always had a problem with booze and guns. In fact, they were the reason he'd done his bits in the joint. For as long as he could remember, he was in constant pain, fear, feeling out of place and insecure . . .

. . . Until he took a drink, and then, man, the world was his. He was somebody, a man who took nothing from anyone, a man who could kill and fight and steal and pimp, whatever he had to do.

It was always easier with a bottle. Finding out about guns was probably the second-best thing that had ever happened to him. Having a gun on him and having a few drinks in him, nothing came close to it. To the feeling of power and invulnerability he experienced when he had both gun and alcohol in and on him. He could not be beat. He was invincible. He was God.

He'd been popped this last time, drunk, minding his own business in his Chrysler Cordoba, driving down the street and the bitch behind him wanted to pass and had started laying on the horn, giving him the business, and her window had been rolled down and she had called him an asshole at a stoplight. Teddy had looked into the rearview mirror, totally amazed, happy now that he was certain that the driver was a woman. He'd pulled away from the light, quickly, got up to speed, letting her get right up on his bumper, still leaning on the horn, then he'd slammed on his brakes, watched as the bitch's head hit the windshield of her car with enough force to crack the thing. He'd listened to the cars behind her smashing into each other and he'd thought about getting out, slapping her around a little, but he could see the blood spattered all over the window, and he guessed that the bitch wouldn't be able to feel it even if he did. He had a pint of Early Times between his legs and pistols under the seat, in the glove compartment and in the trunk, so he'd taken off. She'd learned her lesson.

He hadn't gone a block when the cops had nailed him.

They couldn't lay the accident on him, although that was the reason they had stopped him, and they tried like hell. But the woman had rear-ended him, and the fact that she died—her neck had been broken in the crash—couldn't get laid at his feet. But he'd already been on probation for drunk driving, not to mention the fact that he was a convicted federal felon, and they found all three unregistered weapons. Even with his cousin Guy Bags getting him before a friendly judge, he'd been sentenced to four years. And he'd had to serve eighteen months.

He forgot about blackouts now, forgot about waking up in the morning with Bags on the phone madder than hell wondering where the hell he was, not really knowing himself for awhile. He forgot about the hangover he'd be nursing all day tomorrow, everything else that went along with getting blitzed. He forgot that the great big cop who had made fun of him was carrying a badge that made him much bigger even than he already was, bigger than Teddy, Bags, Bolo, Montaine and the rest of them all rolled into one. He forgot about the heat that could come down after a cop—even a hated stool pigeon rat like Barnes—caught his lunch.

All Teddy could, in fact, remember was the way the cop had talked to him back there. He placed the gun in his lap and took a long pull at the scotch bottle, lowered it and breathed through his mouth for awhile, his eyes closing involuntarily as the tears filled them, his entire upper body on fire. He got his breathing back to normal and felt satisfied, manly. Ready to take on the world. He took another long pull, let the scotch join all the others he'd had that day, starting with the gin in his apartment, and the one in the bar that afternoon when Montaine had more or less told him to get the fuck out of the restaurant.

By the time the two cops came out of the bar, the bottle was almost empty and Teddy knew exactly what he was going to do.

Bigum was driving, as always, looking over at Sean, a little angry about what had happened back at the bar.

"You shouldn't have laughed at what Bolo said," Bigum told him at last, when it had simmered in his craw long enough.

"About the missionaries?" Sean looking all self-conscious and upset. "Sorry, Bigum, honestly I am. But it just struck me as so, so—" And he was off again, trying not to, Bigum had to hand him that, he had tried, but now he was laughing again.

"Sean, I want to tell you something; my people was over here, picking cotton for the goddamn slave owners, while yours were starving to death in Ireland, eating potatoes five times a day."

Sean looked stunned and laughed even harder and Bigum felt glad. The missionary crack hadn't been funny and even if Sean thought that it had been, he shouldn't have laughed in front of all those criminoid punks.

"Hey, Bigum," Sean said, earnestly, after he'd regained control, "I don't play that racial stuff." Going for a smile but not getting one, Bigum concentrating hard on getting them through the driving snowstorm. He was thinking, Bigum was. And it was hard because he couldn't see a yard in front of him or behind and he needed all his concentration just to get them from block to block in one piece. But what he was thinking about was something that had been on his mind for a long time. For years . . .

He said, "Sean, I think I'm gonna pull the plug."

"Again?"

"I'm serious, Sean. I'm sick of it. Acting every day like we're fighting crime, making jokes about it, playing the fools in front of the other guys in the squad room, goofing on each other. Saying all that shit about the war on crime having to be fought, hell, *thinking* it, like what they got us doing is somehow important. I've had it, Sean. Really, man, I think I would have gotten out long ago if it wasn't that the rest of them, the crooked cops, would think they scared me out."

"Take a job where?"

"Man, with my rep, my size, my arrest record, I could get the chief's job maybe one of a thousand towns, right here in Illinois. My experience. Got to be someplace, they need to fill their racial quota."

"Bigum, if you go, so do I."

Bigum turned his head for just a second so Sean could see how seriously he took his next statement, then looked back at the not-yet-plowed streets. The car was trying to turn on him, sway to the left, and he fought it, struggled, got it going straight ahead again. Less than a block away he could see the white snow-covered facade of Sean's building. That was good, because what he had to say was something he wanted Sean to think about all alone for awhile, without Bigum's presence right there with him making him prejudiced or less than objective about what he'd been told. He said, "Sean, *you* ninety percent of the reason I ain't gone yet," then slid into the curb.

Sean looked at Bigum for a moment, angry, hurt, uncertain about how he should respond. His first reaction was to strike out, lash at Bigum, hurt him back, tell him he didn't need some oversized freak to keep a job in order for him to perform his duties. But naturally he couldn't say that. Bigum hadn't wanted to hurt him, had been simply laying out the facts. Sean didn't respond, wanting to think about what Bigum had said first. In the morning, there would be enough time.

He got out of the car and closed the door gently,

danced through the snow to his front door as Bigum pulled slowly from the curb. As he passed the apartment building, Bigum honked, once, as he always did, and Sean caught movement out of the corner of his eye and he looked—heavens, he couldn't believe it—there was some idiot driving ten feet behind Bigum in a big car, driving without lights. In spite of the lateness of the hour, mindless of his fellow tenants sleeping all above him, he shouted, "Lights!" as loudly as he could. Man, the frame of mind Bigum was in, if the dummy rear-ended him, he might just hurt the drunken fool.

Bigum felt good, though sad. It was out at last, all of his feelings about the job and why he hadn't pulled the plug already. If he did, what would Sean do? Sean would get over the hurt; he was resilient, but Bigum was getting older every day, man, pushing forty already, not too many jobs out there for guys his age, even with his experience. He sighed, pumped the brakes as he saw the light at the end of the street turn yellow, determined not to slide through another one. God didn't give guys like him two lucky breaks in one night. He pulled to the light, his wheels locked, and the car shuddered to a stop against the curb. He sensed movement next to him, on his left, before he heard the sound of a car horn blare at him.

Teddy had followed them without his lights on, staying five, ten, twenty feet back, secure in the knowledge that they couldn't see him. Not in this storm. Hell, he was having a hard enough time keeping their taillights in view himself, and he knew what he was looking for. He'd almost lost it when they pulled over in front of the apartment building, but the cop had been pumping his brakes and Teddy had had time to stop and pull to the curb quickly. Snow crunched under his tires and he took the opportunity to finish the bottle as he waited, then opened the window just a crack, for some fresh air.

It was hot and stuffy in the car. Smelly, too. There, the brake lights went off and the jig—yeah, it was the nigger; the white guy was standing in his doorway, looking this way—took off and Teddy put the car in gear and followed the red taillights, turning his head as he passed the white cop, who probably couldn't see anything except the shape of the car in this storm anyhow.

Followed the jig and—there was a God—saw the car's brake lights flashing again and again, then hold as the guy pulled to the stoplight, no other cars on the streets, no passersby in this weather, no one walking a dog, nothing, so Teddy pumped his own, the front-wheel-drive Caddy stopping on a dime, next to the jig. With his left hand he powered his right front window down then beeped the horn, his right hand now holding the .38 Smith straight out, pointed right at the cop's head. There, he had his attention now; the jig was staring at him in amazement, his big gorilla eyes open wide, his mouth just beginning to scream when Teddy pulled the trigger five times, silencing him forever.

Teddy took his foot off the brake and drove away from the light as soon as it turned green.

Behind him the green unmarked police car slid away from the curb as Bigum slumped over onto the front seat and his foot came away from the brake pedal. It smacked softly into the light pole and the engine died.

11 "The funny thing is, Vincent, here you are, living in a *bomb* shelter, and you have no provisions. My God, not even a stove and refrigerator." Evlyn seemed to be trying to make conversation, and if it had been anyone else, Vincent would have told her to shut up, but then again, who else could it have been? Evlyn and Bolo were the only people in the world who had ever been allowed into Vincent's home.

He was trying to think while she puttered around the books, both of them trying to put off the conversation they knew had to be coming. But that was for later.

Barecki couldn't have turned him in. If he had, the heat would have been waiting for him at the Cal City chop shop. It couldn't have been Barecki or any of his people. But no one else had known anything.

Years ago, one of Vincent's earliest memories, in fact, was the sight of a younger Bolo, with a full head of hair, a little paunchy from living the good life, telling him constantly, "Don't trust anyone who don't have the same last name as you." And as far as Vincent knew, he was the last of the clan. In other words, Bolo had been telling him, trust no one.

He'd messed up once, but that had been enough for

him. With Camille. And he'd paid the price. It hadn't
happened since.

Bolo was the only person who knew what he was
doing and Bolo would cut his tongue out before he'd
tell anyone. That wasn't even worth thinking about,
Bolo turning on him. He'd die first. And Barecki could
do it a million different ways . . . so who could it have
been? Evlyn spoke again, breaking his concentration.

"You remember back in the bar with the short guy?"

"How could I forget, Evlyn?"

"Do you know, before you hurt him, when he was
standing there trying to shake your hand and everyone
knew there was going to be trouble and the whole bar
got quiet? Do you know what you said? You said, to
the guy, that he had insulted your father."

"I did?"

"He loves you, you know, just like a real son."

"Come on, Evlyn, will you? All of a sudden everyone
loves me. You, Bolo, how about those two cops, think
they love me, too? Or what about the punk back there,
does he love me? After all, I got pretty intimate with
him."

"You can't tell me you love me, can you? You expect
so much. I'm supposed to sit around and wait until you
decide what you want to do before I even tell my
mother I'm seeing anyone. Waiting for you to make
sure how you feel. In the meantime, it's against the rules
for me to even ask you what the guy was doing there,
walking in with a suitcase. It's against the rules for me
to love you, too, isn't it, because you can't love me
back, you're afraid to love me back."

"Evlyn, do you want me to lie to you?"

Evlyn hung her head, and Vincent could see from the
couch that she was trying not to cry. He wondered if he
should go to her, maybe comfort her. Comfort. How
long had it been since he'd even thought of comforting

anyone? For that matter, had he ever thought of comforting anyone before, ever?

He said, "Shit."

Then got up off the couch and went to her, held her, and Evlyn let loose.

They were on the couch, just staring into the fire. He'd pulled the switch that drew back the blinds and they could look up and see the snow falling onto the large skylight window, melting and dripping down to the roof. Holding each other and trying to keep it that way, both of them feeling safe, comforted, trying not to do anything to break the mood.

But Vincent felt a little phony, fraudulent, as if the whole thing was a sham. The woman had slept with him, had told him she loved him. Had waited for him, giving him all the time he needed to get himself together, patiently waiting for him to make up his mind as to what he wanted from her.

And what did he want? How long could he reasonably expect her to wait for him to figure things out?

"Evlyn?"

"Hmmm?" She sounded like a cat purring, content, happy in his arms. Maybe thinking that because he had come to her when she'd begun crying he was finally loosening up. He wondered if he was, then knew it was so; evident in his next words.

"I love you," Vincent said.

Evlyn sat up, uncurled herself and disengaged herself from him, held him at arm's length. He could feel the strength in her fingers, squeezing his biceps. Her eyes were searching his, trying to see if he was for real or what, and he didn't blame her a bit. She had every reason to see him as a user, a con artist. My God, telling her that she'd lose tips if the guys at the bar found out she was seeing him steadily. If anything, it would *increase* her tips.

Evlyn said, "You mean it, don't you?"

"Of course I mean it, I wouldn't say it if I didn't mean it." Vincent was trying for outrage, a little righteous indignation, show her he was a serious-minded man, but she was smiling at him, breaking his heart with that open trusting smile, and—shit!—those gorgeous green eyes were filling with tears, there they went, they were spinning down her cheeks and he'd told himself almost two years ago that he'd never make her cry, like her ex-husband had. . . .

But she was grabbing him, squeezing him so hard it almost hurt; would hurt if it hadn't felt so good, and she was telling him she loved him, too, for the very first time. She'd never had a chance to tell him she loved him, too, before, she said. Vincent wondered why he felt the lump in his throat, convinced himself he was getting the flu. Running around to train stations before dawn and training to Hegewisch, taking a bus from there to Cal City as the sun was coming up would do that to you. . . .

But he didn't believe that any more than he believed Bolo's warning that he himself was the only person in the world he could trust.

Vincent said, "Evlyn? Listen, I want to tell you something."

And then he told her. Almost everything.

At dawn, when he rightfully should have been standing on a corner in front of a convenience store waiting for some trusting mark to come along, he was holding her, still, the two of them having spent the night talking. She told him she understood things now that had puzzled her from the beginning but that she'd never questioned because she felt from the start that if he ever wanted to tell her about his life, then he would, and now he had. . . .

And as she was thanking him, telling him she understood how hard it must have been, her eyes alight again because they both knew that this was something special here, the start of the real relationship, it came to him.

How the cops had gotten on to him.

He got up and stretched, walked to the closet and went into the bathroom, closed the door behind him. He picked up the phone and dialed Barecki's garage.

"Yeah?"

"Bob, don't mention any names. You remember a Latino dude, young, skinny, hanging around yesterday morning?"

"Yeah."

"He turned you out." Vincent was going to tell him that he'd better move on but you never knew, some guys might take it as an insult, telling them something that obvious. He waited.

Barecki said, "Buddy? Listen, the next thing you take? Make it a Porsche or a Jag, cause I'm dropping my commiss on it. Everything I get on it is yours." And he hung up.

Vincent hung up the phone and went out of the bathroom, out of the closet and back to the couch. His mind was on Barecki giving him the whole pile on a nice new Porsche, handing over maybe twenty or twenty-five grand for ten minutes of Vincent's time. All right.

Then noticed as he came closer that she had opened the bed, made it up, and was lying there nude, smiling up at him from under the covers. Vincent walked over to the thermostat on the wall and turned it all the way up. Immediately the furnace kicked on. He hoped that it had enough juice to kick the heat all the way down to the bed, because suddenly he was seeing this woman in an entirely new light and he wanted to get to know every inch of her all over again and definitely not from feeling and groping under the covers.

He thought it was a pretty good idea that he'd just had and he told her what he'd been thinking, undressing, letting the clothes drop on the floor; unthinkable at any other time.

Evlyn threw back the covers and said, "Hey, for an idea like that, I'd lay in the snowbank outside your door, buster, and let you get to know me."

Vincent smiled broadly, feeling very good indeed, almost glowing, as a matter of fact. Naked, he walked to the sofa bed.

The thing about most women he'd known, all of them had a little thing they said or did, some way that they acted. Something that he always figured for really cute at first but within six months drove him crazy. Darleen, the sociology major at the university who thought it would be so much fun to do a paper on him. She used to get a faraway look in her eyes whenever he'd ask her a question, act like she was giving it deep, ponderous thought, weighing every word she was going to speak before she said them. Even if he'd asked her what time it was or if she was ready for another drink. What horse she liked. He'd thought her to be a deep thinker, heavy. After a short time, she'd get the look in her eyes and he'd want to choke her. There was another girl, what was her name? Genevieve, something French, anyway. She'd say his name with that goofy affected accent of hers and he'd also thought it was so cute, at first. So special. And again, within a couple of months it grated on his nerves like fingernails on a chalkboard. And he knew then that it was time to move on. Even his wife, for Christ's sake, when they'd bought the house and she'd seen the gigantic kitchen that she wound up cooking in maybe three times all told, she'd jumped up on the great big butcher-block table and sat there Indian style, talking to him. He'd thought, How spontaneous. Then later, when she'd do it, he'd think, How unsanitary.

For two years he'd been looking for that flaw in Evlyn, that little thing she did that he knew was unique to her, something that in her case he guessed he could live with no matter how long it took her to get out of it because she was so special. He couldn't find a single thing.

They weathered the storm in his place, ordering carry-out food, six-packs of Pepsi that they'd leave out on the steps, then bring in and set before the fire for a couple of minutes when they were ready for it. She came into the warehouse and watched him work out, marveled as he did a hundred sit-ups and push-ups at a time, watched quietly so as not to break his concentration as he beat the living daylights out of the bag. He'd asked her if she was into working out and she'd asked him if he was nuts. She'd tried jogging once and had puked. He smiled, comparing her again to his wife, who had been so competitive that she'd gone to a gym and taken boxing lessons so she could learn to hit the bag, paid someone to teach her things that Vincent would have been happy to show her for nothing.

He had to stop comparing them. For his own sake if not for hers.

On the second full day, they had The Talk. For the rest of his life, whenever he thought of that conversation, he would think of it as The Talk. The first night, on his couch, he'd told her things he'd never planned on telling anyone, not Bolo, not anyone. About the time as a teenager scoring with Boirand. Inside a warehouse and Vincent had the petty cash but was working on taking all the IBM typewriters when the security guard made his rounds. The minimum-wage son of a bitch carrying a pistol and thinking he was a cop. He'd blown

Boirand away the second he spotted him, and Vincent had nearly killed him, had snuck up behind him and had nailed him in the back of his skull with a typewriter before fleeing into the night.

About fighting. All about fighting. How he had been a tremendous lightweight, truly wonderful. He had the speed and the timing and the talent that nobody on earth could give you if it didn't come naturally. Fighting three-round amateur bouts and going forty-four and two. But then he was growing and what had been a great talent as a lightweight had been only a gifted talent for a welterweight. And then a good solid talent for a middleweight.

Evlyn said, "But I heard you turned pro, didn't I? Didn't you tell me once that you fought pro?"

Telling someone that you used to be a pretty good thief was one thing. Telling her that you'd done seven years was another. But getting into the past so heavily, telling her about his greatest defeat and his greatest heartbreak, that was in a different class altogether. Still, he was on a roll.

"I got busted on a B & E when I was eighteen, the year the picture in the bar was taken. Bolo, back then, he had hopes of managing me, making me a champ. But I was out of control, always violent, in trouble. He tried, he really did, but hell, I had guys coming over to the house who used to bring me new locks to pick instead of toys to play with; what was he going to do, chain me down? The judge gave me a choice. Go to the joint or join the Army. I figured if I was gonna go in the Army, I may as well go all the way, so I went Airborne."

"You jumped out of airplanes?" Shocked, surprised, amazed that he'd never told her about this before. And he couldn't figure out why he hadn't at first. It was a safe subject, neutral. Nothing that could make her lose her respect for him.

All this time he'd labored under the delusion that she would break up with him if she knew what he really did for a living, and had never told her anything. Assuming that she would jump to no conclusions. About a guy who had no visible means of support and who wore thousand-dollar suits and drove a brand new Caddy. Christ. And he hadn't told her the one thing that maybe would gain some real respect. The time was right. If he was going to do it, it had to be now, no matter how the memory bothered him. If it got too bad, he could always skip over things, she'd never know.

He said, "Right away, in Basic, for Christ's sake, I got into boxing. Hundred and fifty pounds at the time, I was whipping everyone in the platoon, then the company, then the division. This was '69, remember, the Munich Olympics were three years away. They started training right after Jump School.

"There was a guy named Basile, used to be a great heavyweight, would have been champion, but he got hurt, run over by a car or something, broke him up. He was still great, but he couldn't get licensed. A good kidney shot might have killed him. He became my father. I lived with him, trained with him, worked out with him every day."

Nick Basile had caught Vincent lifting weights in the gym one day and had slapped him right in the face, the first person to ever get away with it. He'd never lifted another weight again. Nick Basile had given him a robe and a pair of boxing trunks and his first pair of real boxing shoes, not the gym shoes he wore stateside as an amateur. Nick Basile had touted him, pulled strings with his commander and had promised them they had an Olympic contender on their hands that would maybe make the folks back home who were all up in arms about the war in Vietnam forget about it for a little while at least while they cheered on their great fighting soldier.

He'd fought thirty-one times for Nick Basile and had never lost once.

His last fight, and this girl came on to him after, hitting on him so obviously that even Nick had told him to go ahead, he'd see him in the morning. Took her to a guest house in Mannheim, Germany, then pounding on the door at three in the morning, the MPs charging in, the girl's father, the commanding general of the entire United States Army Europe, USAREUR, telling him calmly that he'd raped his last teenager. . . .

He hadn't been able to beat the rap, it was his word against hers and the general's, and he carried a lot more clout than even Nick Basile the civilian Army Boxing Coach. Another choice, another easy decision. They'd drop the charges if he'd volunteer for a transfer to the Nam.

He told her about the battles, the Silver Stars, the A-Shaw Valley. Not looking at her, just staring off, afraid to look at her, in a way. He'd never told anyone any of this stuff before.

"I came home feeling lucky, you know? I never could understand the guys wanting parades, Jesus, I was *alive*." Right away into training, Hank Greely now his trainer. What had been a great talent in a lightweight had turned into a mediocre one in a light-heavyweight. Hundred and seventy-five pounds then and now, and he couldn't lose an ounce if his life depended on it.

"But you look so slender with your clothes off, strong, but almost skinny."

"Most people put me at a hundred ninety, two hundred. Because I got big bones and wide shoulders. But it's one seventy-five still. Five feet, eleven inches. All of me."

"After that, Bolo put you to work?"

"Not right away. Even back then, after I retired from the ring, he wanted me to go straight, set me up in something, give me the money.

"I was bitter, I guess. My dreams shattered. I used to dream all the time about being a champion, being the next champ of the world. I was doing B & Es again, twenty-four years old, when Bolo took me on my first real score. For the next three years I lived like a king, with what I'd known earlier and what he taught me, more every day I worked, too, I learned, I got to be one of the best."

"Until Tino."

"Until Tino, yeah."

"And it's over now, Vincent, all of it? You're through boosting cars and TVs and stereos and you're through scoring the safes and all that?"

Vincent looked at her. She was trying hard to keep her hope out of her voice but Bolo had told him when he was just a little kid that the eyes never lie. And they didn't this time, either. She was looking at him so lovingly, so hopefully, that he *couldn't* lie.

"I got one more thing coming up, Evlyn. I didn't tell you about it because someone else is involved, and I can't put his trust in anyone he doesn't tell me to. One more, then I'm out."

"And you think," Evlyn said, still looking at him the same way, "that I'm not smart enough to figure out that the only person you trust enough to do anything with is Bolo?"

He didn't answer.

"It is Bolo, isn't it."

Still, Vincent couldn't bring himself to tell her straight out. He just nodded.

And after he nodded, and he knew that she knew, then he had told her everything.

Later, she asked him, "So what do we do now?" and he'd told her that they waited for Bolo to call.

"That's not what I mean; I already told Bolo I was

here, I already called him to tell him I wouldn't be coming in to work last night."

"You called Bolo?"

"Yes."

"And what did he say?"

"He said he'd be in touch and if I left you and came
to work, he'd fire me."

"What did you mean then?"

"I mean us, where do we go from here, you and me?"

He hesitated. Still afraid. Still cautious. Then he
plunged in with both feet. "We go to church?"

And there it was, goddamnit, she was off and crying
again. . . .

12 By the third day Vincent was feeling better than he could ever remember feeling before. One of the very few things that had totally amazed him about his lifestyle was the number of otherwise intelligent women who flocked to bad guys. The men that hung around Bolo's were, by conditioning and practice, paranoid, and would never go to a strange woman's house for illicit purposes. They'd take them to motels and hotels and, rarely, to their own homes, so the weeknight action was slow. On more evenings than not, Evlyn was the only female in the bar. The situation was different on weekends.

Gino Papa, Leo, Pez, and even Animal never had a problem getting laid. The girls would flock in on Friday and Saturday nights, legal secretaries, stockbrokers, lawyers, office girls of all sizes and shapes, attracted to the quiet violence that flowed from the personalities of Bolo's regulars like smoke off ice. It was a standing joke, the average crook without even trying got more action than a rich security-trading yuppie could buy.

The women loved it, the tough talk, the gentility that the men showed toward them, the old-world courtliness and manners, the chivalry these men possessed. They ate it up with a spoon. Vincent used to carry a lighter with

him at all times even though he had never smoked a
cigarette in his life, just in case one of the women
needed a light. This kind of thing turned them on.
There was no equality in Bolo's bar, no feminists allowed. Women were to be respected and treated like
betters, not equals. At least for the weekend.

Not so with Evlyn. These last three days had showed
him that she was nothing at all like that.

Although she knew the rules and had never asked him
anything about his work, she was waiting, letting the
walls down, allowing herself to fall in love with him,
but not taking it any further than one day at a time. She
hadn't planned a future for them. Couldn't see one with
him. She explained all this to him during their three
days together. Three glorious days of sex and love and
laughter. Good combination any old time, but special
between them, as they had both waited for so long for
it to happen.

"It wasn't the drinking," she told him. "Although that
was part of it. It was the violence, walking through the
park together and you beating up anyone who even said
hello. The anger within you, it was frightening."

"Why didn't you break it off?"

She'd just looked at him.

Evlyn was waiting for the day to come when he
would make a commitment. And now the day was finally here. And she too let all her hair down with him,
telling him things about her life she had never shared
with anyone before.

By Saturday they both knew that this was it for them.
The real thing. Love, which had evaded them all their
lives.

"I make three or four hundred a night, Vincent,"
Evlyn said.

"I figured you did all right, the way those guys drop
money."

She took a deep breath; her next words would be a

test for both of them. For her because she had never offered her bank account to a man before, for him because she knew he was prideful and old-fashioned.

She said, "I've got seventeen thousand dollars in the bank. We could live on that and my money until you decide what you want to do."

Vincent looked surprised. "You've got seventeen grand stashed?" Evlyn nodded. Her last secret out.

Vincent wondered should he tell her or not. He'd told her everything else, but the subject of money had never come up. What the hell, in for a penny . . .

"Evlyn, I've got three-hundred and seventeen *grand* locked up."

Evlyn said, "How much?"

"You heard me the first time."

"Oh, Vincent, then why take the chance, why risk what we have now by going out again?"

"Bolo doesn't trust anyone else."

"Vincent, listen to me, 'cause I'm stone serious." Evlyn leveled him with her glaring, blazing green eyes and said, "I can't wait for you. You're a convicted felon; if they bust you, you will go away for a long, long time. I am thirty-two years old and I will not wait ten years for you to come out of prison and try and start a new life when you're fifty."

It was happening. The first bad thing that had happened between them in their wonderful three days.

Vincent said, "Bolo has never spent a day behind bars in his life."

"But you *have*. Vincent, please, don't think I'm nagging or whining or trying to tell you what to do. I'm not. All I'm saying is I won't spend ten years of my life sitting around with you in prison, waiting. Do you understand that?"

"Hey," Vincent said, "life goes on, you know?" Even to his own ears he sounded cold.

The second bad thing to happen to them came on the

afternoon of the third day. Vincent had worked out and showered, angry because the great snowdrifts outside prevented him from running, too happy and lazy to go to Hank Greely's gym, where there was an indoor track. He had scraped and shoveled the walkway in front of his building, his driveway, and he had swept the stairs. They were frozen, covered with ice, and now when they ordered carry-out food, he would go into the warehouse on the first floor and pay for it from street level, not wanting to have a lawsuit on his hands if some clumsy delivery boy took a dive on his iron stairway. All together, thirty-four inches of snow had fallen in the past three days. No record, not for Chicago, but coming close. He was sipping a Pepsi, sitting on his couch, relaxed, watching Evlyn light the fire. He noticed that the firewood pile had dropped drastically. Maybe a week's worth left. He'd have to call and order some more. Suddenly the door was rattling, being pounded on from outside. Hard.

Vincent had a thick steel fire door. With two dead bolts and a regular knob lock. The dead bolts had two-inch tongues. Even refrigerator Perry could not kick in his door. He was worried more about the security alarms going off than he was about a break-in. He walked over to the door and flicked the switch on the panel that would turn off both alarms.

"Who is it."

"Police."

Vincent was surprised. He said, "You got a warrant?"

"Don't make me come back with one, Martin."

"Go away."

"Martin, I'll kick this door down if you don't let me in."

Vincent said, "Go ahead," and walked away from the door.

Evlyn was watching him curiously, a slight, puzzled smile on her face.

There was a muffled boom. The door didn't even shake. Three more, one after the other. Then two more, quick, then it stopped and even through the brick walls and the steel door they heard the shout of fear and anger, then the sound of iron hitting something, maybe bone.

Vincent said, "The asshole fell down the stairs."

"Vincent, shouldn't you see if he's all right?"

"Screw him, that's what he gets, kicking on a guy's door like that."

Evlyn was off the floor and over to the door, throwing back bolts and locks before he could respond, Vincent standing by the couch amazed, shocked. She threw open the door and not surprisingly, there was no one there. She looked out.

Halfway down the stairs lay a large form, tangled in the stairs and the iron bannister. One arm was clinging to the railing for dear life, the other under the body, maybe broken. The mass moaned. Evlyn walked down the stairs daintily, her feet bare, patches of skin tearing away as she lifted her feet away from the iron steps.

Then Vincent was there, shoes on, lifting her and carrying her carefully and slowly back up the stairs. He dropped her on the couch and shook his head angrily but said nothing. He stared at her for a second, then turned and walked to the open door.

Standing in the doorway now was the cop, the smaller cop from the other night, a pretty big guy still, looking larger without his partner there dwarfing him.

Vincent said, "You make a grand entrance, I'll say that for you." Surprised because the cop was wearing his full-dress blue uniform. Vincent noticed the clean new sergeant's chevrons on the arms. "Now what's so important you come in here trying to kick in my door?" He closed the door behind him, making a big deal out of checking it on the outside for dents. He locked both dead bolts and turned back to the sergeant. "And where's your partner; don't you guys travel in pairs?"

The cop said to him, "I just came from his funeral."

Vincent was sitting on one end of the couch, the cop on the other. Between them was Evlyn, sort of the demarcation line, the demilitarized zone. As there was no coffee or tea or anyplace to make either beverage even if they had them, Evlyn had offered him a Pepsi and wasn't too surprised when he turned her down. "I could order you some coffee, if you'd like, have it delivered." Evlyn looked sweetly at Vincent, ignoring the heat in his eyes and the dark anger stamped on his face. "You take cream and sugar, don't you, Vincent?" she said, then went to the telephone.

Sean said, "It looks like the main library in here."

Vincent said, "You got a reason to be here besides critiquing the decorating?"

"The cops been here to talk to you yet?"

"You're the first one."

Sean's shoulders drooped, as if he'd suddenly been burdened with an exceptionally heavy load. "That figures," he said, his voice defeated, weary. He looked up and stared Vincent right in the eye, Vincent feeling as much warmth coming off Sean as he'd felt walking down the steel stairway going after Evlyn. This man was cold.

"Immediately after we left the bar, Bigum dropped me off and was on his way home when somebody shot and killed him."

Vincent, visibly shocked, said, "Hey, I'm sorry."

The cop, Sean Kent, looked at him as he said it, trying to see if Vincent was being a wiseass. At last convinced that Vincent was truly sorry, he said, "You didn't hear about it? All three stations blared it for two days, the radios, front page in the *Sun-Times* and the *Tribune*."

"I don't have a TV or a radio and I don't read the papers."

Sean looked around the huge single room, seeing nothing but row after row of books, then nodded.

"Pretty nice digs for a guy makes ten an hour tending bar."

"Where'd you get that?"

Evlyn came back and sat down in her spot between them, smiling. She said, "Coffee's on the way. I had to order five dollars' worth or they wouldn't deliver it, though." Sean looked at her gratefully.

"Thank you," he said.

Evlyn, smiling still, said, "You're welcome."

Vincent, frustrated, said, "How'd you find out about me working at the bar or where I live?"

Sean looked at him and said, "Computers, Vincent, if you know the right questions, have all the answers."

"My work history is in a computer?"

"In the IRS files. They're supposed to be hackerproof, but I've found out that nothing really is, not even the Department of Defense files, where I got your Army history, copies of your discharge papers, your awards. The medals. Hit the right button, zip, there's all you want to know. Hit another button, zap, the FAX machine goes to work, prints you whatever you want."

"So what, you're here because you think I had something to do with your partner's death?"

"He didn't *die*, he was murdered. There's a difference."

"I had no problem with him. Or with you. Matter of fact, far as cops go, I figured you for pretty nice guys, all things considered. See, I've been in the precinct houses before, Sarge. Had my head busted fourteen times, questioning me about murders, bullshit they know I had nothing to do with but bringing me in and hurting me, trying to get some of my action."

"And you never split with them."

"I got a theory, Sarge. If you're gonna be a crook, be Raffles. If you're gonna be a cop, be Kojak. No, I never gave them a dime."

There was a knock on the door and Vincent got up, went to the door and let the delivery boy in, gave him ten dollars and told him to keep the change. The kid mumbled his thanks, as if Vincent had stiffed him, given him a quarter or something instead of a 100 percent tip, and started the treacherous descent down the iron steps.

Sean Kent looked at him as if he were the Savior, no, not at him, at the cardboard box in his hands. There were eight cups of steaming hot black coffee in the box, along with little tiny cartons of cream and a couple dozen packets of sugar. Vincent and Sean added the cream and sugar, Vincent smiling at the relish evident on Sean's face. Christ, the guy could hardly wait to get his hands on the coffee. Sean sipped long and loudly, his face rapturous, then turned to Evlyn.

"Thank you so much, young lady."

"Call me young again, I'll go out and buy a Mr. Coffee for your next visit."

Vincent said, "There won't be any next visit." His face angry, feeling hurt and betrayed by the easy familiarity Evlyn assumed toward the cop. Toward the enemy.

Although even he had to admit the guy was different; there was something about him that wasn't like all the other cops Vincent had known. What was it? In the first place, the guy was out of shape, the buttons of his dress blue tunic straining at the waist as he sat leaning forward sipping the coffee, looking sadly into the fire, as if he were an invited guest. And the man didn't come on like a hard guy, acting like the badge gave him a license to steal and treat you like dirt under his feet.

Sean looked at Vincent, relaxed, sitting there sipping his coffee, his hand under the Styrofoam cup to catch any drops that spilled. He said, "I agree with you."

"That you won't be coming back?"

"No, that if you're gonna be a cop, be Kojak."

"Oh."

"Three days, my partner's been dead. They called me into the office; there're guys there from the OPS, some brass from upstairs, come all the way over from Twenty-sixth and California, politicians, making sure there wasn't a brewing scandal to worry about. I told them nothing, not about you, not about the bar, not about the kid you had the pistol stuck in his mouth when we walked in."

"Not because you like me so much, right?"

Sean grunted, but not unpleasantly. "Hardly. Because as far as our bosses were concerned, we had no business in there after five o'clock."

Sean was wondering about Vincent Martin. He wasn't your typical crook, your average bad guy. In the first place, the guy had a million books—hardcover—lying around the house. Most of the crooks Sean knew could barely write their names, let alone read. But there was something more to the guy. He didn't play games when he talked. Although he was a wiseass, which, considering, could be forgiven. Hell, the guy was a thief. He didn't cop an attitude about Sean's breaking into files—supposedly top-secret files—and learning all about him. But neither did he lie and try to cover up when Sean had told him that he had the IRS file on him, try to bluff and bluster that he was a working man and why wasn't Sean out busting John Gacy or some nonsense like that. He accepted the fact, as if it was no big secret, nothing to worry about. Maybe it wasn't.

What it was, Sean figured, was the guy was basically a nice guy, basically honest. Respectful. He'd apologized about Bigum, and that had thrown Sean for a loop. Already, Bigum not even cold in the ground yet, Sean had gotten hundreds of "sympathy" cards from fellow officers, with handwritten messages telling him just how very glad they were that Bigum had died, some even saying they were angry because they hadn't had the opportunity to kill him themselves. . . .

Hell, this guy, he couldn't be any worse than they were. Probably more of a man than they'd ever be. And although the brass had given Bigum a hero's sendoff, the fact that the law hadn't been around to see Vincent meant that they weren't working too hard to find out who had killed Bigum. Even a brand-new rookie detective fresh out of blues would have learned before now their whereabouts on Wednesday night. . . .

So Sean took a chance. There would not be any arrest or conviction of Bigum's killer. He couldn't allow that. Not if he could help it, not unless he was the cop making the arrest, sending the guy down the river for life, maybe to the chair. And Vincent could put it all together for him. He needed Vincent's help. And so he decided to trust him. Not all the way, just give the facts for now, see how the kid responded.

He gulped the remains of his coffee, put cream and sugar in another one, then started talking.

13 "So now you're on what, administrative leave?"

"Vincent, it's like this. When your partner dies, you get a choice. Ride a desk and see the department shrink, or take vacation. I wanted part of the investigation; it was refused. They know I wouldn't be objective. I'd find the guy; I'd blow him into next week, violate all of his civil rights. I refused vacation time, and when they balked, I told them I wanted to take my pension. I can't even do that for thirty days. After the loss of a partner, you have to give thirty-days' notice, a cooling-off period, let you get your mind right. So the only other options open were medical leave, in which case you give up your gun, or admin. leave. I took two weeks. Vincent, I know as sure as I'm sitting here, they're gonna try and make us look dirty. I told you the story, about Bigum and me; they've been waiting for us to goof up for three years. Now that he's dead, they have the OPS sniffing around, maybe even a couple of dirty cops feeding them garbage about Bigum. They'll sully his memory if I don't get the killer."

"And you think," Vincent said, "that I can help you."

"The last three days, I've talked to everyone who lives within a block of the shooting. Calming people down, listening to them curse me for having to tell me everything they'd already told the uniforms. But when they need us, boy, they don't care how much of our time they waste." Sean took a breath, fighting his resentment at the public at large, and continued. "All we've got, Vincent, all *I've* got, is a black car, big, new, maybe a Caddy or a Lincoln, pulling away from the stoplight moments after the shooting, and not one of the people who claim to have seen it will swear in court that they saw it. No license number, nothing. For three weeks we've been playing our daily game with the department, delivering warrants, talking to burglary victims, garbage, the crap work. We've done nothing. Then we get a tip on you and suddenly Bigum's dead."

The coffee was gone now, as was Evlyn. She'd taken Vincent's Cadillac and gone shopping, promising never to return until she hunted down a small refrigerator and at the very least a microwave oven. Vincent didn't argue with her. He'd been thinking about getting some appliances all winter. He sat on his end of the couch, looking at Sean, listening carefully to his every word. And he knew there was no accusation in his tone, knew Sean did not blame him in any way for his partner's death. Rather than comment on what Sean had said, he sat looking at him, casually, waiting for Sean to speak again.

"You know too much, Vincent."

"How's that?"

"Usually, you talk to a guy and leave an awkward silence, he jumps to fill it in with empty words, make the cop feel comfortable, try and show the cop what a nice guy he is. Or else, with something like what I just said, the guy jumps on the defensive right away, gets indignant. You're a strange breed."

"We both know I had nothing to do with your partner's death, and you keep forgetting, I been inside before plenty of times."

"For no reason other than you were jaywalking, right?"

"Now I am getting indignant. You come here, give me a story, sure, your partner's dead and I'm sorry, but it's obvious you want my help for something you're beating around the bush about. Now you tell me why I should do anything for you?"

"Because a good cop's dead."

"Good pepole die every day, buddy. I can't go running around avenging them."

"But I can. Are you familiar with the term, 'paybacks are a bear?'"

"Yes, I am, and I'll tell you something. Everyone I've ever heard use it was a sissy. Had no intentions of ever getting back at anyone. They say that, like they're badasses gonna lay in the weeds and then attack when the time's right. Bullshit. They say it to ease their consciences, that's all. To stroke their ego. Laying around in bed at night, planning their revenge and never doing it. But talking about it a lot. Like you're doing now."

"Be careful, Vincent."

"Be careful my ass. This is my fucking house, remember? Here you are, supercop, come in here telling me about paybacks, telling me I should help you find your partner's killer, shit, you admit that you and this Bigum guy were planning on busting me, and now I'm supposed to help you? Fuck that, Sarge, and fuck you, too, okay? Cops never did nothing for me but break my balls and bust my head. I'm supposed to help them now because one of them caught their lunch? Forget about it."

"Vincent," Sean said, sitting forward now, not seeming at all angry at Vincent's attack, "I came here because you aren't like the rest of them. Even today, talking, I knew something's different about you. You listen, you pay attention. If I had a nickel for every thief I've ever known in my life, I could retire, and I'll tell you something right now, you ain't like the rest. They talk to the law, all of a sudden they think they're Bob Hope, making with the wisecracks. Always talking down to us like they're smarter because they've served time. Like that makes them smart. Well, I've got news for you, in case you don't know it. Bigum was worth every one of them rolled into one and then some. And all I want from you is a gosh darn address I can't find on a computer."

"Whose address?"

"Fella named Ted King. The punk who was giving your pistol head the other night."

So that was it. This guy wanted information from Vincent about a guy he thinks Vincent had a problem with. Figures a thief will roll over and spill his guts to the cops because he's got a personal problem with someone.

Vincent said, "I'm sorry about your partner, but I wouldn't rat out the guy shot my own mother."

"Just because he's a crook, too?"

"That punk's no crook. If he is, he's one of the kind who give thieves a black eye, a bad name. Maybe goes into old people's homes and burns their feet with matches until they tell him where the good silver is. He's no thief. He's just a two-bit punk who thinks a gun makes him bad."

"And what do you think you have that makes you bad, Vincent?"

"I think it's time for you to go."

"Why are you protecting him, Vincent?"

"Been nice talking with you, Sarge."

"Vincent, there is one more thing maybe we should discuss before I leave. I want an address, nothing more. No information from you, nothing. I know all about this guy, his age, his hair color, his mother's name, who his cousin is and why he did time. All I want to know is where he lives. That the computer can't tell me. That's all I'm asking you to do. Now you're saying straight up that you won't help me, is that it?"

"I'm telling you I can't help you."

"Well, then, I was hoping it wouldn't come to this, Vincent, but if you don't get me the address, I'm gonna make your life miserable. Let's start with the IRS, filing false claims. I can prove you don't tend bar at Bolo's. I can prove you file false claims to cover your behind. I can place you in a hot car in Calumet City four days ago. There're other things, too, Vincent. Not to mention, the second I take care of Ted King, I'm gonna cover you like flies on garbage, waiting for you to make a mistake. And when you do, Vincent, I'll pop you. I'll be with you every minute of every day, always watching; you'll never see me but I'll be there. And you'll fall. Everyone knows me, on the street, kid, you ask. When I go after someone, they go down, no matter how I got to do it."

Vincent said, "The last way on earth to get me to do something. Guess what that is."

Sean sighed heavily and rose to his feet. He said, "Threaten you."

"Good day, Sarge."

Sean looked at him for several seconds, then said, "You call me Sergeant Kent, Martin."

"And you call me Mr. Martin, Sergeant Kent, and let's leave it at that."

Sean walked to the door and threw the dead bolts back. Before he opened it he turned to Vincent. "You want to know something, Mr. Martin? There're cops, a lot of cops, who know as soon as they bust you that they are gonna lose. That you'll walk. So they turn into Hitler while they got you, bust your head, beat you with the phone book; I know all about it. But they do it because they've only got you for a little while, and they know it. So they use their power, the power of the badge, and they make life miserable for you while they can. I never went in for that. But I'll tell you a little story. Awhile back, Bigum and I, we were working a couple of homicides, on our own time, as usual. There were a couple of North Side guys, both with records, both child molesters, got their throats slit in their sleep. Also, as usual, with guys like that the department didn't make too much of a fuss. Before we got to him, he got two more convicted pedophiles. We nabbed him, the guy, his only son was kidnapped and killed by some freak over twenty years back. He's fifty years old and a drunk and he's gotten a divorce and lost his job behind what happened to his son. He was getting the names out of the newspapers, Vincent; when the baby lovers get arrested, it gives their past busts, all that stuff, along with their address. He'd break in late at night and slit their throats. We waited until there was another short-eyes arrest, reading the papers every day, and when it happens, we go to the short-eyes's house, as soon as he makes bail, announce ourselves as police officers and tell the guy what we want to do. He agrees to let us stake his house out, and he is the worst piece of garbage I ever met in my life, Vincent. In his bedroom he's got pictures cut out of the clothing catalogues, hanging all over his walls, little kids in their underwear. No telling where he kept the hardcore stuff. The third night, in comes our man, through the connecting garage door, two in the morning, crying, sniffling, keening, Vincent, hating himself but doing what he feels he has to do. We grab him, and believe me, when Bigum grabbed you, you were *grabbed*, and while we're reading him his rights, this piece of garbage comes out of the bedroom screaming and crying, attacking the little guy, this little white-haired fifty-year-old loser whose life is long passed, calling him terrible, vile names. Bigum looked at me and I shrugged. He let the guy go and handed him his knife."

Sean turned the doorknob and opened the door, was about to step through it when Vincent said, "Wait a minute, Jesus." Sean smiled and stepped back into the gigantic room, holding the door open, his eyebrows arched in query.

"What'd you do, for Christ's sake?"

"Do, well, we left, Vincent, what else could we do?"

"And the guy, the child molester?"

"Oh, he got his throat slashed. Same MO as the others, you know, the cops, they never did get the guy who did it, but right after that, the killings stopped. Funny."

He turned to go again and Vincent said, "Listen, let's order some more coffee, okay? Stick around."

"Say I get you that number. Ted King's address. Then what?"

"You really want to know?"

"Yeah, what would you do?"

"Vincent, I'd whack him."

"Straight up?"

"Straight up."

"See, the thing of it is, I figured you for a cop suffering, going through changes because your partner caught his lunch. I get you this kid's address and you kill him, then your conscience starts bothering you, you come looking for me, try and nail me to the wall so you can sleep at night."

"It's got nothing to do with you, Mr. Martin."

Vincent smiled and said, "Call me Vincent."

"I'm Sean."

"And I've never done a cop a favor before, Sean."

"Tell me about it."

"What if this Teddy, he didn't kill your partner; sometime in the future, some guy gets nailed on some routine bust; he cops to killing Bigum. What then?"

"Then," Sean said, "two pieces of garbage are off the street forever, because I'll tell you something, Vincent, whoever killed Bigum is going to die and I don't care if I have to do a crime, get sent to Stateville to get him, whoever did this is going to die."

"You mean it, don't you?"

Sean smiled. "Straight up, Vincent."

"Let me ask around, okay?"

"Thank you, Vincent."

"And Sean?"

"Hmm?"

"How come, you're a cop, you never say fuck?"

Evlyn was surprised to see Sean still there, but she was grateful. He could help Vincent, she told them, carry up the goods. Behind her came two men struggling with an awkward box, an obviously heavy appliance, and Vincent helped them up the steps and into the building, Evlyn standing way on the other side of the room, showing them where to put things. They brought in a little electric oven and a small refrigerator, while Sean walked up and down twice bringing in double armfuls of groceries. The men left with a generous tip and Sean and Vincent hooked things up, got them working, Vincent quiet, but Sean telling stories, amusing Evlyn, winning her over. When they were done, Vincent stepped back and looked around him.

She had bought a small table and it was covered with pans and pots, canned goods and a carton of Pepsi. The refrigerator was humming and the stove was shining, an entire section of his library blocked out.

Evlyn said, "We need some shelves and a sink, Vincent, desperately."

He smiled sadly. "Welcome to the twentieth century," he said.

"What was that?" Evlyn asked.

Vincent looked at Sean. "They taught me woodworking in the joint, Sean. I made all these shelves. I guess I can make some cabinets, eh?"

Sean, on his way out the door now, said, "Good for you, kid," and they all three knew exactly what he was talking about.

"Do you mind?" Evlyn asked. Sitting on the couch, looking at him sincerely. "I realize it's all of a sudden different. Three days with you and I'm changing everything."

"I don't mind," Vincent said. "What I was doing, I guess, was building the world's biggest prison cell."

"We could partition off just a little bit for a kitchen, maybe another section for a TV room, whatever. A regular home."

"It's going to be rough, you know. For me, I mean. At least for a little while."

"You'll tell me though, won't you, Vincent? If it starts bothering you?"

"I'll tell you."

"You know why I left?"

"So he could talk openly."

"Partly. But because you could tell, he needed you. And I didn't want to be hanging around, make you anything less than objective toward him. As if you'd feel that you had to turn him down because of who and what you are if I was around to witness it. Afraid that I'd lose respect for you. Or something silly like that. Vincent, I love the *real* you. Not the guy who drinks and beats up punks in the park. Not the man in the bar the other night, making some tough guy take his own gun barrel in his mouth. I love you, the sensitive you I got to know in spite of you. The you that I've seen so rarely, but the you that I know is inside."

They were sitting together, gazing into the fire, the wind blowing at the door and the skylight. Vincent was listening, carefully, wondering if he should be feeling resentment or anger at her words or her actions. At her suddenly bringing all these changes into his life. It was worth it, surely, for her company. He could not expect her to accept his nomadic, isolated lifestyle. He knew it was time for a change, for some bright lights, for a kitchen and maybe even a television. And he decided if he had to think about whether to get angry about it or not, then it was not worthy of anger. What he was doing was deciding how he should act. How the person, the Vincent she knew, should respond. And she'd already told him that she loved not that Vincent but the one inside. The one hiding behind walls of mistrust and caution that he'd built up all his life, a brick at a time. Every arrest, boom, a brick. Every woman who'd hurt him, bang, another one. Every time life kicked him in the ass, three more were added to the pile. The walls were too damn high and it was time they came down. A little at a time. Then, after the score, he'd see what he could do about dynamiting the rest of them all at once. If he had to think about his feelings and then decide how to act upon them, then he was being a phony, no better than little Teddy, who acted like a killer when he had a gun in his waistband but who copped out and showed himself to be a punk as soon as the pressure came down on him.

Vincent said, "I love you, Evlyn," leaving all the rest unsaid, both of them knowing that in order for him to be making more than an empty promise while mouthing cheap words he would have to change. . . .

And he could. Goddamnit, anyone could change. He surely could.

Couldn't he?

They made love there on the couch with the purple winter-evening sky showering down around them from the exposed skylight, snow swirling against the shatterproof glass, winds gusting and blowing, making hollow, sinister sounds. And they were safe.

Early Sunday morning, Bolo called.

14 The first night was the hardest for Teddy. After the killing. The first move he made was to drive over the Michigan Avenue bridge and flip the pistol out the car window, and as soon as the weapon left his hand, he wondered if the river was frozen over or if the gun would just smack into ice and lie there, outlined perfectly against the pure white snow. Man. At least he'd wiped the thing off. He had that much sense.

Another problem was, Teddy, all his life, had had fantasies that he would only act out when he was drunk. And then when he'd wake the next day, the remorse and guilt would overwhelm him. Until he was certain that he would not be caught for his drunken act. Inside, they'd told him that over 80 percent of the guys doing time in state joints were there for things they did while under the influence of drugs or alcohol. Teddy could believe it. He himself would never have left the scene of his accident if he hadn't been blitzed. Hell, the dip broad, she'd deserved what she'd gotten. Had it coming. The other 20 percent of the state prisoners were hardcore criminals, recidivist cat burglars, car thieves, outfit guys, whatever. That was state prisons only. The numbers could probably be reversed in the federal joints, where almost all of your outfit guys wound up, along with your politicians and your white-collar-crime guys and your Medicaid-abusing doctors and the rest of the dips who screwed up and were punished with a few years in the sunshine out in sunny California or Florida. Teddy hoped that if they ever got him again, it would be on a federal beef. He hadn't had a tan in a long time.

He drove straight from the bridge to his mother's house on the Northwest side, close to the Brickyard Shopping Center, closer yet to St. Nicholas' Albanian Church, where the picture of the Virgin Mother was still shedding tears and packing in the faithful. It had been one of the first stops Teddy had made after getting home. He hadn't been allowed into the back of the church, behind the painting, and he'd asked the guy in the suit, who was obviously a bodyguard protecting the icon, if there was somebody in back there, with a water can, or what. The guy had just looked at him.

His cousin Guido had set him up in a two-bedroom apartment, furnished, on the North Side, above a dry cleaners Bags's people operated for him. But tonight he didn't want to be alone. He knew the terrors the morning would bring.

His mother came to the door in her bathrobe, fat now; jeez, how the guinea broads packed it on when they got to be in their fifties. He didn't bring a bottle in, that would have been pushing it too far, and he walked in slowly, trying to hide the fact that he was drunk. Unsuccessfully. He told his mother that she had to cover for him; if anyone asked, he'd been there since eleven or so. That was all he told her and God bless her Italian soul and the hot dago blood coursing through her veins, she agreed to do so without argument.

But his father didn't see things the same way. Lying on the couch, in his shorts, a quilt over him, seething with resentment that she hadn't allowed him to sleep in his old bedroom, Teddy listened as they argued. His mother telling his father that he had to get up for work in a couple of hours and to please calm down; his father telling his mother that their son was no longer welcome in his house. Mom telling him that he was blood and Pop saying not anymore. Teddy passed out listening to them fight like a couple of idiots. Hell, he was here already, what the hell was there to fight about.

A few hours later and the banging started. Coffeepot banged against the counter; pots banged on the stove. Head afire and shaking, Teddy opened his eyes and there he was, the old man, standing there in red long underwear, glaring at him from the kitchen.

"Wake up and get the hell out, you don't want to find a job," his father said.

Teddy's pop, having worked as a laborer in the construction trade for the past thirty years, had no use for any man who didn't earn his living from the sweat of his brow.

"Pop," Teddy said, "you want to do me a favor, turn that light off?" Knowing that his pop could clean his clock even if Teddy had a pistol in each hand, and therefor showing respect.

"You got a job yet?"

"Pop, *please*." Not too proud to beg, the thought of what he'd done the night before starting to close in on him. It would shock him into stark-raving wakefulness in a minute, if he didn't get back to sleep.

"You come to my house drunk in the middle of the night and then tell me what to do?" The old man's eyes were blazing fire now, his lips downcast, yellow teeth showing, light glinting off them. A look of disgust. "I raised a piece of trash!" The strongest words Teddy had ever heard him speak in the house.

His eyes were closed and he was drifting off to sleep again when a rough hand grabbed his shoulder and shook him hard. He opened his eyes, frightened, knowing in his heart that it was the police, feeling both grati-

tude and anger when he realized that it was only his
father.

"You get one night, because your mother wants it.
You won't get two. You be out of my house before I
get home, boy." And he was gone, slamming the door
behind him.

Fuck him, too, Teddy thought. Never came up once
to see him on the farm, never wrote or accepted the
charges when Teddy called. A piece of shit, his father
was, thinking that anyone who didn't bust his hump
and take shit from a gang boss ten hours a day wasn't a
real man. When Teddy could buy and sell him three
times over, still fresh from the joint. What an asshole.

What really bothered him was that the asshole had
brought upon him full wakefulness.

And with the waking came the memory. The jig cop
in his tin-can Plymouth, sitting at the light and Teddy
shooting him five times in the head. Oh, God, don't let
me get caught, please.

Teddy cut his deal with God throughout the morning, until he heard his mother banging around in the
kitchen now, Christ, both his parents anxious to get rid
of him. What a family. He felt like his head was about
to burst open, felt the throbbing inside it every time his
heart beat. Thu-*thud*, thu-*thud*, his body pulsating, his
mouth afire, his nerves jittery, his leg jumping con-
vulsively as he lay there. Teddy's prayers were directed
to the God of alibis, a God who turned his back on you
only when you were beyond redemption. But this time
he wasn't. Not yet. Teddy prayed that if God let him
get away with this one, he'd never take another drink as
long as he lived. Ever.

Too jumpy and afraid to sleep, Teddy got off the
couch, dressed and slunk from the house without a
word to his mother. He got into the Eldorado and
drove the couple of blocks to St. Nicholas' Albanian
Church, parked around back and was inside before the

morning crowd arrived for mass. He walked up the aisle, stopped before the weeping Madonna, and bowed his head. Prayed to her that if she would intercede for him, ask her Son to let Teddy get away this time, he'd never drink again. He promised solemnly, then walked to the candle rack, lighted one, and dropped his whole wad of bills into the poor box. Had to be a couple hundred there, at least. Even God, Teddy believed, had his price.

He made it to his apartment without molestation, and broke his promise upon entering. Popped a cold icy Bud from the fridge, drank it in one long, protracted guzzle. This wasn't really drinking. It was only beer. Shaking still, he undressed and took a long hot shower, soaping several times, shampooing his hair twice. Then conditioning it. The stuff was supposed to give you thicker hair. He walked naked from the bathroom and dried himself in front of the mirror, feeling penitent and cleansed. If they weren't watching the apartment, or his mother's, then they weren't on to him. Not yet. He dropped the towel at the foot of the bed and tumbled naked between the sheets. He said a silent prayer, hung over and filled with remorse, terrified that this would be the last sleep he would ever have between fresh linen sheets on a warm, cozy, comfortable bed. He slept until the phone on the nightstand started ringing.

"Hello?" Teddy croaked, hoarsely. His head didn't hurt nearly as much and his heart wasn't pounding anymore. His hand was steady on the receiver. He had a hard-on.

And then he remembered. Jesus Christ in heaven, he'd capped a cop.

"Teddy, where the fuck you at?"

Bags. Thank God. Not the heat.

"I'm here, sleeping for shit's sake, I had a problem last night."

"The thing went off okay; I talked to the guys. What the fuck problem you got, except you're in love with a bottle of White Label?" Disdain in his voice. The fucker. Teddy checked the bedside clock. Ten o'clock. Jesus, he'd slept for twelve hours. And if they weren't here yet, they weren't gonna make it, because one thing was for sure, when a cop got aced, they grabbed everyone they could in the first couple hours, even if they had to invent a suspect. So even in his drunken stupor of the night before, he'd been right. The Chicago police department wasn't about to waste manpower searching for the killer of Bigum Barnes, the stoolie.

Into the phone he said, "Hey, cuz," smiling now, feeling his oats, believing that everything was just fine, "I got some good news for you, but I can't say it over the phone."

"What the fuck you call me?"

Teddy grinned. "Cuz, like, short for cousin. Listen, I got to catch the news; I'll see you tomorrow."

"You want to ever watch the news again, you'll see me now, you understand?" Bags's tone of voice telling Teddy he meant every word.

"Where at?"

"At the joint," Guido said, and hung up.

Let him wait, Teddy thought. He rolled over in bed, the hangover just a mild one now, the pain and anguish of that morning for the most part past. Never knowing that a psychopath fears nothing but exposure, that a sociopath feels remorse only upon getting caught, Teddy King began to play with himself.

The joint mentioned by Bags was the hot night spot for the gangsters in town, Tony's Tempo Lounge, a big flashy joint on S. State Street. The girls worked there, rubbing and copping and handling whatever the boys wanted rubbed or copped or handled. High-class girls, too, none of the saggy-titted low-lifes the outfit guys filled the strip joints with, the burnouts who had gradu-

ated from places like Tony's into the houses, from there
to the dance halls or even worse, the factories down
south where they never got a chance to get out of bed
except to wipe themselves out before another customer
climbed up there.

Teddy walked in jauntily, swaggering, his two-inch
lifts bringing him up just that far but the knowledge of
what he'd got away with making him ten feet tall. He
spotted Bags far over in the corner booth, as usual, a
boozy blonde with him, the girl wearing a low-cut satin
and sequins thing that showed about 90 percent of her
titties. There were maybe fifty booths in Tony's place,
another forty or so tables for two, the bar having
twenty-five or thirty stools to sit on. Not a spare seat in
the house tonight, though, and it was only Thursday.
Tony was raking it in.

He made a drinking motion with his right hand as he
passed a cocktail waitress in what was really more a
swimsuit than a uniform and she nodded, smiled, knowing who he was or rather whom he knew, and what he
drank. Teddy sauntered over to his cousin's booth and
sat down, winking at the girl with Guy Bags.

Bags said to him, "It's about time." Teddy could tell
from his tone of voice that he wasn't in trouble; Bags
was about half-drunk already. His eyes were glazed; he
was looking around the room like a real gangster, looking for trouble. He wouldn't get it here. Everyone here
knew their place. The bit on the phone had probably
been said to impress the bitch with Bags. He'd probably
called one of the waitresses over and told her to bring a
phone to him, like she didn't have enough to do already
with the joint packed rafter to floor, and he'd gone
tough with Teddy to show the bitch he was a killer.

Teddy said, "I had a lady to take care of, you know
how it is."

Bags laughed. "Nothing like a nut to take the edge
off a hangover, eh, Teddy?"

"Only thing good about a hangover, Guido, is getting a nut."

Bags gestured at the girl with him. "You wanna take Mary Jane here into the back and try for another one? My pleasure." Teddy seeing the girl turn her full attention and all her charms on him, anything to impress a big shot like Bags.

Man, what a slut. Maybe a ton of makeup, her eyes gone, the girl high on something. Rubbing her nose every couple of minutes. A walking disease farm.

He said, "No thanks." Winking at the girl to show no hard feelings, then added, "Guido, there's something maybe you and me should talk about."

Guy Bags noticed the tone of voice Teddy was trying so hard for, the businessman set, one man to another. He told the chick to blow and she got up without another word and took her bag with her, sashayed over to the women's can, her own can swinging in rhythm with the music coming from the jukebox. They watched her until the door swung shut behind her, then Bags said, "You shoulda took me up on that one, Teddy; she'd suck the cream out of a Twinkie and never leave a tooth mark on the cake."

Teddy's drink came and he forgot all about his promise, his vow to God that he'd made that morning. He'd got away with it now, he was sure of it. Cautiously, watching Bags carefully, he said, "Did you hear about the cop getting whacked last night?"

And there it was, proof again of God's existence. Bag's eyes filled with delight and he was smiling, then chuckling softly. He said, "I'd like to find the guy capped that nigger son of a bitch, give him something for going to all the trouble. Shit, shooting someone for free when we'd give him a hundred grand for the job. What a set of balls he must have on him."

Teddy playing it coy, cool, knowing how to do it now, said, "Like to shake his hand, eh, cuz?"

Bags eyeing him, going hard again. "I don't like that cuz bullshit, Teddy, you hear me?" Then softening, adding, "Yeah, I'd like to shake his hand, me and the rest of the boys, we'd have something in our hands, too, show our appreciation."

Teddy stuck his hand out above the table, giving Bags the eye, serious now, letting him know he wasn't playing, this was for real. He said, "Shake, Guido."

Guido looked at him for about ten seconds, hard, the realization setting in, the reality of Teddy's words hitting home. He said, "No shit."

Teddy said, "For real. Right on the corner of Hudson and Webster. Guy was sitting at the light, big ugly stool pigeon nigger with a mouth as big as his ass, likes to insult people. Gave me some shit after I delivered the cash to the burglar. I gunned him down and went to my ma's, got an alibi in case I need one."

Bags was staring at him as if witnessing a miraculous occurrence, his eyes wide, his mouth half-smiling, half-trembling. Then the smile won, and he reached over and shook Teddy's hand, pulled him right into him, hugged him hard there in the booth with maybe 500 people watching, and Teddy was no longer ten feet tall, he was Paul Bunyon, a giant, because Bags was telling him how he'd always said that good old Teddy, he had real balls.

"You got rid of the gun, right, Teddy?"

And he saw his chance. Now that he'd earned the respect he had coming all along, he felt that it was time to take his rightful place at Guy Bags's side. He said, "It's in the river, wiped and clean. And the name's Ted." He said it smiling benignly, not being a tough guy, half-expecting Bags to take off on him.

Bags said, "What did you say?"

Teddy said, "You don't like cuz, I don't like Teddy. The name's Ted, okay?"

Guido's eyes were on him, staring hard. Probably

knowing that anyone who would ace a cop had to have the balls to shoot his own cousin for insulting him. He showed his respect, all right, making Teddy feel alive and powerful and righteous.

Bags said to him, loud enough so everyone around them could hear, "I salute you, Don Ted," and he raised his glass and waited for Teddy to lift his. They touched rims, lightly, and, staring each other in the eye hard, then drained their glasses.

Bags drank his drink, his mind racing. His face showed good cheer and respect, but he was thinking, Good God Almighty, this dumb shit had capped a detective.

This was against Montaine's strictest rules. You never, ever brought heat down on the gang, no matter what. Even if he himself, Guy Bags, had shot a cop, stoolie or not, he would have to go down, as a lesson. The rules were not made to be bent, let alone broken. And if Montaine would kill his loyal right arm for killing a cop, what would he do to a drunken shit like Ted King?

It made Bags shiver to think about it. What would happen was, Montaine would want Ted's head in a hat box, to take out and show to other young up-and-comers who might do something stupid to try and impress him. And he'd want Bags's balls right in there with Teddy's head, to show everybody what happened to guys who sponsored people they shouldn't have.

Bags thought of all he had told Montaine; how Ted was loyal, gutsy, stand-up, a tried-and-true button who was ready to move up to better things. He had single-handedly pushed Ted's promotion through, over the heads of guys more worthy, because Ted was family, and therefore, presumably, could be counted on above the others.

Bags now knew what a mistake that had been. Then immediately saw a way to correct his error.

He would play Teddy like a violin. He would make sure Montaine did not become aware of who had whacked out the cop. Montaine would be happy that the jig was out of the way, the same way Bags had been when he heard the news. It was good that the guy was dead; it was bad that one of their own had done the job. If Montaine remained ignorant, all could work out. He could get through this in one piece. And then, when the dumb shit picked up the tapes, as soon as he hit the old thief in the head, Bags would have the backup crew put a couple of slugs in Teddy's dumb fucking head.

Plans had a way of going wrong. He had seen the future, with Montaine in the top-dog spot and himself in the top-underboss position that Montaine now held. Ted would have been his chief of security, smart enough to know that he was dumb and that without Bags's blessing, he would wind up breaking legs down on the docks. Bags would never have to worry about getting hit, because his head bodyguard would be blood.

Oh, well.

It was a shame but there was no way around it. The kid had made his bed, and now would have to sleep in it. He turned to Ted and put a man-to-man tone in his voice, and whispered: "Just one thing, Ted." Teddy raised his eyebrows, his glass held in his hand, his pinky out. Bags said, "There might be some ferocious heat about this. Don't say a word to anyone, and I mean nobody, until I explain things to Montaine." He saw the quick flash of fear pass across Teddy's face, and knew he had him in the palm of his hand. He pressed on.

"Montaine finds out you did it, without me calming him down about it, Ted, and believe me, he'll kill you without thinking about it. Give me a week, ten days to plant some seeds. Jerry figures out what a good thing it was that you did, he gets a chance to think about it calmly, and I guarantee, you'll get a spot right under me." Teddy was nodding eagerly, hanging on his every word, and Bags figured that he'd said enough. He held out his freshened glass, and they touched rims. He said, "You fucking wild man," and Teddy grinned.

Later, Bags told Teddy, "After you take the guy, whatever you find is yours. I told my friends we'd get our dough back, part of the bargain, but after they find out who aced Bigum Barnes, once Montaine sees our point of view and puts the word out, they won't have no problem with letting you have it, especially after you give us the dead thief and whatever he comes up with out of the safe. A million bucks, cost us all a hundred grand each. Me and Montaine put the million up, but after the other guys find out how he saved their asses, we'll get a hundred grand each from them as tribute. So what you find, Ted, is yours. A small price to pay to get two of our worst enemies out of our hair."

Teddy was on his fourth drink now, and they'd been talking business. He was getting a kick out of it whenever one of his cousin's associates would come by to pay his respects and Bags would introduce him as "Ted, he's one of us," letting Teddy know he was in now, that he had remade his bones and was a man to be admired. Teddy got off on the way the guys would look at him, sizing him up, and he showed respect, although with a slight touch of arrogance. After all, he was a man to be feared now. The women kept their distance, seeing the two tough guys in the back booth with their heads together talking low, but when he caught one of them looking at them, he saw the way they checked him out, gazing at him as if they were from South Africa and he was a steak they couldn't wait to sink their teeth into. He liked the way they looked at him and knew that his masturbation days were over. It would be pussy every night, any night he wanted. Any girl he wanted.

If he hadn't been the guest of honor in a joint full of

outfit guys, Teddy might have broken down and started to cry, that's how very good he was feeling.

But he was and so he didn't. But he didn't stop himself from drinking it all in, from accepting the praise of his cousin. Not yet an equal, but working on it; Bags had already told him as much. Maybe even, someday, a superior. Anything was possible when you had a gun and the balls to use it.

Before they left, staggering from the booth, ready to go out into the freezing January night, Bags told Teddy that he could take a few days off, rest up for the job ahead of them come Monday. When Teddy would make a million dollars tax-free cash . . .

Sunday morning, the last day of January. Vincent did not believe the weather. The wind was howling around him, gusting at him madly, ripping at his clothing, trying to pull the garments from his body and freeze him on the spot. The streets were passable; the plows had made their rounds and now tons and tons of snow— snow that was rapidly turning dingy gray—was piled at the curbs. It took him a full half an hour to shovel the solid piles away from his curb; the stuff was pushed a couple of feet onto his driveway. The warehouse was icy, even the thick stone walls had ice on them. He scraped the ice from his windshield and swore that next year he would have a larger furnace put in. One that would heat the warehouse, too. Forty-five minutes after he'd stepped from his apartment, Vincent pulled to the curb before Bolo's bar. The inside of the car still was not warm. He could see his breath clouding in front of him. The radio said that the windchill factor was seventy-two degrees below zero, the temperature itself twenty-one below. And that was not even a record for the last day of January. Vincent shut off the engine,

locked the car, hoping the lock would not freeze, set the
alarm and walked toward the bar.

The only window in Bolo's place was the one in the
front door. A diamond perhaps eight inches square.
Vincent knew that was for a very good reason. No one
could train a camera with a zoom lens on the front of
the joint and see who was inside. And many of the customers, the regulars, came and went through the solid
six-inch-thick steel back door. He saw the sign in the
tiny window now, hand-lettered, clear only if you were
standing in the recess leading to the door. It read,
CLOSED DUE TO BLIZZARD. Vincent grinned and
turned his key in the lock. The door swung open on
well-oiled hinges. He entered and saw Bolo playing
around with the safe under the bar. He quickly locked
the door behind him and stamped his feet on the rubber
mat set at the entrance. Pounded them until the snow
was off and he could feel them again. Then he walked
over to see what Bolo was doing.

What Bolo was doing was taking out the suitcase that
the kid, Teddy, had brought him the other night.

Bolo threw it on the bar and closed the safe, spun the
dial, then put the false bottom back in place under the
bar. The fit was perfect, seamless. The most thorough
search from the most professional of thieves would not
find it. A square had been laser cut into the ground, and
into the surrounding foot of mahogany that was part of
the bar bottom. The safe installed there, the wood replaced, whole. Only Bolo and Vincent knew the combination. Not that it mattered all that much. If a pro ever
found the safe, he could beat it almost as fast as Vincent
could with the combo. The way it was hidden was all
important. Along with the fact that every regular solid
patron of the bar knew that Bolo kept a safe upstairs in
his dwellings. If word ever did get out about his having
come into a windfall and some reckless fool tried to take
him off, all he'd get for his troubles would be the couple

of grand salted upstairs in the barrel safe behind the large painting of a street scene in Venice, Italy.

Bolo said, "That's yours," pointing his chin at the bag there on the bar, a cheap little thing at that, didn't even have a lock on it.

Vincent went to it and unzipped it, threw it open and looked for the first time in his life at a million dollars, all in one chunk, packed tightly inside the cheap canvas suitcase. He didn't say anything for a long, long time.

They were upstairs in Bolo's apartment. The place was furnished like a distant memory of the old country. Heavy Victorian furniture with fringed bottoms. All the chairs and sofas having large, almost overbearing wings. Vincent would sit in one of them and get paranoid, thinking that the damn thing was going to devour him like in a teenaged science-fiction flick. The suitcase with the million dollars was on a heavy oak table in the dining room. Bolo's apartment had six full rooms, two bedrooms, a living room, a dining room, a sitting room and a full kitchen. Every room was filled with antiques. There wasn't a book in sight. Bolo wasn't into reading, unless it was a copy of the locksmith's manual.

Vincent was staring at Bolo, hard, waiting. Bolo hadn't said a word since telling him that the money was his, and Vincent wasn't about to play the anxious kid with Bolo. Jumping up and down, saying, tell me, tell me.

At last Bolo broke the silence. He was looking at Vincent with a funny grin on his face, like the cat caught with his mouth full of feathers. Caught in the act and enjoying it, too late to try and cop a plea, nothing to do but sit there and chew, swallow, and hope the owner liked him more than he had the bird.

"You make up your mind about things, kid?"

"I'm ready."

"You're sure, now? No second thoughts?"

"For that kind of money, Bolo, I'll break into hell and steal the devil's fucking pitchfork."

"Well, kid," Bolo said, the feathers swallowed, the grin full out, a hundred-watter, "breaking into hell would be a piece of cake next to where we're going to score."

Vincent said, "Where's that, Bolo," smiling himself now, enjoying Bolo's sense of drama and his impeccable timing.

"Vincent, me boy, we are going to break into the ninetieth floor of the Sears Tower."

Vincent grunted. "What's so hard about that?"

"We got to go in from the outside," Bolo said.

"From the *out*side?"

"You heard me, Vincent."

"And when are we supposed to commit this simple little magic act?"

Bolo smiled full out now, his belly shaking with laughter he was trying desperately to control. He said, "Tomorrow afternoon." Then broke, laughing at the look on Vincent's face.

Vincent said, "Tomorrow afternoon. It's supposed to be thirty degrees below zero tomorrow, Bolo. Up that high, the windchill, it'll be like the top of Mount Everest. We don't get down and inside within maybe two minutes, they'll find us dangling up there, a couple of ice cubes, before we know it."

Bolo said, "What do you want for a million dollars cash money, Vincent, a stroll in the park?"

"Just assuming now, that you don't have Alzheimer's, that your mind isn't totally shot from syphilis or whatever, say you are serious, Bolo. Just for a second. We, meaning you and me, are going to climb Sears Tower tomorrow afternoon in subzero weather with maybe a hundred-degree-below-zero windchill factor, and go in through the glass, into some stiff's house. From there supposedly to the safe. And then back out the same way, into the cold, up the rope. Your ancient ass blowing in the wind. Just suppose I agree to do this thing with you. You want to tell me whose crib we're going to take?"

Bolo said, "The number-one guy in the entire Chicago Mafia, that's who."

"Raymond Parilo," Vincent said.

Bolo said, "Raymond Parilo."

"You're out of your fucking mind," Vincent said.

Bolo smiled at him, knowingly.

15 What Bolo explained to his protégé there in his antique-laden apartment were the facts of life as the Mafia understood them. At first he stared at Vincent as he spoke, right in the eye, letting him know how important this was and making sure he understood. But soon his mind wandered, and he was staring at the ceiling as he ran it down to Vincent, this once-in-a-lifetime score that most thieves dreamed about. A score like he had never been on before; one without any risk of arrest. That would be taken care of. The risks were terribly high in other areas, however. And Bolo pulled no punches as he explained them.

Even with the state-of-the-art equipment he had ordered, equipment that they would be picking up that evening, the risks were as high as the rewards. He wanted to hear the objections now, because once they were hanging almost a thousand feet in the air, there would be no time for second thoughts. As he spoke Bolo remembered that Vincent had not been on a real score for almost ten years. He had been locked up for seven and home for more than two. Bolo himself hadn't been on a score for several years; and this was a fact that fazed him not in the least. He believed that once you were a thief, then that was that; you were a thief for the rest of your life. The fact that neither man had been active in their profession lately would, in fact, work in their favor. If they pulled it off, no cop that might somehow be brought into the investigation by the Parilo mob, for whatever reasons, or, for that matter, any Parilo loyalists who did any investigating, would suspect them. They were last decade's news.

Bolo was no stranger to either violence or sudden death. He'd seen and been involved with both these brutal facts of thieving more than once. He laughed, for example, when "Hill Street Blues" was on the recorder, seeing all the cops so gentle and careful with suspects. He himself had been beaten by the law so many times he had lost count. Had had pistols pointed at his head while the hammer was back, seconds from death and standing unafraid and ready.

What he told Vincent at first was all about how they'd work it, the way it would happen if it was to happen at all. He'd been planning and watching and setting things up for weeks, in contact with Baggio on a near daily basis. Meeting with Montaine had been a formality more than anything else. He'd had the score laid down and rolled over with its legs up and spread and ready to be entered days before that meeting, before the money was truly guaranteed. Before he'd had to meet a slob like young Teddy who would drive for them, or rather, for him, for Bolo. Teddy would know nothing about Vincent's involvement. He and the rest of the goombahs would believe that Bolo had undertaken and completed the Herculean task all alone, just in case . . .

What Bolo told Vincent about after he ran down the basics of the score was a tale as political as it was anything else, a story of greed and lust for power that could only happen in a city as divided and uncivilized as Chicago. In New York or Cleveland or Florida, such a thing could never happen, but in Chicago it was considered a real coup, a real act of class and cunning.

It started with eleven men, and would end up with ten.

Tommy Campo had, in the last years of his reign, given his orders directly to his right-hand man, Angelo Paterro, who then gave his own set of orders to one of twelve underbosses. Like Christ, Campo felt safe with a dozen apostles. Unlike Christ, all twelve of Campo's disciples were in their hearts a Judas. Would gladly cut Campo's throat and take all that he had if the opportunity arose. He did not begrudge them this, in fact welcomed it. He wanted them jealous, angry, wanted them bickering amongst themselves. If they got along, if they were friendly, they might well have plotted together to overthrow him.

The underboss named Mikey Barboza, the only non-Italian of the bunch—he was a Portuguese—was now dead. Angelo Paterro was on an Army base living in relative luxury compared to how he had been living, in true luxury when compared to Tommy Campo, who was now languishing in the state joint down Joliet way. Which left the eleven, the underbosses, the supposed equals.

But there was one who was the most powerful of the equals and his name was Raymond Parilo. He did not reach his exalted position due to his intelligence. As a matter of fact, of the eleven, Parilo was probably the dumbest, the most brutal, the one with the least amount of imagination or guile. But, conversely, he was the one more than any of them who stood the best chance of walking away from the collapsing building with not only his body undamaged, but holding mortgage and title to the thing, free and clear, with a license from the national commission to rebuild.

All because he was Angelo Paterro's brother-in-law. Angelo was married to Raymond's sister, and that made all the difference in the world. It was not in the least unusual within the mob's ranks for one to rise above another of superior quality and intelligence due to the union of matrimony. Men had been marrying Mafia women for centuries, hoping that the joining would put them in a position of power. What made this case unusual was the simple fact that Paterro had never heard the name Raymond Parilo in his life before falling in love with his Carmella. It was Carmella who had introduced her future husband to her violent and unruly brother, and it was Carmy who had begged Angelo to help him. Angelo had taken one look at the wild-eyed beast of a man that Raymond had been as a youngster and he knew that if he gave him his break, Raymond would repay him with undying gratitude and loyalty. He was far too stupid to do otherwise.

From the start it had been a bringing together of two of the men who, in the violent world in which they lived, were the very best at what they did. Paterro with his cunning, logical and calculating mind, Raymond with his violence. Brutal, deadly, cold and unforgiving. Raymond would have tried to murder Tommy Campo himself if Paterro had so ordered it. Paterro had made it clear while dealing with the underbosses that Raymond would open his own veins, gladly, if Paterro asked him to.

But Montaine's decision to oust him from their ranks was for reasons much deeper than jealousy, resentment or fear.

It had been proven to Baggio's and Montaine's satisfaction that Raymond had more tapes stored in his wall safe in his apartment than even Paterro himself had.

Raymond, as the brother-in-law and right hand of Angelo Paterro, was in no danger of being arrested due to Tombstone's rolling over. It was widely known that Carmy and her brother were closer than even Italian men thought to be possible; they were as one. Even if

Paterro wanted to give the feds enough to put Raymond away, Carmy would not allow it. He was, in Paterro's eyes then, and now in the eyes of the other ten underbosses, the heir apparent.

And now that it was proven that Paterro had kept his incriminating tapes in more than one spot, then Montaine, to solidify his position as Parilo's heir after Raymond's death, had to get, then use to his own advantage, the devastating tapes.

Bolo had to hand it to Paterro, he knew his stuff. If a man were to try and find a place to keep something hidden from his enemies, what better place indeed than the safe of a family member who had sworn undying fealty? A thousand feet above the ground in a near burglarproof, secure and strongly guarded fortress in the sky? What Paterro had never counted on was Raymond's suddenly getting himself a mid-life case of ambition.

Raymond had begun to see his brother-in-law as a stoolie and nothing more. A man to be loathed and looked down upon. Bolo suspected that this attitude came more from Raymond's growing accustomed to the trappings of power and wealth than to any old-country dago ideals. He had something from Tombstone that would make him the king of kings, the boss of bosses. The Man. And the rest had better listen and do as they were told.

Montaine and Baggio would take the tapes and become unbeatable. With the six underbosses whose voices were on tape behind them, the other four would fall in line and serve Montaine as their new leader.

As it was, at the moment, the authorities were working Paterro night and day to ensure that Tommy Campo never breathed free air again in his life. His death sentence and other life sentences made Campo a nonthreat to anyone, ever again.

But after they were through with Campo, then what?

Even if Montaine could somehow avert the bloodshed and convince Parilo to just hold off and wait, what then? Would Paterro someday call the man he thought to be his loyal brother-in-law and order him to bring the other tapes to him? Would the other ten mobsters fall as Campo had, leaving the city of Chicago wide open to a lifelong reign by Raymond Parilo? Or, worse yet and probably closer to the truth than anything else: Was Angelo Paterro, with his fine Sicilian mind, preparing himself for a return to power, all alone and singularly the top man in Chicago, using Parilo as his pawn? If Paterro served even the full ten years, using that time to put the opposition behind bars, cementing Raymond into the top spot and locking him in, he would still be only sixty-five years old upon his release. When he would quite possibly move Raymond out and take over as the single most powerful outfit man in the United States. The national commission never messed in Chicago's business. They were the outsiders, violent outcasts who were beneath contempt with their killings in the streets, their propensity to use violence first and reasoning afterward. The commission might well forgive even a stool pigeon who brought order out of this chaos. Who secured the national idea of the mob in Chicago well and firmly. Paterro might indeed be doing just that.

And Montaine and Baggio, with knowledge of the tapes, could not afford to wait and see.

It would cause a bloodbath, the killing of Raymond Parilo and the burglary of his apartment. People loyal to him, and there were many, would want to know who had done it and would thirst for justice. Even Montaine, with all his power and strength, would have a problem holding on to the top spot.

Unless he had the tapes in his possession, and the men whose voices were on those tapes in his pocket.

And so he had turned to Bolo.

Monday afternoon at precisely twelve, a luncheon
meeting was being held in one of the banquet rooms of
the Ritz Hotel, to be attended by all eleven of the surviving underbosses. There would be food and drink; at-
tendance was mandatory, and Raymond had assured his
fellow underbosses when he had called the meet that
this would be one of the few occasions when he would
leave the safety of his clifftop nest and mingle with the
rest. His plan, as told to Montaine and Baggio, was to
immediately upon his arrival have his men murder, in
full view of the others, the four underbosses whose loyalty could not be guaranteed by the tapes in his safe. He
would then, while the bodies of the dead mobsters lay
at their feet, tell the remaining six precisely what he expected from them from that moment on. It was a plan
that Montaine had refined for him, had, through repeated efforts and arguments, turned into a plan that
worked to Montaine's advantage.

He had convinced Parilo to wait. To let the wine flow
and the food be eaten. Had assured Parilo that the scene
would be more graphic, would remain in the minds of
the surviving men forever as if carved in stone if he first
allowed the doomed men to eat and drink, become soft
and comfortable, before having them brutally slain.

Parilo had agreed to wait until 2:45 to commit the
actual murders. Then, while his men carted the bodies,
stuffed into trash cans, down the service elevator, he
would get their attention and only then tell them what
their roles would be from that day on.

And everything would go almost according to Parilo's plan, except with one small change.

He would never return from the meeting.

But before it ended, before the 2:45 killing time,
Montaine would have to have assurances that he indeed
was in possession of the tapes. Everything hinged on
them. If he killed Parilo without them, the other underbosses would fall upon him like sharks on a wounded

swimmer. The underbosses were Montaine's only concern. The bodyguards had already been reached, and had been assured high positions in Montaine's new army after they went along with Montaine's treachery. But without the tapes, without good, sound reason for whacking Parilo out, he, and Bags along with him, were dead.

It was up to Bolo to give them these assurances. He had nearly three hours to get in, break the safe and get back out to the street, where Teddy would supposedly take possession of whatever tapes were found in the safe; any valuables, including jewels or cash, would belong to Bolo. Teddy would drive from there to the Ritz Hotel in Water Tower Place and simply nod to his boss and cousin Guido Baggio, and then the matter of Raymond Parilo would be considered solved. They would take care of him.

"So that's the scoop?" Vincent asked.

"The straight, all the way."

Vincent said, "I'll be goddamned."

Bolo said, "You probably will be, but what do you think?"

"From what I heard on the street, Paterro taped his conversations with Campo. The other guys, even if their names were on the tapes, wouldn't that be considered circumstantial in a court of law?"

"Vincent, I know personally maybe a thousand guys, doing hard time because of convictions where the prosecutors only had circumstantial evidence. And besides, doesn't it stand to reason, if he was taping his conversations with Campo, that he would take it one step further and tape his underbosses, too, if only to keep them in line if they started getting too big for their britches?"

"Why pay you two million?"

"Us, two million, kid."

"I know, Bolo, but they don't know about me. Why don't they just send in a bunch of their goons, go in and bust the safe, whack the guy right there in his apartment?"

Bolo sighed, as if trying to explain relativity to a retarded child. He said, "Didn't you understand what I just said? Parilo is Paterro's brother-in-law. Word would get back to Paterro, right now, that someone had gotten to him. If the tapes were there, Paterro knows about them because he put them there, and you can believe he's got a cadre of his own people guarding the place, with orders to kill anyone comes up there who isn't Parilo. Paterro doesn't know about Parilo's treachery, dummy. And do you think Montaine wants Paterro knowing he killed a member of his family for no reason? That's where Teddy comes in. He tells them we got the tapes; they whack Raymond and then they don't give a fuck what Paterro knows.

"See, Vincent, these guys, Baggio and Montaine, they suffer from the same disease every gangster in this city has contracted since the time of Al Capone: They're greedy. They've decided they will run the city together, as equals. Split it up between them. And hell, not just Chicago. They got Missouri, they got Michigan and Wisconsin, they got Minnesota. Chicago takes care of all these states; they control them. There're billions involved here. They can afford to split it up. All they got to do is get rid of the tapes and Raymond, and they think the world is theirs. Anything Paterro says in court then will be nothing but his word against theirs. A good lawyer, and they walk.

"Another thing is, Vincent, the joint is secure. With a capital S. Raymond keeps them outside, no one but him and his broads get into the apartment, but there're two guards sitting on a couch outside the door twenty-four hours a day. A half a dozen more are constantly roaming the stairways and lobbies, wearing security uniforms and carrying pistols. These guys figure it ain't just for looks. Hell, security in Sears Tower is the best in the city, even without the damn mob guards. They're rolling the dice with everything they got, based on the fact that the tapes are there, man, and they think I'm the only guy good enough to get in and out with them without getting my ass blown into the middle of next week."

"Bolo," Vincent said, "what if the tapes are in there, but the guy's got dupes made somewhere, sitting in a box at the bank?"

Bolo smiled. "That's the first thing I asked Baggio, even before he saw the tapes himself. He said that, one, Parilo's too stupid to dupe the things. Two, the guy's too paranoid, wouldn't leave a dupe anywhere but in the safety of his own apartment, and the originals are already there, so what would be the point? No, this guy thinks he owns it all, Vincent, and even if we go in there and there ain't a dime in the safe, we're scoring two mill of the mob's money. We can't fucking lose."

"Unless the wind blows our asses off the building."

"Not much chance of that, with the goods I got for us to climb down with."

"This is crazy, you know that, don't you, Bolo."

Bolo said, "Kid, I warned you about that crazy life, twenty-five years ago. It didn't do any good then; you wanted to play badass then, so now you're stuck with it.

"But this is it for both of us, kid. We take the money and run. Rest easy from here on out. A million apiece and whatever we score out of the safe."

"It could pay for a nice wedding, you know?"

Bolo didn't answer.

"You hear what I said there, Bolo?"

Slowly, Bolo's face broke into a wide, wide grin. His eyes danced with merriment. Vincent could swear that Bolo's eyes filled with tears. Bolo didn't say anything, he just nodded. Vigorously.

"The pipes are frozen."

Vincent was on the phone, talking to Evlyn, telling

her he wouldn't be seeing her until tomorrow afternoon, four at the latest. He figured if he wasn't home
by then, he never would be. And now she tells him the
pipes are frozen. Heavy goddamn industrial-sized pipes
that had held water for fifty years without a leak or ever
freezing up one damn time and there you were, when
you needed a mind free of trouble and problems, boy,
something always came up.

"You know," Vincent said, "those pipes, they're
wrapped with enough insulation to keep goddamn Alas-
kan pipes from freezing, and here it is Chicago and the
damn things block up."

"Vincent, I'll take the Mercury or a cab and go over
to my place and wait for you there, okay?"

"No, no, don't do that. Listen, I'll reserve you a suite
in your name at the Pick-Congress; you take a cab,
go to your house and get some clothes, wait for me
there."

"Vincent, I have maybe three hundred dollars in my
purse. The Congress won't take good looks and I don't
own a credit card."

"Evlyn, go over to the R section of the bookcases.
Find the 'Religion' section, then grab the second Bible,
the King James one, the big one with all the hand let-
tering and the pictures. Open it up and there's ten
grand inside. Between the pages, in hundreds. Take it
all for shopping for your wedding gown or whatever
when the weather breaks, okay? Pay for two nights at
the hotel. A good suite, not one of the dinky ones. Get
the one the president stayed in, the one Sinatra stayed
in. Go first class for a change. You deserve it."

"Vincent, this is it, isn't it?"

Vincent looked at Bolo sitting at the kitchen table,
waiting for him. He said, "I love you," softly. Then
hung up.

"Call the hotel and then let's eat and get some rest.

We got a big night ahead of us," Bolo said, and Vincent began to dial Information. . . .

Many burglars defecate in the homes they are working in, and these thieves are referred to by the police as "shitters." It is a common misconception that the thieves perform this act due to their disdain for the people they are robbing, or the police, or both.

This is untrue.

The fact is that the sphincter muscle loosens when you are inside a place where you do not belong, doing things that you know can put you behind stone walls for a long, long time. They loosen sometimes so rapidly that you cannot get to the bathroom, and so you let your pants down and do what you have to do wherever you happen to be.

Now some thieves get creative. As long as they have to go, they decide to get cute and do something the people who own the homes will remember for a long time to come. Something that cops will talk about in cop bars for years and years, something that will make them semilegends in their own time. They shit on plates and then put them in the refrigerator. They shit on pool tables and then place the eight ball directly in the middle. They shit on top of the toilet seat and then write "Whoops," in lipstick on the mirror. They shit on ice cube trays and in coffee cans, on pillows on the beds and in shoes. No place is sacred to them.

Bolo considered them beneath contempt, and classless to boot. The point of scoring was to make money, period. Not to cause any problem for the tenants, other than having to call their insurance company in the morning, or maybe their locksmith and order a new safe. This time a burglarproof one! He never trashed a house or even took a drink, which was a rarity in his line. He left the house as neatly as he had found it, with the single exception being that every dime and all the jewelry in the safe was gone. Forever. And he had instilled these values in Vincent.

He had never wanted Vincent to follow in his footsteps. He had wanted Vincent to be a square John, a working stiff, someone he could be proud of. But Vincent was a hardhead, had started pulling down scores on his own, so Bolo had taught him the right way. Bolo had made of him a thief with a capital T.

And so on Sunday afternoon they ate big greasy broiled porterhouse steaks in Bolo's kitchen, with plenty of grilled onions on them. The steaks were covered with butter before they were cooked, and they drank plenty of coffee after they ate. They would not eat meat or drink coffee again until after the score. This would ensure that they would have good solid bowel movements that evening. Before leaving in the morning, they would eat plenty of cheese to constipate them, and would share a bottle of Pepto-Bismol to control their stomachs. And their nausea, as they would be climbing. Before they went out to the roof, they would enter a men's room and force themselves to urinate.

They were professionals, and acted as such.

Bolo had also taught Vincent to get rid of any tools used on a score immediately afterward, saving nothing that wasn't strictly nontraceable. Bolo would order the equipment he needed and pick it up before a score, usually a week before, but in this case that night, as it was a rush order. All they would take with them and bring back to the bar would be their own selves and the set of locksmith's picks that Bolo took out of the safe when he put Vincent's money back in. And the money. The loot.

Vincent was used to asking no questions. This, too, had been instilled in him early on in life. As he hadn't asked questions that night when Teddy had brought in the suitcaseful of money. He hadn't asked Bolo what was in it, though he'd wanted to. On countless other

occasions he'd kept his mouth shut, even when he was
dying of curiosity or when it looked to him as if Bolo
were doing something unusually dangerous. It was a
matter of respecting each other's privacy, showing respect and, more importantly, trust. Without trust there
was nothing. And so he didn't ask now where Bolo's
million was. Didn't ask about the maybe ten holes he
saw in Bolo's plot; knew even as Bolo lied to him or
misled him that it was for a good reason. He had to
trust Bolo, 100 percent, all the way, or he'd be breaking
a sacred bond between them. A bond deeper than that
of a father and son or a mother and daughter.

The bond that crime partners had between them.

Guys who would lay down their lives for each other
and who lived by a code so far apart from any known to
the civilized world that to them it was everything they
had in the world. More important than the money or
the thrill of danger. Far more important than any
woman or outside relationship. The strange bonding of
thieves who lived their lives knowing that there were
indeed things much worse than death. Things like getting a rat jacket. Things like losing face. Things like
being branded a coward. These were the things they
could never give up for anyone, at any cost. They would
cut their tongues out before they squealed, ratted each
other or anyone else out. They would die before they
would allow someone to step into their chest or get into
their face. Show they had lost their balls. Because balls
were everything, heart a close second. And so Vincent
didn't ask about the money, didn't pursue the parts of
Bolo's story that didn't ring true. Honesty was just a
word to them, important only at certain times and then
only when it was demanded by the code. And he put
these things out of his mind; they no longer existed,
and he followed Bolo's lead and listened to him and
concentrated on every word. Because within twenty-
four hours each of their lives would be in the hands of

the other, and this was a thing neither took lightly. If one of them didn't make it out, it would be as if neither had. The one who escaped would live the rest of his life with the sure knowledge that he'd let his partner, his crime partner, down. And this was not allowable. Instead of asking, or questioning, Vincent put the questions and his doubts in a compartment in the back of his mind, to be dealt with tomorrow, as soon as they got back from the score. To do any less would be to break the code, to doubt Bolo's wisdom, to question his heart and his balls. And this just could not be done.

Instead, he rested on the bed in Bolo's guest room, eyes never closing but staring sightlessly at the white ceiling. Thinking and trying not to. Thinking of over nine dry years, two of them spent boosting; *boosting*, for Christ's sake, when he'd been trained as a thief, as a professional stand-up ballsy thief with plenty of heart. Thinking of how it must have broken Bolo's heart to see him stealing cars and stereos and the rest when he had information that could put him on top of the world if he would only use it.

He thought, too, about how good he was feeling, how alive, knowing as he thought about it that the feeling would intensify a thousandfold tomorrow, when they were doing it, actually scoring.

Thought for what seemed like minutes but was really hours because suddenly Bolo was in the room, all business now, shaking his arm, and he hadn't even heard him walking through the house. Telling Vincent softly and firmly that it was time to go; they had equipment that had to be bought and paid for and inspected. Vincent knew it was stuff their very lives would be dependent upon in the day to come. He rose from the bed and put on his heavy leather coat quickly, anticipating, feeling vibrant, dangerous, and vitally alive.

*   *   *

They met the toolmaker at the Oasis on the Tollway. He was a tall, broad-shouldered, bald man dressed for the weather most elegantly. He greeted Bolo warmly in the smoking section, seated amid the very few who were out this Sunday evening in the most horrible of winters in memory. Truck drivers smoked and drank coffee slowly. A couple of punks acting like players, lounging casually in the ash-wood chairs, stared sullenly at the few in the restaurant, being ignored for the most part, but sometimes a tired trucker would catch their eye and grimace menacingly, and the self-styled badasses would look away. They were jackals looking for game and coming up empty.

The toolmaker, like Bolo, was not alone. He had a second with him and Vincent and the second went out into the frigid near-deserted parking lot and transferred the goods from one trunk to another.

In the eerie silence, Vincent felt almost afraid. No sounds of traffic were coming from the Tollway beneath them, no one was walking from their cars to the Oasis; there were just the sounds of diesel engines idling in the truck parking lot, hundreds of feet away from them. Still, he made the transfer and the eyeball inspection as quickly as possible; the State Police patrolled the Tollway, and they could be expected to drive through several times this bone-chilling night for a cup of coffee or perhaps to call home and see that all was well. He nodded at the second and they stuffed their hands into their coat pockets, ran back to the restaurant and sat with their elders, drinking coffee, the two older men smoking as they talked of times long past; the two younger men playing with their coffee cups, of a generation that did not grow up believing that sucking weed smoke into their lungs was fashionable or manly. At last the two older men shook hands and wished each other well,

Vincent and the second nodding at each other cordially, friendship still light-years away.

Vincent and Bolo walked to their car, hurriedly, their shoulders hunched against the wind, collars up. The windchill factor at seven-thirty that Sunday night in January was sixty-two below zero. And falling. The Tollway itself was nearly deserted, with drifts of snow twenty feet high on the shoulders. It swirled into their path, driven by the killer wind, biting at the windshield and dying a quick wet death in the blackness of the January night.

Vincent drove them home and they inspected their equipment. There were two pairs of strange-looking boots, mountain-climbing boots with large hard-rubber attachments clamped to the right toes. They were specially made and weighed ten pounds a pair. There were built-in clamps inside the boot that would tighten when the outer straps were pulled tight, ensuring that the boot would be secure and solidly attached. Hard-rubber two-inch-thick soles on the bottom of the boots would guarantee a good grip. The boots were insulated and warmth assured up to fifty degrees below zero. They looked good on the ground, but their actual value would not be known until the next day. If they did not work at that time, the entire score might have to be scrubbed. Next they checked the ropes, black waxed hemp with a breaking strength of one and a half tons. It would serve. The rope had double knots tied at three-foot intervals. There were no cuts or breaks in the rope. It was new and would serve its purpose and a double one if the boots were a bust; they might have to use it to climb down as well as back up. But doing that might sap their strength and leave them without the energy for the climb back up. . . . Enough of that, Vincent thought, no room for doubt, the shoes would work.

The heavy black canvas knapsacks were perfect; they would hold everything and still look to the casual eye as

much smaller than they actually were. The drill with its
suction attachments and its collapsible muffler was
looked over quickly; both men had used the same kind
before and knew its worth; it was checked mainly to
make sure that any numbers were scraped off and then
soaked with acid; no one would be getting the numbers
from it ever again. Two wigs, a fake mustache and
beard. Alligator clamps and a more sophisticated D. B.
III model Soundenhancer were all right and unnum-
bered. The electrical-voltage-current-flow device would
be used if they had to bypass an alarm inside the safe,
the only detail about the inside of the apartment that
they were not already sure of. Skin-tight black wet suits
were fresh and brand-new, as were the surgically thin
but warmth-keeping gloves that would fit up to their
elbows, only their hands from the wrist out not under
the wet suit. Over their eyes they would be wearing ski
goggles, matte black around the rims, the lenses darkened enough so there would be absolutely no reflection.
A rubber suction cup with a round piece of glass with a
handle attached to its center was stored in Vincent's
bag, as were all the other tools. Part of his job would be
to do the mule work. Bolo was the brains. Bolo would
carry only his own equipment up to the roof. Nothing
more, just what he would be wearing. Lastly was a
large, glazier's glass cutter.

And that was it. Maybe one hundred pounds of
equipment strapped to his back, not counting the ten
extra pounds of his boots. Another question Vincent
would not dare ask was if Bolo was in shape for this,
but Vincent certainly wondered about it often enough
as they worked.

Until midnight, they studied the charts. Blueprints of
the building, facts—at this point unimportant but you
never could tell—about the Sears Tower. The many
thousands of miles of wiring inside the building, the
thousands of tons of concrete and steel and glass, the six

year-round window-washing machines—this they paid close attention to—that would wash every window in the world's tallest building eight times yearly, each machine run from power sources independent of the other seven.

They quit at midnight. Vincent rose and stretched, listened to some last-minute advice from Bolo.

"After we leave, you get back here, take the suitcase out of the safe and the suitcase under it, too, that's mine," answering one of Vincent's questions, the one about the money, or so Vincent thought. "Then you hightail it over to your place and wait for me to call, froze pipes or no froze pipes. I ain't talking through the switchboard at no hotel. You got it?"

"We expecting trouble?" Vincent asked.

Bolo said, "Kid, when it comes to these guys, don't ever expect nothing less than trouble."

And he went off to his bedroom to rest for the day ahead.

Surprisingly, and in spite of himself, Vincent slept.

16 They ate bananas and cheese for breakfast. Followed by Pepto-Bismol at seven in the morning on a tremendously cold and overcast Monday morning, the first day of February. Record cold engulfed the city. Trains were running three hours behind, a traveler's advisory was in effect; many businesses were closed due to the blizzard and the now record-breaking cold that was devastating Chicago. Bolo's radio informed them that the city of Chicago had canceled classes in all school districts, grade schools and high schools. The Chicago Archdiocese had closed the Catholic schools. To date, twenty-nine people had died from heart attacks and exposure, that number being overly cautious, not taking into account the people who died from fires that had begun when they burned newspapers in gasless stoves, all utilities shut off due to lack of payment. The number also didn't include the homeless, who were frozen stiff beneath snowbanks, under crawl spaces in private homes where they'd huddled for shelter and a warmth they were never to know again; those who had lain hidden in abandoned buildings with many filthy coats over them, yet not even close enough to save them. These were not mentioned on the radio and never again would be mentioned, even when they were found. They would be quietly carted away and buried in pine boxes, alone, without mourners, their number legion but never to be known by a public with eyes and minds tightly and voluntarily shut against such unhappy sights and thoughts.

At 8 A.M. that Monday morning, the temperature was at an incredible thirty-three degrees below zero. The windchill factor, the temperature that exposed skin would truly feel, was a never-before-recorded and mind-numbing 106 degrees below zero. Exposed skin would be subject to frostbite within two minutes.

Vincent and Bolo put on their wet suits, dressed casually over them, Vincent wrapping the rope tightly around his waist and chest. As he carefully packed his gear, putting the things he would need first in last, Bolo walked out into the arctic cold and started Vincent's Cadillac. They had warmed it upon awakening at six-thirty, again an hour later. By ten o'clock, the Caddy gave Bolo no trouble; the antifreeze was doing its job, the engine still warm. The street and the sidewalks were now slick with ice, almost hockey-rink quality; the crews dispersing the salt would be doing the North Side and the other trendy areas of the city. The South Loop would have to wait. Michigan Avenue might be clear, and State Street, but down here it was conceivable and quite probable that the first warming winds of spring might bring the first sign of anything but hazardous driving conditions.

Which was just fine as far as Vincent and Bolo were concerned. The more hazardous the better. Especially in the streets surrounding Sears Tower. If people were giving every ounce of their concentration to the road, they would not be noticing two men in black crawling down the side of the building like bizarre overgrown spiders.

When the car's defroster was blowing nothing but hot heavy air, Bolo turned the key in the ignition and shut it down. They would not be needing it until later.

Vincent went out the door as Bolo slammed the car door shut, and they began walking north on Clark to West Adams Street, then they turned west.

Bolo kept his eyes down, Vincent noticed. Most likely not wanting to see the huge structure until it was right there. Vincent kept his eyes straight ahead, or tried to, but the score called him, was in his blood now, waiting, singing its siren song, demanding that he look up.

He did.

And saw the monolith there above him. Way, way, *way* above him. All the way down Adams, he could see it. Looking as if it were right in front of him, bigger than any building was ever meant to be, half a mile away but looking as if they would walk right into it at any second.

One hundred and ten stories of dark glass and black steel. Rising, rising, swaying in the wind on the upper floors, the building took up one entire square city block, the world's tallest man-made structure, the offspring of the words *high rise* and *skyscraper*. The upper floors were in the clouds today, for which Vincent was grateful. Even with the promise of no police interference, he would feel less naked, more secure up there, knowing for a fact that no one could possibly see them from street level.

The middle third of the structure was in sight now as they approached. The building began at street level, encompassing nearly the entire block, a marble walkway leading completely around the building, with iron tables with umbrellas and a wishing well on the west side for workers to eat their lunches at in decent weather. Today, and until the thaw, that area would be roped off. From there it began, ever so slowly, to taper. Rising into the heavens inexorably, unstoppable. Tapering slowly, engineered and designed ingeniously to survive brutal winds and raging storms. Up to the ninetieth floor. The top twenty built separately upon the first ninety, looking to the world like a tall stately tuxedoed groom upon a gigantic wedding cake. The first five floors from this level, from where they would begin, were impossible to see with the naked eye. There was a flat roof surrounding the upper twenty floors at "ground" level. The top twenty floors were one fifth the size of the ninetieth, one eighth the size of the first, seemingly miles below on street level.

They approached the building, each wearing his wig, which were mostly hidden by the ski masks rolled to their eyes. A wisp of gray-red hair hung down the top back inch of Bolo's parka, a little more of jet-black hair hung down Vincent's. With the heavy gloves covering their thin superwarm pair, with their heavy outer clothing covering their wet suits, with Vincent's black mustache and Bolo's thick fake beard, and with their backpacks, they looked like a father and son hippie team roaming the tourist attractions, enjoying the solitude that the arctic conditions gave them.

They entered Sears Tower at the main entrance right on North Wacker Drive, going through the revolving doors like they owned the place, talking in normal tones about how much they hated making deliveries on days such as this.

The lobby was nearly deserted, the place uncannily quiet, the few workers roaming the lobby, as well as the few security guards in their understated navy blazers, paying them no attention.

The worst-kept secret about the world's tallest building was its elevator positions. In the lobby, signs directed tourists down the 2 flights to the express elevator that would whisk them in 70 seconds to the 103rd floor, the observation deck. The elevator went up with such astounding speed that no one ever spoke as it rose; even jam-packed, an eerie silence overcame even the most boisterous crowd as the speeding hollow bullet as-

cended. Moving from side to side quickly, even the
most jaded of people were left breathless. On the first
level below the lobby entrance were other elevators. Elevators that would take you express to the sixty-first
floor, where you would have to switch to another that
would take you higher. These elevators were for the
working folk, the low-level employees. Sears itself oc-
cupies the lower half of the building, the upper half devoted to private business, and on the ninetieth, two
condominiums, both owned under separate names by
Tombstone Paterro, who leased one to his brother-in-
law. If you were at Tombstone's level in the mob, special zoning ordinances were passed quite easily. Naturally, the regular elevators did not ever stop at the
ninetieth floor. There was no button for it, or, as a matter of fact, in any of them. Raymond Parilo had a special key that, when inserted in the lock and turned,
allowed the machine to stop on the ninetieth floor. No
bodyguards or security men had the key; just Raymond.
He would allow them access and let them down as he
saw fit. On the ninety-fifth floor, another such arrange-
ment occurred, for the private men's club there, the
members having keys that were stamped and supposedly
safe from being copied. But their keys did not allow
them access to the ninetieth floor, only the ninety-fifth.
Around the north side of the first lower level was another bank of elevators, the executive elevators, which
would whisk the top gunners to their executive suites,
or so the theory went. In practice, many of the lawyers
and other businessmen who operated above the fiftieth
floor used this elevator, along with models, delivery per-
sons, and, on more than one daily occasion, hookers.
The elevators went straight to whatever floor was
wanted, without delay or switching. This was where
Vincent and Bolo headed.

Above the 103rd floor, the entire inside of the building was gutted. This was the machinery area, holding

the tons of cables and wires and switches and hydraulics
and robotics and generators and energy banks that allowed such a massive structure to operate. These were
heavily guarded. No one was allowed up past the 103rd
observation deck without authorization. The only access
to these floors is by stairway, and the doors to these
stairways are kept locked and alarmed. From the 102nd
floor down to the 91st, the truly prime office footage,
private security was in force, paid for by the tenants. If a
tourist were caught wandering, he would be politely but
firmly shown to the elevator and warned that these were
private suites and that no one was allowed on these
floors without security first calling up and getting clear-
ance.

Bolo and Vincent stepped into the first executive elevator they came to and hit the button marked 91. With
a silent burst of power, the bare cubicle ascended, quite
rapidly, swaying gently to the left and right, back and
forth, powered by air and electricity and hydraulics. Up
and up; every tenth floor flashing in a digital display to
the left of the door. Vincent was trying not to fidget
and squirm. Bolo was humming. The elevator began to
slow down at the seventieth floor, and rolled ma-
jestically to a perfect and even stop on the ninety-first.
The doors opened and they exited, talking about the
poor and sorrowful passing of their dear friend Morris
Bloom.

Fortunately there was no one to see them, hear them
or challenge them.

Morris Bloom was the key to it for them. Without
him, the score could never have been pulled off. At
least, not this way, which, when all other possibilities
were explored, was the easiest of the bunch. What Morris Bloom did for them was, he died. On January 4,
poor Morris Bloom had had a heart attack on his yacht
moored in Fort Lauderdale, Florida. His wife, the second one, forty years younger than Morris, and hungry,

had been delighted. As a gesture of spite more than anything else, she had remained in Miami, in her grief telling the executive director of the building that as long as Morris had paid for his suite until March first, then it would, in memory of him, remain in his name until that time. She'd made this remark after learning that she could only get half the rental amount back, as stipulated in the lease. Two thousand square feet of space was sitting, with a waiting list full of prosperous lawyers begging for it, unattended and unmanned.

Mindful of their luck, which was good, knowing that good luck generally brought bad luck in its wake, Vincent and Bolo rushed down the heavily carpeted floor to the door to Morris Bloom's office. Vincent stood watch as Bolo bent and in a second beat the lock. They hurried in, breathing heavily now, the moment upon them.

Scoring time. The moment of truth.

Across the room, behind the receptionist's empty dark desk, stood the windows.

Like most of the others on the upper floors, they were heavily draped. At this level, the temptation was too great to look out upon the lake to the left of the windows. The window faced south, and if one were to look to the left on a clear day, one could see all the way to Michigan. On a clear day, four states can be seen from the Sears Tower sky deck.

Without a moment's hesitation, the men began to strip. Hurriedly, yet cautiously. The two of them breathing deeply and slowly, in controlled even breaths. Drawing it in and blowing it out.

Vincent's skin tingled, gooseflesh rising already. His heart was in his mouth. It had been nearly ten years. And he'd never, ever been this high before. As a matter of fact, no thief ever had.

Over the years he'd climbed down the sides of buildings before. Hanging on ropes, using boots similar to the ones they were wearing now, the heavy rubber toes and soles giving them good traction even on glass or marble.

But never in broad daylight. And never this high. And never in this kind of weather.

He pushed the creeping terror from his mind and tried to do what he used to do, become a nonthinking emotionless machine.

But it wasn't working; he was thinking of Evlyn, thinking—oh dear sweet Jesus Christ in heaven, he was thinking of falling ninety floors to the ground.

Bouncing off the glass and steel as the building widened and he fell . . .

"The fuck's wrong with you?" Bolo hissed.

"I can't do it, man, I'm froze—"

Bolo hit him an open-handed slap, right across the cheek, then again with the back of his hand. "You cock *sucker*," he whispered venomously, "you gutless piece of *shit*, you can't *do* it, you fucking *can't do it!*"

Vincent stood there staring at him, near shock due to both his terror and Bolo's behavior. Murder was in the older man's eyes and Vincent took an involuntary step back.

"I was right," Bolo said, his voice calmer now, "you lost your fucking balls and heart in the joint. You goddamn *sissy.*" This last was spat out; sissy to these men not meaning a male who was slightly afraid or effeminate, as it did to the general public, but something beneath contempt, a man who had taken it in the ass in the joint for protection—a sissy, a punk.

"Gimme that bag!" And Bolo was pulling the straps hard, trying hopelessly to rip the extra-strong knapsack from Vincent's shoulders.

Vincent stepped further back, his face red, ashamed. "Hey, I'll do it," he said.

"Hell you will," Bolo whispered. "I'd rather you punk out on me now than when you're swinging ninety stories above the fucking ground." He took two deep breaths and seemed to control himself somewhat. Maybe, Vincent figured, getting his mind set upon doing it alone. "*Now*, Vincent; don't argue with me about it, give me the tools."

Vincent said, "Bolo, you can't do it alone," trying for stern control in his voice and not making it; even to his own ears he sounded as if he was whining, his voice breaking on the last syllable.

Bolo stared hard at him, right in the eyes, searching, seeing what he must have expected. He spit dryly at Vincent's feet. "At least," he said, "I got the balls to try. Now gimme the bag!"

"Not yet," Vincent said, "it's too early, Bolo. It's only ten forty-five. Jesus, don't rush it, you'll walk in there with the guy laying in bed with some broad."

"Bullshit. By the time I get set up, get out there, get the rope set, secure, it'll be eleven fifteen. It'll take at least a half-hour to drive to Water Tower Place in this weather, lunchtime traffic will be terrible. These guys, they get to these meets early, consolidate their power, play politics." He turned away from Vincent and Vincent could see him taking long deep breaths, controlling himself.

Bolo turned back around slowly, and what Vincent saw scared him. The old man's eyes were dead, cold hard ball bearings there on either side of his nose, staring death at Vincent. He had never seen Bolo look at him that way before in his life.

Bolo said, "I'm going to the bathroom. When I come out, that bag better be ready for me to take out there with me, or I swear to Christ, Martin, I'll kill you." Bolo turned and hurried to the other office, shut the door quietly behind him.

Bolo. His father. Christ, the only family he had left in the world. He'd asked him, too, days ago, if Vincent had what it took. Even waited, didn't rush him at all, had given him all the time he'd needed to make up his mind and Vincent had told him that he was ready, that he could handle it.

And now he was punking out. Sending Bolo out to his death, which was certainly what the result of his going out there alone would be doing. All alone but willing to fight his fear and use it, feed off it.

Kick its ass.

Moving with a speed born of desperation and terror, Vincent tore off the rest of his remaining outer clothing, stripped down to the wet suit and groped on the top of his bag for the shoes, the goggles. Put them on and uncoiled the rope and strapped the black-canvas bag to his chest; he'd be needing quick and sure access to it shortly.

Vincent walked to the corner and unzipped the front of the wet suit, fumbled around in the tight Damart long-underwear bottoms for his penis, pulled it out and rapidly pissed against the wall. He put himself back together and went to the window and got the first item out of his bag.

The suction cup attached to the piece of glass with the handle. He pulled back the drapes and pushed the cup hard against the black-glass window, let it go. It hung there without movement. He reached into his bag without looking and removed the large glazier's cutting tool, reached out and used both hands to cut a wide circle around the cup, leaning into it, putting his shoulder into it. The glass was a quarter of an inch thick.

He heard movement behind him and spun quickly, the cutting tool still in his hand.

Bolo stood staring at him the same way as he had before, his hands at his side but now balled into fists. Vincent beat him to the punch by speaking first.

"You old bastard," he hissed with meaning, anger and resentment in his tone, "you ever touch me again and I'll rip your hand off your arm."

For a second it was touch and go. Vincent could see Bolo's indecision, saw the older man get ready to jump him as he held the tool loosely in his hand, ready to drop it and swing if he had to.

Then Bolo smiled. The smile tight, controlled, but still and all, a smile.

"What'd you expect, you asshole?" Bolo said. "A pep talk?" He looked at the deep scratch in the glass behind Vincent. "Well, get to work, huh?" Bolo said.

17 Vincent knew all about the difference between fantasy and reality. Going all the way back to when he was fighting lightweight amateur bouts, he could remember guys with solid natural muscular physiques, kids who had never had to work for a second to look sculpted. Their fathers would show them a few things, tell them how tough they were, tell them they were the next Ali. They'd come to the gym, these kids, and Hank would work them, show them some things, teach them what he could, then match them. And some skinny black kid with long arms and a gawky style would slap hell out of them, giving them a good first taste of reality. Most of them lost the heart for fighting right then and there. Other guys, real workers, they'd spend months training, looking great in the gym, look even better sparring with the safety gear on. They'd be ready, willing and able to do what had to be done to win. Against a real opponent, the second the bell rang for the first round of their first real fight, they'd fold. No left tit. No heart. It was all, when you came down to it, a matter of heart. Watching John Garfield in a movie was one thing; getting in the ring and really doing it was another.

Then there was the war, young men joining up, brag-

ging day and night how they'd told the recruiter that
they just had to go to Vietnam, had to go and kill
something. Vincent had looked at them in boot camp,
wondering if they were crazy. When the time came and
he'd been forced into the war, it was guys like them
who suddenly learned that combat wasn't a John Wayne
movie. They were the men who, if they lived, spent
their year buzzed, in a heroin high, proving themselves
undependable to their fellow soldiers and to themselves.
They, too, had no heart. Later, back in the world, after
the pro career had begun, he'd see the guys in the bars
who spent hours in gymnasiums wearing sweat suits
with men's names on them or worse yet, names of gyms
stenciled in. They had the bumper stickers with their
karate schools advertised on them attached to their cars.
They had nice bodies, hard, tight, heavy muscles. Flat-
ten their noses just once for them, really splatter it for
them, break a bone one time, and they would hide in
their beds or under them for two weeks. No heart.

Vincent had no use for guys who needed to work out
to elevate their self-esteem so that they could kick sand
in the faces of the bullies who had tormented them in
their youth. He figured, if someone he thought could
whip him ever kicked sand in his face, he would find a
brick, a bottle, something, and split the guy's head open
for him.

That, to him, was the meaning of heart.

Like for instance, there wasn't a man alive, being of
sound body, having the use of both of his legs, who
couldn't walk through a three-foot hole in a glass window and drop two feet to the roof of a building. Or any
man in any gym anywhere to whom climbing down
hand over hand twenty feet, with the use of thin rope
with knots tied in it, would pose a problem.

But let them try and do it hanging from the upper
stories of the Sears Tower and see how they made out.

Walking through the hole had been harder for him

than anything he could ever remember doing, and he'd done a lot of dangerous things. It was harder than climbing into the ring with a guy who was the odds-on favorite to knock you out. It was harder even than going into the joint that first night. At least in there he'd had a pretty good idea of what to expect.

He climbed through the hole and the wind hit him, caught hold of him, driving white clouds around his head, swirling like smoke that had no smell. Dense, thick, those clouds were. Bolo was right behind him, going right to the metal eight-inch beam that secured the massive air-conditioning unit that cooled the ninety-first floor. Bolo tied the rope around it as Vincent walked slowly to the edge of the building, looked down.

There was nothing to see but ethereal whiteness, drifting and swirling. Good. He wasn't sure if he could go over the edge if the air was clear and he could see the ground.

One of the advantages of their going over the south side of the building was what it faced, which was mostly nothing. From the sky deck, the observation tower, you could see a couple of buildings, way below you, so far down that no one working there could look out the window and see any more than maybe the first fourth of the tower. Railroad tracks and open space dominated most of the land southward. Further on were the expressways, but they couldn't be seen with the naked eye, nor could the thousands and thousands of homes and projects to the south. Thank Christ.

Bolo was behind him with the rope, lying right there on the edge and looking over, and Vincent got down to his knees beside him, helped him edge the rope directly down following the black-metal beam that held the windows together. Raymond Parilo's windows. Ten, fifteen feet, that's all it really was, an easy climb. He had to get it out of his head that he was here atop the world's tallest building. If he hung on to the rope with one hand with even half his strength, it would be good enough to handle him as he cut his hole in Raymond's window.

Piece of cake.

It came to him then. The reason he ever stole at all. A feeling he had forgotten, mostly, catching only small glimpses of it from time to time when he walked right past a uniformed security guard carrying a hot VCR on his shoulder and acting as if it was paid for. Comparing the two, though, was like comparing making love to a woman with masturbation.

His confidence came back as his asshole tightened. There was no other way for him to put it. The blood was pounding in his ears; he could hear it, roaring like the ocean. He felt powerful, fully alive and aware. Brave and secure. He could do this thing with his eyes closed. It was a building, that's all. And inside the building was a safe, that's all. And there wasn't a building made that the right man couldn't climb, nor had the safe been invented that couldn't be beat.

Getting over. He was getting over on them all, beating them. The law. The screws. The judges. The mob. He was smarter than they were, better, quicker, and he would get over or die trying, no, no die trying bullshit, *he would get over*.

He'd had this feeling before, leaping out of airplanes. And going into high rises. And in the joint, knowing they were out there trying to get him and he had to beat them one way or the other. It was not a feeling he had ever read about, nothing crept along his spine, although that was where the feeling began. What it did, was, it fucking *surged* through him, in waves growing ever stronger, like a continuous electric current, and every time it passed through him the voltage was turned a little higher. Great spasms of all-knowing pleasure surged through him; he felt it tingling in

his toes and his fingers and the top of his head. Felt
it in his balls and his heart and his ass, and he knew
that he was smiling now, ready, on the edge like no
one had ever been before and he knew that he had the
heart to go through with it; it was nothing, it was a
piece–of–fucking–cake.

"It's mine," Vincent said.

Bolo looked up. "You're fucking right it is."

"I own it, Bolo."

"Then get your ass down there and take it."

Vincent turned around, adjusted his glasses, his feeling, that exalted, almost narcotic spasming, getting
stronger as he turned his back to the vicious wind
and the great drop. He adjusted his goggles, pulled
the ski mask down over them, made sure he could see
well, then got to his knees. He crawled backwards, to
the edge of the building, gripped the rope with one
hand and kept going, feeling his right knee fall off into
space and then his left, knowing without even having
to look where the beam was, holding on to the rope
now with both hands and falling free, out there, doing
it.

Vincent's right foot hit the beam and gripped, not
sliding at all thanks to the heavy-rubber toes. He put his
left foot beneath the right and leaned back, placed both
feet flat. If the building fell over, he would land two
blocks away from where he now dangled, but he didn't
care; he had it; he wished it were higher still. He allowed the rope to dangle between his legs and slowly
slid down it, his feet pressing into the beam, slowing his
descent. At three feet his hands grasped a knot, slid past
it, and he dropped another three, then another, then
another. Then he stopped.

Vincent hung there for a full minute, taking deep,
deep breaths of the frigid air, wondering how long he'd
been out against the wall, thinking that the skin that
wasn't covered by the wet suit, under the ski mask, his

forehead and his nose and chin, these areas might well now be frostbitten and he would not know it until they were turning black. He smiled there a thousand feet above the ground.

"How you doing?" Said from above him. Bolo.

"I own it," he said softly, wondering if his voice carried upward the ten or twelve feet or so to where Bolo would be hanging over the rooftop, staring into the milky whiteness. He reached into the bag hanging from his chest, his left hand grasping the knot in the rope, his feet now wrapped around the knot six feet farther along. He got out the suction cup and attached it to the window. Around him the wind was howling, sounding like a banshee in a horror movie. There was nothing around to break the wind and it buffeted him, tried to pull the foreign entity from its perch here but this, too, was no contest. Although his teeth were now beginning to chatter softly, he paid them no attention and began to work on the window.

It wouldn't cut.

He didn't have enough leverage to get any muscle behind his strokes; the goddamn thing would do nothing more than scratch maybe a third of the way through.

"Hey!" he hissed loudly.

"What's the matter?" Bolo's voice was a stage whisper without the least bit of fear.

"This apartment here, is it soundproofed?"

"Course it is, shit, it's the Sears Tower."

"I break the window, those goons out in the hall won't hear it."

"You can shoot off a thirty-eight in there, they won't hear it."

Hurriedly, freezing cold now, his body temperature dropping, shivering in great heaves with his teeth now threatening to break against themselves from their incessant rapid chattering, Vincent began to run the cutting tool along the window with as much strength as he could muster. He could barely feel his fingers now and he was afraid that he was going to let go of the rope and not even be aware of it until he noticed that the window was rising and he was going down, down, do—STOP! he ordered himself, and continued making a huge slashed X in the window.

Out of breath and feeling weak, frightened but kicking its ass real good now, he put the tool back in his pack and gratefully grabbed the rope above him, the knot, with both hands. Resting the left a little. He forced his tongue from the roof of his mouth; he'd read that this action would stop shivers, but he was wrong, it didn't stop his shivering at all. He reached down with his left hand and held the rope tightly with his right, let his feet fall away from the knot they were resting on. He dangled now by one hand 950 feet above the wide city sidewalks and the street. He grasped the next knot, inched it up with his fingers until he had the bottom one. Three feet of rope left and then nothing. He began wrapping the rope around his right wrist, dangling from it, and when he was done, he grasped the rope firmly with his left, allowed his right to fall free and grab the short loose end of the rope.

Vincent didn't want to think now; it was too late for that. It was time to act. He brought his knees up into his chest, put his feet flat against the beam, inched his feet over a little at a time until they were in the center of the X he had cut, his soles resting on either side of the suction cup with the handle.

Vincent took a deep breath of arctic air and pushed off as hard as he could, out into space, hanging on to the rope for dear life as he swung out maybe twenty feet, then came back, quickly, and he tucked his chin into his chest and held his legs stiff—straight out in front of him—and they hit the glass and smashed through and the glass shattered around the X and he was going in.

Vincent let go of the rope, or else it would catch and grab and he would cut himself to pieces on the broken glass around the edge of the hole. He fell into the apartment and landed heavily on his back, windless, shaking, terror creeping in now with thought.

Christ, what if the window hadn't smashed and he'd been—STOP! Again, his mind following the order as it had so many times before in tight situations. Breathing heavily, trying to get his wind back, he heard Bolo climbing through the window and looked up.

In time to see Bolo race to the door, checking the edges, running his fingertips along the frame. Bolo sighed, turned to Vincent with a sheepish smile. Vincent had noticed that when Bolo's fingers ran along the doorway, they were shaking.

Bolo said, "Soundproof all right."

"You didn't *know*?!" Incredulous, angry, his mind not about to listen to orders now but running down what would have happened had the room not been soundproofed. He stared at Bolo who still hadn't stopped smiling.

Bolo said, "Well, I was pretty sure."

Usually, the first thing he would do upon invading a home would be to check for two alternate ways out of the place in the event of an emergency, but here, where was there to go? So that was out. The two of them did give the apartment a thorough search, though, in case their information had been wrong and Parilo did sometimes leave a woman in the house when he was gone. He hadn't.

In the bedroom, Vincent and Bolo stepped to the painting behind which they knew they would find the safe. They didn't touch it, but turned their backs to each other like dualists and paced off four steps each. The steel joists would be four feet apart in the apartment, and they would both work through two of them if they had to, taking turns with the drill and the heavy cutting bit. Vincent removed the backpack and took out the cutting tool, ran it into the top of the dry wall at ceiling level and twisted, ran it down to the floor. Then threw it to Bolo as he pounded the dry wall, pulling it out and away from the wall. When the hole was big enough, he stepped into it, and—thank God; there was room, they wouldn't have to cut at all—stepped around the joists, pressing his chest against the steel and forcing himself through. His back was against the steel shell of the inner wall that would lead to the hallway. He looked at the safe and saw Bolo smiling back at him over the round cylinder of the cheap barrel. They stepped back through the holes they had made and grinned at each other, slapped each other on the back, both of them knowing they'd be out of there in half an hour because this cheap son of a bitch, this arrogant bastard who put all his faith in fallible men, had not even bothered to alarm his goddamn windows and to top it all off had only installed a small round ancient Mosler barrel safe. Without an alarm anywhere to be seen.

Still, Bolo took nothing for granted.

He approached the painting slowly, pressed his head to the edge of it, looking around, then he smiled and stepped back. He pulled the picture from the wall and they were looking at the face of the safe, maybe two feet around and another three feet deep.

"Small little jimmy bar was all we needed," Vincent said.

"Rather safe than sorry, kid," Bolo said, the drill attached to the wall now, pulled down and running; they didn't even bother with the muffler. It was a two-minute job, tops.

As Bolo worked, Vincent went to the dresser and found a handkerchief, began unpacking his tools from the case, then wiped them down thoroughly. He lined them up neatly at the base of the wall. If there was anything of value in the safe, the tools would be left behind. Vincent fervently hoped there was plenty of loot. He didn't relish the thought of climbing that rope in that wind with all this weight on his back.

It was something they had talked out the night before, leaving the tools. It would further the mob's cause in the event that something went wrong and they could not kill Parilo. There had been precedent set. Thieves had taken on the mob hierarchy before. Anthony (The Fish) Accovina had once had his River Ridge home burglarized while he was away in Palm Springs, golfing. His safe was a walk-in baby built into the concrete of the basement walls. The thieves had escaped with millions, but within weeks bodies began turning up—with the hands cut off of them. That had been the last time anyone had questioned the superiority of the mob in Chicago.

Until now.

It was a logical assumption that it was due to happen, what with the war going on, the power struggle. It was safe to assume that some overzealous professional thief would see it as an opportunity to show the gang what he thought of them, having been forced to pay tribute to them from almost every score he'd ever taken down. They could get away with it and no one would even glance their way because Bolo was long retired and everyone knew that Vincent was a booster these days. Paterro or anyone else with a mind to would not know whom to chop up.

Vincent heard the drill stop and looked up as Bolo threw open the safe and stood there staring into it, smiling again. He got to his feet and looked in.

Then started smiling right back himself.

The safe had one shelf dividing it. The top was filled with little microcassettes wrapped in hard plastic cases. Maybe fifty of them. The bottom shelf was filled to the back of the safe with bundles of tightly stacked and highly piled hundred-dollar bills.

Vincent stuffed the money into his pack, nearly filling it. There had to be several million dollars there. Bolo took the tapes.

They left the tools and walked rapidly to the broken window, Vincent helping Bolo up and through, and he stuck his head out and watched the old pro scurry up the rope as if he was climbing in someone's backyard at a Fourth of July picnic. Seeming unmindful of the wind and the vast height, he didn't even use his legs; he grabbed the first knot and pulled hard and reached with the other hand and grabbed the next and pulled himself up, and before Vincent knew it, Bolo had disappeared over the roof's edge. He climbed through the window and repeated the feat.

They scurried across the roof, leaving the rope, went in through the broken window and hurriedly dressed in their street clothes. Bolo walked to the door and put his ear to it, as if it wasn't soundproof and he could hear someone walking in the hallway. One of the guards, maybe. Vincent doubted it, as the guards were human beings and would be sloughing off now that the boss was gone and they were under no one's thumb. But Bolo waited, with his left hand held up for silence. Then suddenly he turned the knob and stepped through, with Vincent right behind him, and then they were at the elevators and into the first one that came.

And from there, it really was a piece of cake.

Bolo turned left at the entrance to Sears Tower, out on the street, and Vincent turned right. Heading home with his backpack full of hard cash while Bolo went off to hand over the tapes.

Vincent didn't know it as he walked, but there was a jaunt in his step that was not usually there. At all times he walked like a thief, appearing to move slowly, but going quickly. Now he did a little ditty-bop as he sauntered. Heading home.

And there was a grin splitting his face wide open. . . .

18 Teddy King had a problem. He was sitting across the street from Sears Tower, his heater running full blast, the climate control on his cousin's Caddy turned all the way up. Thirty feet or so behind him, the backup car idled in the freezing air. He had resented their presence at first, had felt that he was man enough to handle an over-the-hill wise-ass booster like Bolo on his own, but Bags had explained something to him that made sense. Montaine was not about to hand out another million dollars, not to a guy who was about to die, so if Bolo got cute, pulled a stunt, and Ted had to chill him there on the street, the backups would report back to the Ritz and Parilo's execution could commence.

Teddy forgot about them, sat staring out the windshield. He was warm and comfortable, thinking of Mary Jane, and considering his problem.

The street, no matter how you looked at it, was ruled by the black guys. When the term *streetwise* was used, what was really being said was *blackwise*. Street talk, no matter who spoke it, was definitely black. The ghetto slur, the drawl, that was street. And considering himself a pretty street guy, he had always incorporated the black ghetto drawl into his speech pattern.

But Baggio, Montaine, and the rest of the mobsters hated the blacks. Teddy wasn't sure why. He thought maybe it was sexual jealousy. And their hatred confused him.

For most of his life, even in the joint, the only color that seemed to matter was green, for dollars. Teddy had been a wild-eyed drunken teenager when Martin Luther King, Jr., had been killed and the ghettos had burned. It hadn't affected him either way. In his neighborhood, the Supremes and the Temptations and Curtis Mayfield and the Impressions were the groups that were hip. The Jackson Five, too. In high school, before he dropped out, his gang had caught the freaks, the Beatles worshippers and lovers of other psychedelic narcotic-music-playing groups, in the toilets, and had beaten their heads in for them. His peers wore tints and knit shirts. And spoke the street lingo. Black talk.

And these guys, these mobsters, they didn't go in for that. Sure, he'd killed Bigum Barnes, but that wasn't a racial thing. He was the enemy, one of the big shots trying to force their rules and regulations on the rest of them and make them live like the Germans used to when Hitler was the head man. Any black cop with a badge was a nigger, in the same way any white cop with a badge was an asshole. It was just a matter of knowing your enemy.

But man, did Baggio get upset when Teddy talked. "Why you want to gimme that nigger jive for?" he'd ask, looking at Teddy real funny like. "Why don't you talk like a man?"

Teddy would gladly oblige him, but man, the way those guys talked, it was like they just stepped off the spaghetti boat. All dees dems dose and dats, dropping every *g*, throwing in all the *madrones* and *saludes*. As soon as they got half in the bag, they'd start in talking the dago language, like they were all from some little village in Sicily. Teddy couldn't think of one of them who was born in the old country, off the top of his head. They'd all been born here.

But Mary Jane, God, how she went for that stuff. Baggio had been right, she could indeed suck the cream out of a Twinkie and never touch the cake. Or at least she'd never leave a tooth mark in it. He'd never had anything like it before, and now she was all his, a gift from Baggio. A present showing Teddy how highly he was held in their world.

But Mary Jane, she didn't like the street talk, either. Always nagging, asking why he had to talk like "one of them," like they weren't real people. So he'd play the part for her, and not slap her around for being disrespectful. She was the only woman he had ever known who could suck him hard when he had half a bag on. He wasn't about to lose her. At least not yet.

He was smiling, sitting in his cousin's car with the climate control turned all the way into the red, relaxing, the pistol between his legs, hidden by his thighs, when someone knocked on the car window and he jumped so high his head hit the car roof.

It was Bolo, wearing a beard that looked real.

"Get in the car," Teddy said, going for the rough-and-tumble dago sound, not quite making it. Probably because he felt so foolish trying to talk like an old man. And Bolo, he was making rolling motions with his right hand, as if a brand new Eldorado had cranks to lower the window. Teddy powered the window down.

Calmly, he said, "Get in the car, will you?" And the old son of a gun, he just stood out there smiling, shaking his head.

"Where's the rest of the money?" Bolo said.

"I got it, I got it, just get in the car and let's see the tapes, huh? Then you'll get the dough."

"Let's see the money, first, Teddy."

"Don't call me Teddy." Going for the tough on-the-muscle tone, making it, too, in his anger over being called the dreaded child's nickname.

"Okay," Bolo said, amiably, and Teddy felt his self-esteem rise at the old man's backing down.

"Let's," Bolo said, "see the money, *asshole*."

Teddy pulled the pistol out from between his thighs and pointed it at Bolo's head. "Get in the *car*, old man."

"You shoot, you never get the tapes." And he was holding up the empty knapsack, showing Teddy that there was nothing in it, and Teddy forgot the street, forgot the dago inflection, forgot it all as his voice raised into a high-pitched squeal.

"Where's the fucking tapes?"

Bolo was grinning at him, broadly, and it took all of Teddy's self-control to lower the gun and put it back between his legs.

"The tapes are safe. As a matter of fact, I put them in a safe-deposit box right there in Sears bank. Under a phony name, of course. Once the heat comes on about the score, the cops, they'll be checking new accounts, I bet.

"Listen, it's cold out here, Teddy. You want to maybe come on out, go into the bank with me, make sure the tapes are there? Then you can go back and tell your superiors, they can whack Raymond, but they don't get the tapes until we make the switch and I get the dough."

"You put the tapes in a box?"

Bolo nodded his head vigorously. He said, "It's cold out here, you know it?"

Teddy had to admire him, the old dip, he'd figured it all out and he wasn't even mad that they had planned to rip him off, let alone waste him. But that admiration didn't lessen his anger.

Teddy said, "I got to tell you something, Bolo, I ain't got no superiors, but you want to come along, talk to

Mr. Baggio himself, maybe you can straighten things out between you."

"Listen, Teddy?" Bolo said, then he waited, the dip son of a bitch of a puke, he waited there in the goddamn cold until Teddy said, "What," before he would finish it. Teddy did and Bolo said, "Tell your *masters* I'll have the tapes at the bar in one hour. They can bring the money, all alone, just Montaine and Baggio. I don't want to see your sissy ass around me no more, understand? And tell them I'll be covered three ways from Sunday. If any other punks come in or if I see you or anything happens except for Baggio and Montaine walking into my bar with a million bucks, the tapes, they are going to get passed to the FBI before anyone can even get the front door open. And then, see, I'll be pissed off, and there's no telling what'll happen."

He was smiling again. Making fun of me, Teddy thought. Telling me what he thinks of me. Well, let's see how smart he really is. Teddy checked his watch. Man, only 12:45. Plenty of time to roll a couple of miles north and give the big shots the word. The nod. Maybe he'd just wink at them, nod his head once, show them how cool he was under pressure.

But this guy, he was too much of a wiseass to get away with this. All the "Teddy" shit, and the "asshole" business and the "kid" talk. He thought he was dealing with a two-bit player or one of the scumbag dip boosters who hung around the gin mill he owned. Well, it was cold, but you did what you had to do. And what he had to do now was, he had to shake this guy up a little.

Teddy powered the window shut and turned off the engine, got out of the car, and the wind and cold hit him like a hammer blow. Man, it was *freezing* out here. Casually, he placed the gun in his coat pocket and squeezed the butt tightly to reassure himself. He smiled as the old buzzard backed up a few steps, cautiously, fear right there on his wrinkled old face.

Teddy chuckled. "Don't worry, old man. I ain't gonna kill you. Not yet, at least. Your million's in the trunk. But you got to come on like a tough guy, play games, shit, you act dumber than the Sicilians. Now you and me, we go take a look at the tapes, all right, and if they're there, if this ain't some kind of game you're trying to run, beat us out of a million bucks when maybe you didn't have the balls to go into the apartment, then we'll switch."

That got him. The old dip, his chest swelled proudly and he looked like he was going to spit on Teddy right there he was so mad. Good for him. Teddy decided to rub it in a little more.

"And we can make the switch right here, in broad daylight, out on the sidewalk, so's you don't poop your diapers, okay? I mean, it's obvious, you're scared of me." Smile. Show him who was boss.

"You show me the money, first." Bolo said it through clenched teeth that were chattering now. He had taken Teddy for a chump, and now he was paying. The old guy was scared. Well, he ain't seen nothing yet.

"No deal, old man. You think I'm stupid, don't you? You already beat us out of a million, now you think I'm gonna hand over another one to you before I see the tapes? You been out of circulation too long." Teddy thought of something, pictured this old guy hanging over the side of the tower all alone and knew it hadn't happened. He was too old. Too long out of the game. He threw a parting shot in the dark at Bolo, more as a joke than anything else. "You and your badass kid. The booster."

And there it was, he'd hit home because there was no denying it, the guy's eyes narrowed and he turned all the way around, looked up at the tower to see if maybe Teddy could have spotted them up there. When he turned around he was trying for the cocky grin again, but not making it. It wasn't working. He knew that Teddy knew.

And that wasn't all Teddy knew. The thing about the kid was only the smallest part of it all. Because when Bolo turned, Teddy had heard the undeniable sound of plastic cracking around something. Like maybe the old fart, he had the tapes in a garbage bag underneath that heavy coat of his. Oh, God, let it be so.

"Hey, old-timer, I'm freezing, you know? So show me the tapes and I'll give you the money and we'll get out of here, go our separate ways. Like I got time, play around with some washed-up booster. I got better things to do."

That had torn it, right there. The thief's ego was too big, too goddamn big to make him keep his mouth shut. Bolo reached under his coat and ripped away a black garbage bag that had been taped there. Inside, Teddy could make out the distinct shapes of little boxed cassettes.

He heard a car door slam down the street behind him, but paid it no attention, because Bolo was shaking the bag in his face.

"I got the tapes right here, punk. Now you show me the money."

Teddy smirked, hiding his pleasure behind a cynical facade. He ought to ask to see them, make it look even better, but it was just too cold. He looked up and down the street, reaching under the gun for his car keys. He saw that his uncle's boys were standing by the side of their car, their hands under their coats. That made him feel good.

The way he saw it, he'd open the trunk and step back, let the geezer get close to it and then he'd pop him, two in the head, right there in the street. Shove him into the trunk and adios, get the hell out of there. Bags would know how to get rid of the body and clean the trunk out so no one would ever know.

Teddy King walked to the rear of the car and popped the key into the lock, turned it, holding his hand firmly on the down curve so it couldn't open. His right hand went into his coat—no problem there; the man would have to expect him to cover himself; he was supposed to have a million bucks in there.

And that was when he spotted the great big white cop who had been in the bar with the jig cop he'd offed last week. The cop was crossing the street.

He pressed the trunk closed and grabbed the keys with his left hand, the right coming out with the pistol, and he fired off two shots, quick, at the cop, who ducked back across the street, crouching down behind a parked car.

People were coming out of Sears Tower now, looking, trying to see where the shots had come from. Teddy raced to the driver's side of the car, and was in with the key turning the engine over before the cop even grew the balls to peek over the car he was cowering behind. Teddy hit the unlock button, the rear doors unlocked and Bolo hopped into the backseat just as the rear window exploded into a million glass fragments and he heard the bee buzz of a bullet whiz past his ear, close. Cops! As he threw the car in drive and was racing down the street as fast as he dared with all the ice around, he shot a glance into the rearview mirror and saw that it wasn't cops at all, the bullets that were now whacking into the back end of the car were being fired by his cousin's two men. . . .

He turned the corner and a cab swerved, ran up onto the sidewalk as Teddy, too, swerved, and still nearly hit it in the ass end, jumping the line, getting back into his own lane and pouring it to her now, driving away, leaning on the horn.

He looked again into the rearview mirror. No blue flashing lights spinning. No squad cars or even green damn Plymouths coming after him. If they were setting

him up, if they were watching him, there would have
been more than one cop, a shitload of them would have
been waiting and he never would have seen them until
they nailed him. And he never would have got off even
a single shot before they iced him, capped him fifty or
sixty times to make sure he was dead.

Jesus Christ, could the guy have been working
alone?! Was it possible? And what was worse, why in
the name of Christ had the two guys who were supposed to be backing him up been shooting at him?

He pulled to the curb and slammed the car into park,
a couple of miles away from the scene. On a side street
in the South Loop. He had to keep cool now, had to
stay calm. He had to get his head together and figure
things out. First, he had to get the tapes, take care of
this old dip and get the news to Baggio and Montaine.
Let them know that their men were fucking up, shooting at the wrong guys. And if the other guy, the cop,
was alone, the outfit could cool any heat the shooting
might bring down. It would be Teddy's word against
the cop's. But he had to get through this first. Then
figure out why in the hell his own people had fired
upon him. He would have to do that first, before he
entered a hotel room filled with the same type of people.

He turned around and looked at Bolo, who was still
staring out the back window, like he expected the entire
department to be racing after them. Too stupid to have
figured it out, that the cop was working solo. Trying to
even the score for his partner.

Teddy leveled the gun and said, "Yo."

Bolo turned and spotted the gun and went cross-eyed
staring into the barrel. It was almost comical.

Bolo said, "Now, be careful with that thing, Ted."

"Ted, eh?" Teddy felt victorious, on top of the heap.
This dip had finally shown his respect, had called him
by his righteous name.

Teddy said, "I'm not Teddy anymore, eh? Or what about asshole? Or kid?" But Bolo wouldn't say anything, just kept staring into the barrel of the gun.

"Well, Ted ain't good enough, old man." Teddy smiled. "Call me Mr. King."

Bolo looked at him.

Teddy said, "You heard me, call me Mr. King."

Bolo said, swallowing hard first, "Mr. King."

Teddy laughed wildly, shaking his head from side to side.

"Mr. King, sir," he said.

Bolo was still staring at the gun; Teddy had changed from a .38 to a fourteen-shot 9mm Berretta automatic and he was taking no shit from man nor beast.

Bolo said, "Mr. King, sir." His voice was quivering.

Teddy threw his head back and began to laugh in mighty brays, when he felt his finger being twisted back, then his wrist and—shit—his finger popped out of the guard and Bolo had the gun now, was staring at him with a no-bullshit look on his face.

Teddy shut his eyes.

Bolo said, "Get out of the car," and Teddy obeyed, getting out, not thinking anything was funny anymore. The look on Bolo's face told him straight up that he was a dead man. The guy would take one look in the empty trunk and would cap him right in the head.

Bolo took the keys from the ignition, sliding in backward, his eyes never leaving Teddy, who was quivering now, afraid that he was going to shit himself, the cold biting into him and he stood there clamping his legs together tightly.

Teddy said, "Please." A tear streamed down his face and left frozen tracks in its wake. "Please, don't kill me."

Bolo smiled at him and slid out of the car, quickly walked around the rear and opened the trunk. He slammed it shut right away. Teddy watched him move as if in a blur, because his eyes were misting over and he was having a very hard time focusing.

Bolo said, "I ought to, you fucking piker, but why waste a bullet? Way it looked to me, your masters there, Bags and Montaine, are gonna do the job for me. Hell, those two sons of bitches, they were waiting for you to kill me, then they were gonna kill you. Just like a wop, panic and fuck things up."

Teddy squeezed his eyes shut. My God, the man was right. His own cousin had set him up for execution. He said through shaking lips, softly, "Please."

He felt his nose smash and something hit the back of his head and he guessed that he was shot. The old man had shot him in the face and then in the back of the head. He shrieked and then something had ahold of his coat lapels and was dragging him to his feet. He felt his back hit the car; he didn't know what part of the car. He opened his eyes.

He wasn't dead. That was the important thing. But he felt the warm stream of liquid down the front of his pants and knew that he'd pissed himself. He opened his eyes. The man must have punched him in the nose and what he'd felt after that, on the back of his head, was the crunch as it made contact with the street. He hadn't even known he had fallen.

All sense of time and feeling was leaving him; all he knew now, with a certainty, was that he had to live. He would beg.

But he didn't have to.

Bolo was standing away from him, maybe five, six feet away. He was shaking his head and chuckling softly. Teddy decided it would be best to laugh along with him. Bolo looked at him and he stopped laughing, reached a tentative hand up and wiped at his nose. Stung like a son of a bitch. He didn't know if the touch made his eyes water, because he was crying.

Bolo flipped the button on the side of the pistol and

the clip bounced into his hand. He threw the clip across the street, into a vacant lot. There was no traffic on this lonely ice-ridden side road. The only witness to Teddy's humiliation was an old white-bearded wino shuffling through the refuse in the lot. He looked up when the clip landed near him and stepped over to it, slowly. Bolo threw the keys and the wino backed up, stared hatred across at them. Saw the gun and backed away. Bolo handed Teddy the gun.

"One hour, *Mr.* King. My place. You make a call, tell Montaine. Then, if you got any sense, you better start running before the cops or the mob catch up to your sorry ass. One hour and five minutes from now, the tapes are with the Gee, along with your name and description and the license plate from this fucking Mafia staff car." He turned his back on Teddy as if Teddy was a sissy in the joint who wasn't important enough to worry about, and started walking away.

It took Teddy a couple of minutes to control himself. He got into the car and sat there shivering and crying, wiping the blood away from his mouth and nose, getting snot all over the sleeve of his three-hundred-dollar coat. He smelled of urine and fear. He slammed his fist on the steering wheel so hard that it cracked under his hand, cutting into him deeply. He cried out in pain and covered his eyes with his left hand while he sucked the wound in his right and shook and sobbed.

He'd killed a cop and that was supposed to set him up for life, and now his own people were trying to kill him!

At last he reached into the glove compartment and found some napkins, sniffled and moaned with self-pity and pain as he wrapped a couple of them around his naked freezing hand. He used the rest to wipe at the urine stain on the front of his pants. He got out of the still-warm car and ran to the sidewalk, grabbed handfuls

of freezing dry snow and rubbed it vigorously up and
down on the stain. Heard a laugh and turned to look
across the street and there was the wino standing there
pointing at him and laughing. Talking to someone only
the wino could see. Wrapped in maybe three coats and
as many layers of pants. He was shaking the keys at
Teddy and offering—Jesus Christ, he was offering to
sell them.

Teddy did what he had to do. He raced across the
street and punched the wino right in the mouth with his
right hand as hard as he could, and he was sure as soon
as the punch landed that he had broken it. Blood
spurted from the cut near the underside of his palm and
his knuckles were blood-covered as he pulled his hand
back, but it didn't stop him; he grabbed the wino's
filthy collar with his left and brought him forward, the
wino screaming in shock and pain, the keys dropping to
the ground as Teddy hit him again.

The wino fell to the frozen ground and Teddy kicked
him again and again in the head, changing feet when
the one he was using started to ache.

When the wino's head was busted watermelon, Teddy
stepped back, breathing heavily, exhausted. He felt better now. He bent down and got his keys, reached into
the wino's outer pocket and found, right off, the clip to
his 9mm. He crossed the street at a run, shivering from
the cold. Picked the gun up off the concrete where he'd
dropped it in his haste to find warmth and a quiet place
to cry. He jammed the clip into the butt and felt even
better still, almost whole. A bottle, that would help. He
would make a phone call and tell a lie and maybe buy
some time. Then, as soon as he aced that son of a bitch
Bolo and his kid, got the tapes in his possession, he
would show that dirty bastard Bags something about
playing in the big leagues.

*   *   *

The spot Teddy had decided to pull over at was less than three blocks away from Bolo's bar. Thank God, because man, it was cold. Somehow, Bolo'd managed to keep his hands on the tapes, a miracle when you thought about it, what with renegade cops making unscheduled appearances, then psycho mob killers shooting at them. Shit, for a day that had started out so fine, with the successful score and all, it was sure going to hell in a hurry.

But still, he wasn't complaining. How many other sixty-year-old guys, with tumors on their asses, were able to do the things he'd done that day? Not many, he'd bet.

His cheerful mood broke again as he hurriedly turned the corner onto his block. Down there in front of the bar were two figures, big, wearing overcoats. As he neared, his suspicions were confirmed. Cops. Christ on a crutch, when were these guys gonna learn?

He strode right up to them, got right in the chest of the big idiot, Sean Kent.

"You dumbass," Bolo said. "For the first time in my life I make a deal with a cop and you gotta go ahead and fuck things up."

Bolo looked at Sean and shook his head with disgust. He ignored the second man with the big cop, didn't bother to even acknowledge his presence. He opened the door to his bar with the key that was hidden under the garbage can in the alley. He and Vincent had gone out to score without one piece of ID between them. They took nothing that might accidentally be dropped anywhere along the way. He walked into the place and went directly to the bar and poured himself a stiff double shot of bourbon. He drank it down and shivered. He pulled off his gloves and dropped them on the bartop, poured another drink but didn't drink it until he removed his coat and threw it against the wall. It landed in a heap in the back booth. He drank his drink and lit a cigarette. He looked at Sean Kent standing there staring at him as if nothing was going on.

"You fucked up," Bolo said, "you big fucking stupe."

The second cop—it was obvious the guy was a cop—spoke up. "This is a detective in the Chicago police—"

Bolo said, "You shut the fuck up, cop. You ain't even supposed to be here."

Sean said, "Look, I know how you see it."

Bolo glared at him. "The deal was, you were supposed to wait here. Not out there, *here*." He slammed two rock glasses down on the bar and without asking poured freehand into them, motioned for the cops to go ahead. Sean picked his up and drained it; the other cop left his sitting there.

Bolo looked at him. He was a big guy, too, maybe the same height as Sean but in a lot better shape. Athletic-looking but no rookie dick, he'd been around awhile. Bolo said, "Vic Perry, MCU, right?" Getting a respectful nod from the cop, Perry. Bolo looked at Sean.

"Why'd you bring him in? Worried you can't get me killed all by yourself?"

Sean sighed. He said, "Bolo, if I hadn't followed you, believe me, you would have died out there. The kid was getting ready to pop you right in the street. He knows he can get away with it. He did it to Bigum. And the mobsters, too, don't forget them. If King didn't kill you, they were gonna."

Bolo felt a stirring of hope. Sean hadn't mentioned Sears Tower and neither had he. Maybe Perry didn't know. There were a lot of ways to find out, beating around the bush, but time was running out. He turned to Perry.

"How much you know?"

"I know you're dying and you're having a fit of conscience. Gonna give us a couple of top mobsters. You turn them over, you walk away."

Bolo nodded. Good, straight answer. And he hadn't mentioned anything about a score. Maybe he *didn't* know. Hell, the odds were good that Sean himself didn't know anything about the score, although he would have known something was up when he saw them walking around with wigs and—

Bolo reached up and ripped off the wig and the beard and threw them against the wall. His hair, what was left of it, was flattened against his head and in spite of the frigid temperature outside, it was slick with sweat. He'd left the wiped-down diving suit on the floor of the dead lawyer's office.

Taped once again to Bolo's chest was a large black-plastic trash bag that made strange sounds when he moved. As he did now, pouring himself and Sean another drink. He held his glass up and drank it down, noticing that Perry still didn't touch the drink sitting in front of him.

"You call him because you fucked up?"

"Because, Bolo, he's the only man on the department I trust."

"How about *you*?" Bolo said to Perry. "How many guys *you* bring in?"

Perry looked at him for a second before answering, then he smiled. "I've got fifty-two guys working for me these days. I trust every one of them. But Bigum Barnes was my friend and Sean here said we had to go it solo for Bigum's sake. I'll back him up and be corroborating witness at the trial, but this is his show."

Bolo nodded, glad this wasn't turning into a department free-for-all party. He ripped the tapes free, handed them to Perry. "Take these. My going-away present to the law. Sean can handle the pinch himself. They'll be alone, Montaine and Baggio."

"You're sure?"

"Sean, I'm sure. Just like I'm sure I would have got them over here even sooner if you hadn't tried to play supercop, come racing across the street like a big damn stupe."

"I saved your life, a stupe like me did."

"I would have got away."

Sean took a sip of his drink, put it down, rubbed his hands together. "I bet you would have, too."

Bolo turned to Vic Perry. "And it ain't no deathbed act of conscience, either; I want you to understand that. This guy comes to me, tells me about his partner, I figure, what the hell, I'm blowing town anyway, going away for my health, I better give it a shot, help the guy out. We can't have guys running around, gunning down cops in the street, you know?"

He turned back to Sean. "You played gumshoe following me around today; you lay low over the weekend, like you said you would?"

"I left here and went straight to Bigum's brother's house. He's a doctor over on the North Side, got a nice place."

"Yeah, yeah, fine. You didn't go to any of the outfit joints, make a jerk out of yourself, make any of them suspicious?"

"No." Sean was smiling, obviously enjoying the interplay.

Perry said, "Look, Mr. Rubolo, we appreciate the help and everything, but I'll tell you something, we are Chicago police officers and you're gonna have to learn that we don't listen to that kind of talk from your kind of people."

Bolo looked at Sean and asked, "Is he for real?"

Vincent couldn't help himself, he had to showboat a little. As soon as he left the score, he had gone directly to Bolo's and let himself in, then locked the door behind him. He had a shot of brandy to warm him, just

one, then opened the safe and got out his suitcase and
Bolo's. He closed and locked the safe, went right back
out of the place, locked the door and put the key back
under the garbage can. He went to his Caddy and felt
around under the seat, got his keys out and started the
car up and drove away.

Straight to the Pick-Congress. Where the president of
the United States had stayed. Where Sinatra had stayed.
Where hundreds of lesser lights had spent nights and
weeks when in town, paying a couple of grand a night
for a suite and getting their money's worth because
everybody knew that the Congress was the place to stay
when you were in town. They had the best service, the
classiest suites. The best accommodations. He parked
the car in the heated garage and hauled both suitcases
up himself, waving off the garage attendants, and the
bellhops after he entered the hotel. He asked the stiff in
the monkey suit behind the desk what suite Lynch was
in and was told there was no Lynch presently in any
suite. He fought panic for a moment, then got it and
smiled. He asked for the Martin suite and was directed
to suite 2305. Not the presidential suite but close
enough. The Secret Service had been billeted in 2305
when the head man was in town. Maybe a half a dozen
of them. The guy behind the desk was looking at his
clothes with disdain and Vincent turned and walked to
the elevators, waving away the bellhops who swarmed
around him, the hops still dressed in the old style, wearing the red uniforms with the brass buttons and with
the little round hats on their heads. Waiting for the elevator, he had to fight the urge to shout out, Call for
Phi-lip Mor-ris. He smiled.

She answered after his first knock and stepped back to
let him into the room. Vincent came in carrying both
bags under one arm, smiling broadly, in a hurry but
taking the time to show off a little.

Jesus, talk about putting on the Ritz. Old furniture

with wings on the back, a fireplace blazing away. Not a
book in sight. He walked to the low coffee table and
placed his—their—suitcase atop it.

Vincent said, "Keep this warm for me until I get
back, will you? The fire starts going low, throw a couple
of bundles in. I hear they burn slow."

He dropped Bolo's suitcase and swept her into his
arms, laughing. "It's all over, Evlyn. We're free." He
kissed her, trying with all his might to climb right
through her mouth into her body, show her how much
he cared. He broke away from her. Bolo had told him
to go straight home and that was where he had to be.

"I love you," Vincent said.

"Where you going now?" Evlyn said, looking confused but happy. She looked relieved more than anything else.

"I'll be back in an hour, maybe two. With some
clothes and some cold champagne."

Evlyn was smiling now, still looking a little confused,
though. "Aren't there clothes in your suitcase?"

Vincent winked at her. "Check those threads out,
baby, and keep warm. Don't open the door for Bolo
even. Just me." Then, carrying Bolo's suitcase, he left
the suite, making sure she locked the door securely behind him.

19 Evlyn locked the door behind Vincent as he had instructed, bolted it and slid the chain into its slot before she turned to the suitcase there on the table. She was far from stupid, had deduced what it held by Vincent's cavalier attitude toward it and his remark about throwing a couple of bundles into the fire. What amazed her, though, was the fact that there were no clothes inside of the bag. It couldn't possibly be filled with money. That much money didn't exist. Or did it?

He'd told her it was over and they were free. Now her question was if a man with over $300,000 did not consider himself free, what amount would give him the reassurance he so obviously needed?

She opened the suitcase and stared at the piles of banded hundred-dollar bills. She didn't have to count it to know there had to be at least a million dollars there. Maybe even more.

Evlyn laughed lightly, several short giggles that surprised her. To her ears the laugh sounded almost maniacal. Certainly frightened. As if she'd come upon a corpse in the forest and was trying to convince herself that it was only a discarded mannequin. She ran her hands through the piles of bills and lifted a double handful up, then let them drop to the floor. It did not appear to even make a dent in the amount of money in the suitcase. She picked up a banded stack and saw a five followed by three zeros. She'd dropped maybe $50,000 onto the carpet and it hadn't made the money left inside look even $10 less full than it had looked before she touched it.

Evlyn was thinking thoughts that she knew were wrong, but nevertheless she was thinking them, consciously; they hadn't popped into her mind of their own volition. She was wondering, rationally, if that was the end of it. If they were indeed truly free.

Vincent was without a doubt a man with a drinking problem, three weeks dry or not. She'd been married to an alcoholic who had beaten her severely and then the next day acted as if he did not remember anything. Acted shocked as all get out when he saw the bruises, then he would fall on his knees and beg forgiveness, tell her that it would never happen again. She loved him and so she had tried Alanon, the support group for the loved ones of alcoholics. And she had learned a few things about compulsions. Even if Vincent didn't have a drinking compulsion, even if he wasn't an alcoholic, he certainly had a compulsion to steal. He was a thief, born and bred. Would she be waiting up at night terrified of where he was and what he might be doing, shaking with fear every time the phone rang because she would just know that it was the law telling her he was dead or, worse yet, back in prison? Could she deal with that?

She loved him, she had no doubt about that at all. But she had her doubts about him.

Could she live through it again? Married to a man she loved but whose compulsions ruled him and therefore her?

The Alanon ladies had been nice, but they had given her one bit of bum advice. At least she thought it was bum advice, then and now. They told her that his drinking was his problem, not hers. And she asked several of them, alone, drinking coffee at restaurants after meetings, the question that had made them glare at her and then talk trash in sweet, holier-than-thou voices. She'd asked, "If his drinking affects both of our lives, isn't it both of our problems?"

Within six months of her first meeting, she'd taken at least part of their advice and she'd detached from him. But she'd done more than detach emotionally. She detached completely. She left the brutal son of a bitch.

Evlyn remembered back to those days with a smile on her face, staring at more money than she had ever seen before in her life.

This could be her shot. Her way out. Every man had his price. Maybe next time someone would offer Vincent 2 million, 3, and he'd come out of retirement and go back to the life. Maybe it wouldn't even be money that lured him. Sugar Ray Leonard had more money than he ever knew what to do with and he'd come out of retirement for "one last fight" against Hagler, hadn't he? Would Vincent miss the excitement, the adrenaline rush?

Could a man like him ever be truly free?

Evlyn picked the fallen money up and placed it back in the suitcase, then zipped it tight.

She went to the master bedroom and got her coat. She sat on the bed there and picked up the telephone. She called down to the main desk and asked that her bill be prepared, told them she'd be paying in cash. She asked the desk clerk to please call her a cab.

Sean was holding his service revolver in his right hand, staring at the clock. He turned his right wrist a fraction and checked his watch. He said, "C'mon," under his breath. Bolo had gone upstairs a while back and had come back down, shook his hand and said goodbye, had wished Sean luck. He'd left the front door unlocked when he left, carrying two small suitcases. All he had in the world after living sixty full years.

There were only fifteen minutes left in the hour now, and it seemed as if Bolo had left days ago. For the first time, Sean allowed the thought to enter his head: They weren't coming.

Teddy looked a mess but there was no help for it, he didn't have time to go home and change. He would be cutting it close as it was. With the time it had taken him to shoot the breeze with Bolo, then escape from the cop, then get damn near killed, and then what with killing the wino and gathering himself together, having a couple of double shots for courage, time had gotten away from him. It was already almost two-thirty and he was just dropping a quarter into the pay telephone outside a North Side gas station. It took another couple of minutes to get the arrogant punk desk clerk at the Ritz to understand how important the phone call was, and even then he had to talk his way through a couple of flunkies before Bags's voice came over the line.

"Ted," Bags said.

Through the fog of alcohol that was fighting to control Teddy's emotions, came hatred. Black and bile-filled, at the sound of this bastard's voice.

"Hey, cuz. Little smarter than you figured, ain't I?"

"Whaddaya mean?" There was cheer in Bags's voice, surprise, as if the prick wasn't sitting on pins and needles wondering what the fuck to do with Parilo.

"Cut the shit, cuz, or I'll hang up. Tell you what, maybe I'll do that anyway. Let you and Montaine explain to Mr. Parilo why his boys aren't whacking out his enemies right now. Better yet,"—a burst of inspiration had just come to him, and he couldn't help himself, he had to rub it in. "I think I'll just go on back to the Sears

Tower, give Mr. Parilo his tapes back, tell him who set him up."

He heard Bags sigh. "It wasn't my idea, Ted. I just now found out that someone put the hit order out on you, for the cop thing, you know what I'm talking about. There wasn't nothing I could do."

"Bullshit me again, Bags, and I'm hanging up. Those were *your* boys out there. They don't listen to Montaine because Montaine don't fucking pay them."

Silence, shameful and confessional silence, came back at him.

He said, "You set me up, your own flesh and blood. Now tell me, Bags, why should I cut a deal with you, trust you, instead of Parilo himself?"

"On account of that a crazy, paranoid piece of shit like him, Ted, he'd cut your throat in a second. That's the first reason. The second is, we couldn't wait any longer. As soon as the guys reported back that Bolo had the music, the cheese took his retirement. We, the other guy and me, kid, we're the only game in town."

Teddy was proud of the way he handled it. Instead of whimpering inside, he'd come right up with a solution, another lie to cover his ass and keep the guys off his ass for a little while.

Even in the mental and emotional state he was in, he had to hand it to Bags. The guy hadn't said shit over this open line that could land him in trouble if the Gee were taping it. Maybe Bags was smarter than he gave him credit for. Hell, all this trouble had started because some goof had talked too much over the phone.

He said, "Bolo's gone, and I got the goods. They're in a safe place. Anything happens to me, Bags, they get turned over to the heat. You go home, wait for me to think up a nice, public place for us to meet. Not Tony's, either, so forget about it. Then we'll find a way, work things out between us. By the way, cuz, how'd the other guys take it, Parilo's retiring?" He asked the question because he knew that Montaine and Bags would have played hell convincing the others that Parilo was working against them, without the tapes for evidence. He'd asked the question to rub it in, but that son of a bitch Bags, he'd already hung up the phone.

"Time's up," Sean said aloud. Then said, *"Hell!"* They weren't coming.

Sean was devastated.

Vic Perry had taken the tapes back to headquarters, along with a signed statement from Bolo that he had stolen them under contract for the mob. It would be up to the State Attorney's Office as to whether they could legally use them or if they would just be able to listen to them, maybe build cases from things they only heard.

That might be good enough for Perry, but it didn't ease the aching in Sean's heart. Nothing short of emptying his pistol into Teddy King's head would ease that ache.

It had been a shot, that's all. Coming to Bolo after leaving Vincent the other day. He knew he could have followed the kid from one of the all-night taverns the gangsters frequented; he had a record as a DUI artist, a rum head. But that wouldn't be good enough. The punk had to be sober and terrified and staring into the barrel and knowing damn well why he was going to die.

But he couldn't get a line on him. He was on admin. leave and anybody else could have used the computers and found out an address but he was persona non grata around the department, even more so now that he had allowed his partner to die.

Vic Perry had gotten him a line, had given him the punk's home address, but it was the King family residence and the mother wouldn't even speak to him and the father had told him that he had no son. Even then,

Sean had spent the night in his car freezing and staring at the front door, waiting.

He had used the documents he had gathered on Vincent and had gone to him, seeking his help. But that hadn't panned out.

And there was Bolo, acting all sympathetic when Sean approached him, listening to Sean and nodding his gray balding head and pursing his lips, and Sean had thought it was just another game. Until Bolo had asked him how he'd like to bust a couple of Teddy's bosses. Sort of as a going-away present from him.

He'd followed them against Bolo's wishes that morning and he'd had every intention of waiting, waiting until they got back to the bar. He'd just had to see Teddy face to face, though.

And when he saw him, he'd almost pulled the trigger right then and there. Murdered the punk in the street. Sitting in a big Cadillac acting like he owned the city. But he waited, and then Bolo had come out, and when there was no doubt that Teddy was going to shoot Bolo in the head, he'd started across the street, running around the marble wall in front of Sears Tower, behind which he'd been hiding in the subzero cold for a couple of hours.

The kid had taken a couple of shots at him and he'd run back and hidden behind a parked car, not wanting to return fire, and was amazed when the mobsters behind King's car, whom he hadn't noticed due to his tunnel vision on Teddy, began firing at Teddy instead of at him. He himself did not want to kill the little runt until he was sure that the punk knew without doubt why he was doing it. Even if it cost Bolo his life. Which, of course, it hadn't.

Sean looked at his watch. It was getting late. My goodness, after four-thirty and it was dark out now.

He sighed heavily and got off the bar stool he was

perched on, finished the drink in front of him. Three glasses lined up before him. His, Bolo's, and Perry's. Perry hadn't touched his because he was a recovering alcoholic with what—fifteen years without a drink behind him. Sean picked it up and swirled the brown liquid in the glass; downed it in one gulp. Ahhh.

He tried to tell himself that you won a few and you lost a few, but it didn't help. Even through the alcohol fog, he knew it wouldn't end until Teddy King was dead. There could be no other way for it to go.

He wondered about Bolo. Man dying of cancer and asking him about cures. My goodness.

He left the bar and locked it behind him. He hoped Bolo would make out okay. Maybe Bolo was the lucky one.

Vincent waited patiently in his chair, reading. He had the closet door open and the bathroom door, too, so he could hear the telephone on the first ring. The large satchel was on the floor beside him and every so often he'd stop reading and look down at it, wondering. He'd killed some time downstairs, after he first arrived home, banging on pipes, holding burning newspapers under the spots that seemed frozen. At least the water was running again. He'd left the bathroom hot-water faucet open just a fraction, dripping steaming water into the sink. It would keep the pipes open. The toilet flushed. That's all he needed.

He spent an hour counting the money in the backpack, Jesus, 2 mil even, then thought about Evlyn and the money. He was afraid to call her and ask her to put it in the safe. She would think he was having second thoughts, doubts about trusting her. They couldn't start off on the wrong foot, so he didn't call her.

When the skylight overhead darkened, he figured it would be safe to give her a ring. It would be the polite thing to do, let her know he was going to be late so she wouldn't worry. The hotel safe he could throw in as an afterthought. Better yet, let her bring up the money; she'd have to be worried about it by now, or curious or scared or something. The subject would come up.

The desk clerk told him that the Martin party had checked out.

He called her apartment. No answer.

He told himself to be calm. There had to be a rational explanation for this. But he couldn't think of one. It couldn't happen to him two times; it just couldn't. He couldn't be dumb enough to make the same mistake all over again, could he?

He sat back down in his chair and felt a bubble of resentment. The little refrigerator was humming, a strange and alien sound. He began to dislike it passionately. Thought that if he had a window, he would throw the thing right through it, along with all the other nonsense she had bought—with his money—and had invaded his privacy with. Changed his entire lifestyle on a whim.

That *bitch*!

To take his mind off his anxiety, he looked at the satchel and wondered about it. It was much heavier than his own. And Bolo hadn't called yet to tell him what to do with it. Another thing to worry about. But Bolo had told him to stay at his place and wait for the call. Shit.

He hefted the case onto his lap and unzipped it. Inside were gobs and gobs of money, tightly stacked, crushed into the case so tightly that he doubted that even another bundle could be stuffed in there. Atop the pile were three sheets of folded paper. Vincent removed them and unfolded the sheets, and his name jumped out at him from the top line of the first page.

Dear Vincent:

Now you know why I never write to you at the joint,

as the only reading I do is the racing form. (ha!) This is the first letter I have ever wrote and it feels funny. There is cancer on my spine and I am dying. I signed deeds and papers giving the tavern to Eddie, as he earned it. I was gonna give it to him and Evlyn but I know you will take care of her in more ways than one. There is 3 million here and that is about all I have left from a lifetime of stealing and hustling. It is for you and you have to give me your word that you are threw stealing cause it would kill me faster than the cancer if you go back to the joint. I never wanted this life for you but you had your own mind and had to find out the hard way that it aint glamorous. You can trust Sean Kent, he is a good cop and a buddy. He told me about a guy in the fillipines who rubs cancer out of the body and I am on my way to see him now if the mob didnt kill me all ready. If that dont work there is a place in Mexico where they sell you lay-a-trill. Kent tells me that works for some guys with cancer. I will make out okay and if I die thats okay too cause I had a good life and have no regrets or apologies to make. So this is it kid and I want you to no that I aint never written a letter before this and I aint never tried to think about mushy stuff too much but I got to say something else. I aint never been married or had no kids. But if I ever did I always new that if I had a son I would want him to be just like you. You have made me proud especially when you was a army hero and when you was fighting. You were real good. I never told you this stuff before and maybe I should but I just want you to know before I die that I love you. There. Another first thing for me. So do me a favor and take the money and quit kid before you are a old man dying who aint never told no one that you loved them.

The letter was signed Enrico Rubolo.

Vincent read the pages over and over, putting things together, reading between the lines. Remembering the changes Evlyn had told him about, how Bolo had gotten thoughtful and reflective suddenly in the past several weeks that Vincent had been dry. Out there boosting and his best friend in the world was dying with no one to talk to about it. Jesus Christ.

Finally, when the words were almost memorized, Vincent allowed the pages to flutter to his lap. He covered his eyes with his hands and rubbed his forehead roughly. A low, quiet moaning, almost a keening, came from somewhere deep in his chest. Slowly it built to a loud hum, then a cry, then a trembling rage-filled shout that tore from Vincent's soul with a shattering impact upon him.

He jumped up out of the chair and ran to the nearest bookcase and began ripping books from the shelves, scattering them around the apartment, throwing them behind him, then grabbing more, trying to empty the cases, kill the books, in his mad drive to bring destruction down upon something, anything at all.

He was shouting and screaming and pulling books off the shelves and throwing them when someone started pounding on the door.

20 It could only be Evlyn, Vincent thought, and ran to the door with tears streaming down his face. He threw it open and there was Sean Kent standing there bigger than life, staring at him as if seeing him for the first time. Vincent left the door open and turned away from Sean. He walked rapidly to the closet door and walked through into the bathroom. He heard Sean locking the door behind him as he threw handfuls of cold water onto his face, making a conscious effort to control himself. Maybe Bolo said he could trust Kent, and if Bolo said it, then it was so, but that didn't mean Sean still wasn't a cop and therefore the enemy.

He walked back into the room and waved a hand at the couch. Sean sat down and Vincent walked to the other end of the couch and sat on the edge.

"I forgot about the address," Vincent said.

Sean said, "That's all right." Looking around, confusion in his eyes. And compassion. Maybe even empathy.

"So," Sean said, "you're human, eh?"

Vincent looked at him. "You didn't think I was, did you. You thought I was an animal." Sean's ears and face were a bright red. Vincent said, "What did you do, hang around outside for a couple of hours, or what? You look like hell."

"You don't look so hot yourself, buddy. But I walked here from Bolo's place. Woke up this morning and the car was gone, towed or driven away from outside Bigum's brother's house. I guess they figure, I'm retiring, I don't deserve a car."

"I got two of them, you want to borrow one."

Sean smiled for the first time since entering. "I guess," he said, "you really are human after all."

Knowing Sean would have already seen the open satchel filled with money, Vincent didn't bother to try and cover it up, zip it or anything. It would be an insult to do so now. A sign of mistrust and Bolo had written that Sean was okay. What Vincent did do was to pick up the letter and fold it away and go to put it into his shirt pocket. He'd removed the wet suit and the outer garments he'd worn that morning and now was wearing his heavy gray sweats and the sweatshirt didn't have a pocket. It made the gesture seem overly obvious. Like he had something to hide. Sean was just sitting there looking at him pleasantly. As if Vincent were an uninvited guest in Sean's home instead of the other way around. Vincent dropped the letter onto his lap and left it there.

"Privileged communication?" Sean asked, and Vincent nodded. "From Bolo?"

Vincent looked at him squarely. "How'd you know?"

"I," Sean said, "know a lot more than you might think." He paused to light a cigarette and Vincent looked around, trying to remember what he'd used last Saturday for an ashtray when Sean was here. Jesus Christ, he couldn't remember. Two days and it seemed like a lifetime ago. A century. A lot of things had changed in the past two days. Two days, hell, in the past two *hours*.

He got one of the empty fruit cans Evlyn had thrown

into the small lidded garbage can she'd bought, and took it to him. As he handed it to Sean, the phone rang and he dropped it into Sean's lap. Pear juice ran onto Sean's overcoat and pant leg. Vincent didn't notice, as he was racing to the bathroom.

"Vincent?" In a wee small voice, Evlyn was speaking his name.

"Where are you, Evlyn." Flat, emotionless. Cold. He tried for these emotions but his relief sounded strong and clear in his voice. He sighed heavily, feeling empty and tired. "You're calling to say goodbye."

She was crying now, trying to cover it up but he could hear her sniffling on the other end of the line; she couldn't fool him. Shouldn't even try.

"I was going to . . . going to leave, Vincent, but—I love you and I can't." The last six words came out in a rush, in a steady stream sounding like one long word in a foreign language, but he got it all right.

"Where are you, Evlyn, I'll come pick you up."

"Oh, honey, forgive me, I'm at the airport."

Vincent thought about Bolo's letter. About all the things Bolo had said and done for the very first time in his life after sixty years on this earth. He also thought about everyone deserving their chance at freedom.

And about the 3 million in the satchel in the other room and the 2 million in the backpack.

He said, "If you got to get on a plane, if you really have to go, I'll understand," and damnit, now he was fighting to keep control; there was a heavy, choking lump in his throat and a weight in his chest. His eyes were filling up and he was trying to remember how to pray so he could ask God to intercede for him. He could live without the money but he wasn't sure if he could make it without Evlyn, who'd waited.

"I don't want to try it without you, Vincent."

"Me, either."

"There's a cab right out front; I can see it from here."

"Hey," Vincent said, "I'll be waiting." He began to hang up the phone when he remembered where she was calling from and he called her name, trying to get her to not let the suitcase with the million dollars in it out of her sight, but she was already gone. It didn't matter. As long as she came back, he didn't care if she burned the money or threw it out the cab window a bill at a time. As long as she was coming home.

Home.

He walked out of the closet and checked out home. It was a mess. Wow.

"Sean," he said, "listen, why don't you and me go down to the garage and get you a car, okay? I got something I got to do right now but you come around, what, Wednesday, and I'll have an address for you."

"I know you will."

"What makes you so sure?"

"Bolo told me I could trust you," Sean said.

Teddy was filthy and he stank, but there was nothing to be done about that just yet. Montaine would have people watching his apartment, his mother's house, everywhere they might figure him to show. He knew how they operated now. They would grab him, squeeze him, torture him to get him to tell them where the tapes were.

That's what they would do to him if he *had* the tapes. He didn't even want to think about what they would do if they knew that he didn't.

His only chance was to get them, gain possession of the tapes, then get them into the hands of someone, a lawyer maybe, that he could trust. Someone who would turn the tapes over to the Gee if anything happened to him.

The Gee. The FBI. Christ, why hadn't he thought of it before?

He could walk right into the Federal Building, hand the tapes over and demand a spot in the Witness Protection Program. Hell, the feds, they treated the guys in the program like saints. Let them do whatever they wanted. My God, there was a way out.

But first he had to get the tapes. And he had to kill Bolo and the punk kid of his, cover his ass.

He knew now that he was right, that the son had indeed been in the condo atop Sears Tower with Bolo. He knew it was so because of the way Bolo had turned to look at the tower, before the shooting started. Okay, he'd play with Bolo for awhile, find out where the kid lived, then ace Bolo and go take care of the kid.

Teddy left the car in the South Loop and found a package store, bought a quart of scotch and walked slowly through the dusky bone-chilling early-evening winter to the gin mill that Bolo owned. And found it locked due to the weather. Weather, my ass, he thought. The guy was shit-scared is what it was. When the two big shots hadn't shown, he'd probably freaked and closed shop, maybe even he'd run away. Teddy ran through a howling wind to the back of the place, found the door there to be even more solid than the one out front. He walked around to the corner, stood there trying to get out of the wind, wondering what his next move should be. It was full dark now, and too cold to be outside, and if he didn't get the tapes and take care of business soon, he might freeze to death before finding his way to the Federal Building.

He was wondering whether he should kick the door down and charge in, guns blazing, when the door opened and—oh, man, this was his lucky day—the dip cop came out and without even looking either way at the street locked the door and turned into the wind, pulling the collar of his coat up around his big burly red neck. Smiling, Teddy followed him. The guy had a key. The drop, buying the tapes, it was obviously a setup.

Hell, it might even be easier than he planned. He knew that somewhere inside he would find Bolo's home address, on the liquor license or something. Then he could go to Bolo's house and do what he had to do. But now, it was obvious to him, this cop had the tapes. And even if he didn't, at least he had a key to the front door. It had been a burst of inspiration, telling Bags that Bolo was dead. That would keep the mob away from the tavern, as they would figure that the heat would be around. But he hadn't figured on the door being fireproof and made of steel. So he would follow Kent. He would take him down, too, and solve all his problems at once, would not even have to worry that the feds might not allow a guy, suspected of killing a cop, into the WPP. With Kent dead, there was no one to tell them anything. All Teddy had to do now was follow the lone-wolf big shot who was planning on busting the mob single-handedly, the dip, until he wound up alone someplace. Then he could kill him, get the key and go back and take care of business.

It would be easy.

He walked a good half-block behind the cop, the bottle in his left overcoat pocket, his hand on the 9mm pistol tucked away into the right pocket. He had a .38 in a belt holster on his right side, under the coat and the suit jacket. In case he needed more firepower. Things would probably get rough later. He ducked into a closed storefront alcove, took out the bottle and sipped deeply. He coughed, capped the bottle, and replaced it in his pocket as warm shivers raced through his body, spreading outward from his gut. Ahh, how he liked that stuff.

He walked back out onto Van Buren and the cop was gone.

He had to have turned right; there was no other way he could have gone. Teddy ran to the corner and made a skidding right, slipped on the ice and went down,

hard. On his right side. Thankfully, the pistol did not
blow off his right leg and the bottle did not smash. Before he even hit the ground, he knew that the cop had
disappeared. He was nowhere to be seen.

There was only one building there that he could have
gone into. A big stone thing, two-story, looked more
like a building in the joint than a place where someone
lived. There were empty lots on both sides of the building. A Maacco paint shop was on the left of it, past the
lot. The corner was to the right of it. There were only
abandoned buildings past the body shop. Teddy could
tell they were abandoned because the windows were
busted out. But why in the hell would the cop duck into
that building in the South Loop seemingly miles from
anyplace of importance?

A thought struck Teddy, and he smiled. Maybe, just
maybe, this was where Bolo lived. The cop had staked
out the gin mill and when no one showed up to pick up
the tapes, he had decided to walk over to Bolo's house
and talk things over.

Which meant the cop had the tapes on him. Even if
he didn't, it was cool as long as this was Bolo's house.
Bolo would have the tapes and Teddy's million bucks
somewhere on the premises. He couldn't believe his
luck. But it looked like the kind of place the old dip
would live in. A goddamn loft. Less than a block away,
Teddy could see the large white public housing unit
down there, where the welfare mommas lived. A guy in
the joint, a black guy, had told him never to try and
fuck any of the project bitches because they'd suck you
and then bite it off if you didn't hand over all your
money. Mean mothers, those welfare mommas.

Teddy walked hunched over into the wind, toward
the large truck door at street level. Man, talk about paranoid. This had to be Bolo's joint and Bolo had to be a
lot less of a badass then he acted because there was a
recess cut right into the ground, into the concrete, for

the truck door to close into so it couldn't be pried or jimmied. Okay.

Around the side of the building, the iron steps leading up to the second floor, where, presumably, Bolo lived. A big heavy steel door sitting up there, impossible to break down; Teddy could tell that without even going up a single step. Couldn't shoot through it, either. Man. He'd have to wait in the empty lot and when the cop walked by on his way home, he'd have him, drag him into the dark there and blow him away and who would hear it? The project bitches? Hell, shootings had to be a pretty commonplace thing around this neighborhood.

He'd rather do it inside, though, where he knew no one would see him. But you couldn't complain; you had to do what you had to do, and what Teddy had to do now was to wait in the cold with his bottle and his gun and kill a couple of people. Starting with the cop. Two in one week. He wondered if even Dillinger had ever shot down two cops in separate incidents at different times within one week. Probably not. Teddy was about to make history. He'd be a legend. Kill two partners within what, five days.

He stood there in the dark cold night sipping his bottle and living in his mind the act he'd give the feds. Take him and his million in, and he'd give them the tapes. The bottle was half-empty. By the time he would finish it, he'd bet he'd feel right and good for the first time since the man he'd assumed to be an old, washed-up thief had gotten the drop on him just a couple blocks away from this tenement area that very afternoon.

But he never got a chance to finish the booze. He heard sounds, then voices, happy voices, then the sound of feet coming down the iron steps.

Teddy smiled and lowered the bottle to the ground,

reached into his coat and pulled out the 9mm pistol, then flattened himself against the front of the building.

When nobody came around the corner, he hesitated, then turned the corner with the pistol extended and his lips snarling, ready to start blasting, but there was no one in sight. He stepped forward, holding the gun in both hands in front of him, and saw the open door.

How the hell could he have missed it? Under the stairway, a concrete-framed solid man door. It wouldn't have mattered because Teddy was no whore of a booster, and he couldn't have picked the lock or broken it down even if he had noticed it. It was steel, like the door upstairs. Suddenly he heard a car engine cough, then come to life. He slowly walked forward until he could see through the doorway, and when he saw the two of them standing there, he could not believe his luck.

The cop and the son, what was his name, the name Bolo had called him the other night in the bar? It didn't matter. He had them now. Neither man had a weapon in sight and Teddy had a pistol with ten shots still left in it in his strong right hand, and their asses belonged to him.

He stepped into the gloomy warehouse and shouted, *"Freeze!"* and both men dove for the ground and Teddy went in, kicked the door shut behind him and fired two shots into the area near the two cars where he'd last seen the men.

"You're both dead!" he shouted. "Come on out with your hands up and you might live. I only want the tapes!" There was the sound of pistol fire and he threw himself to the floor, scared, this wasn't in the game plan, they weren't supposed to fire back at him.

Shivering more from fear than the cold, he aimed under the wheels of the Cadillac sitting there purring and blowing white exhaust from the pipes. They had to be under that one, on the other side. He fired three times and saw the car rock down as a tire burst. Damnit. But maybe he'd shot one of them.

There was only the light now from the bare bulbs hanging from the wires in the roof, and gloomy shadows encroached his position, frightening shadows. Bad things were in the dark. Aiming carefully, he fired again at the black space under the car and still no shout of pain, no cry of anguish. "Fuckers!" he shouted.

He heard a voice, the cop's voice, call out to him.

"You killed Bigum with that same gun, didn't you, Teddy, you asshole."

Teddy shouted out, "Yeah, and now it's your turn." Then he waited. He wouldn't fire again until he saw them for real.

And he saw one of them sooner than he expected, because the big fat cop was rising now, pistol extended, not even bothering to hide behind the car anymore.

Teddy, lying on the ground, smiled. He steadied the gun and took careful aim at the center of the cop's chest. Slowly, he began to squeeze the trigger. . . .

Sean counted the gunshots as Teddy fired them off, hearing the bullets zing between him and Vincent, the two of them curled into little balls behind the Cadillac's tires. Trying to make tiny little targets. If it was the same gun the punk had used to kill Bigum, it was a .38 Smith, and even if the kid had a live one under the hammer, he'd only have six shots. When the sixth shot sounded, he called out to make certain and, sure enough, the little arrogant punk reassured him. Before Teddy could reload, Sean stood and began to search for Teddy in the dark, not expecting him to be lying on the ground, and the pistol pointed at him was a lot bigger than a .38, and good God, he could see Teddy smiling.

Then a shadow was crossing his path and something hard knocked him to the ground and he heard the sound of the pistol shot at the same time that he heard

Vincent, who had gotten up and thrown himself upon
Sean, grunt loudly, in pain.

God. He'd allowed Bigum to die and now Vincent
was lying atop him and not moving or saying anything.
He couldn't hear the kid breathing, either. Heedless of
his own safety, he rose to his feet and threw himself
across the hood of the Cadillac, shooting his pistol as
fast as he could pull the trigger at the form of Teddy
King who was advancing, smiling like a sap, like he was
on top of the world.

Well, that was not the way it was anymore, at least
Teddy wasn't atop *this* world anymore, because every
single shot Sean fired hit Teddy in the chest, all four
remaining bullets hitting him in a pattern around the
heart that you could cover with the palm of your hand
and Teddy was flying back, his face shocked, still with
the trace of a grin on it but there was surprise and pain
there, too.

Sean thought, Good.

He shouted, "That's for Bigum, you cocksucker!" and
he wished that he was one of the cops who carried a
bunch of extra loads around in his jacket pockets because he would reload and shoot this little piece of scum
a hundred more times if he had the bullets.

Teddy was slumped over in a kneeling position, not
yet certain that he was dead. He slowly raised his head
up and their eyes locked. Teddy's showing shock and
fear—no—terror, not fear, and confusion. Sean smiled
at him and said right to him, "That's for Bigum, you
son of a bitch."

Teddy slowly fell forward until the top of his head
was on the concrete ground. He rolled over onto his
right side and the life went out of him and he lay there,
dead.

Sean felt a cold wetness on his face and realized that
he was crying. And he remembered Vincent. Brave Vin-

cent who had taken a bullet and died for him. My God. He turned to him—

And saw the dead rising as Vincent leaned against the trunk of the Mercury, pushing himself to a standing position. He stood and swayed for a second while Sean stood there shocked, Vincent holding his right arm with his left hand, up high, over the hole in the sweatshirt.

"You big fucking stupe," Vincent said and Sean couldn't help it, he laughed out loud in his relief and gratitude. Vincent said, "You're a big dumb fat ugly stupid. Believing a goddamn-piece-of-shit drunk like that."

Sean started to tell him that he was an officer of the law and then demand to be treated with respect, but that wasn't really true. His papers were in; he'd be retired in twenty-five days. Smiling, he said to Vincent, "Call me mister, son."

Vincent stared knives at him, then looked away at the blood on his hand. He put the hand back on his arm and said, "Mr. *Stupid*, that's who you are."

"Shot you in the upper arm?"

"No, he shot me in the dick and I'm just holding my fucking arm because it's closer, you goof."

"Need an ambulance?"

"In Vietnam, we'd piss on a wound like this and keep on humping, Mr. Stupid." But he was grinning now, enjoying himself, because for the first time in his life he was saying anything he wanted to a cop and the cop had to take it because, by God, Vincent had saved his life.

Sean said, "Let's get upstairs."

"Now you're gonna tell me what to do, eh? Stoop! Big ugly Englishman stupid, that's what you are."

"Hey, Vincent," Sean said, fighting a lump in his throat but feeling good, "I don't play that racial stuff."

And then he was turning and spinning at the sound

of footsteps, Sean thinking what an idiot he was; the mob wouldn't send a hit man out without backup, and it was too late because the door was opening and they'd be coming in firing and his gun was empty. "No!" Sean shouted.

"No, what?" Evlyn asked. Then she put her hand to her mouth as she almost stepped on Teddy King and she stepped back, ready to scream.

Vincent was walking toward her slowly, holding his bleeding arm. He said to Sean, "You want to shit your pants, Mr. Stupid?" And Sean had to hand it to him, his timing was perfect. Sean watched the bleeding booster who had just saved his life step over Teddy King's body and smile at the woman standing there with the suitcase in the warehouse section of the building. He watched as the kid put a cavalier expression on his face; along with the smile, he looked like Rutger Hauer trying to satirize James Bond. He heard the kid say, "How you doing, Evlyn?" as if there wasn't a dead body three feet away from them, and then Sean Kent smiled as the woman threw herself into the kid's arms and by golly, they told each other "I love you" at the exact same time. . . .

Upstairs, the wound cleaned and bandaged—the bullet had gone straight through the flesh of the bicep— Vincent was drinking a can of tomato juice, still playing the mind game with Sean.

Vincent said, "You broke your own rule."

Sean said, "How's that?"

Evlyn was staring at them both as if they had just stepped out of a spaceship.

"You called Teddy an—and I quote—'asshole,' and a 'cocksucker.' And, if I remember right, a 'son of a bitch.'"

Sean, trying for indignation, said, "Well, he *is* an asshole. Or, he *was*."

And for some reason Evlyn couldn't figure out and

never did get around to asking about, the two of them, with a dead body twenty feet below them cooling rapidly in the winter night, laughed.

She heard Vincent say, "A cop, retiring, he could use a good sum of money to get him through his golden years."

She heard Sean say, "That Mercury down there, it's got a trunk big enough, fit ten Ted Kings in. Say they found the guy on the steps of the Sears Tower, what would the cops and the mob think?"

She watched as Vincent nodded, deep in thought. Then saw him smile.

She heard Sean say, "Man with your connections, he could round up a couple of passports, get himself and his girlfriend out of the country awhile, just in case some outfit guy put two and two together"; then heard Vincent say, "I'll bet a guy with my connections could do just that."

She heard Vincent add, "I figure a million, it might set that cop I was talking about up for the rest of his natural years, huh?" Then she saw Sean nodding in agreement.

Straight-faced, perplexed, she asked, "Well, are you two going to call the cops?" And she watched as the two of them really broke up over that one, and as soon as Vincent could control himself, he said, "Why, *sure* we are . . ." Then he broke up laughing again.

About the Author

Eugene Izzi was born and raised in Chicago and, except for the two years he spent in the Army, has lived in the Chicago area all his life. He took jobs as a steelworker and a construction worker prior to devoting himself to writing full-time. His short stories have appeared in several magazines. He now lives in a suburb of Chicago. Three of his previous novels, *The Take, Bad Guys,* and *The Eighth Victim,* are available from St. Martin's Paperbacks.

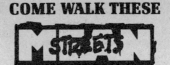

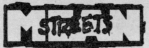